CHEESE WAR

Cheese War

Conflict and Courage in
Tillamook County, Oregon

MARILYN MILNE AND LINDA KIRK

Oregon State University Press   Corvallis

Cataloging-in-Publication data is available from the Library of Congress.

ISBN 978-0-87071-195-4 (paperback); ISBN 978-0-87071-200-5 (ebook)

♾ This paper meets the requirements of ANSI/NISO Z39.48-1992 (Permanence of Paper).

First published in 2022 by Oregon State University Press
Printed in the United States of America

Oregon State University
OSU Press

Oregon State University Press
121 The Valley Library
Corvallis OR 97331-4501
541-737-3166 • fax 541-737-3170
www.osupress.oregonstate.edu

Contents

Preface vii

Key to Organizations xiii

Field Note 1 — Treasure Hunt at the Museum 1

CHAPTER 1   AN IMPORTANT VOTE 3

CHAPTER 2   THE WHYS AND WHEYS OF DAIRIES
AND CHEESEMAKING 11

Field Note 2 — From Milking Pit to Ice Cream Counter . 23

CHAPTER 3   STRANGE BEDFELLOWS 26

Field Note 3 — Farm Chores 41

CHAPTER 4   HARD TIMES 44

CHAPTER 5   TOO MUCH MILK, TOO MUCH DIXON . . . 59

Field Note 4 — Books and Pipes 71

CHAPTER 6   BITTER DISCUSSIONS 73

CHAPTER 7   BAD BOOKKEEPING 86

Field Note 5 — Once Again to the Courthouse . . . 95

CHAPTER 8   STRIFE BUILDS 98

CHAPTER 9   THE CRUSADERS 117

Field Note 6 — Cheese War Truce 138

CHAPTER 10   THE LEAN YEARS 140

Field Note 7 — Tourists Swarm the Factory 156

CHAPTER 11   THE END 159

Field Note 8 — I Was a Teenage Creditor 169

Epilogue 171

Notes 183

Bibliography 203

Index 209

Preface

BY MARILYN MILNE

When I drive through Tillamook County, Oregon, these days, it is easy to see the influence that dairy farming has had on the region. Outside of the county's few towns, large farms cover most of the acreage. Timber—or clear-cuts—blanket the hills, but that industry has taken a back seat to producing milk for dairy products. Tillamook farmers have a uniform goal: to create value from dairying.

In the 1960s, though, their common purpose fell apart when the farmers disagreed vehemently with each other. In *Cheese War*, my coauthor sister and I take a look back at the period of turmoil that created great change in Tillamook's cheese industry. The causes of what she and I call the Cheese War can be traced many decades later. They include insults, lies, personality clashes, lawsuits won and lost, nonpayment for milk, human weakness, stubbornness, fear of change—or acceptance of it—and financial skullduggery. It was a fight sparked by the discovery of wrongdoing, and it resulted in relatives who didn't speak to each other for the rest of their lives as well as improvements to the statewide and local dairy industries.

Cheese War takes the reader through the history of Tillamook County, Oregon, and its cheese industry. While others, including the victorious current producers of Tillamook Cheese, have written about the Cheese War, this book focuses mainly on the courageous losers who fought for change when compromise wasn't possible. Our father, George Milne, was one of the leaders on the losing side of the fight.

From grade school into high school, the Cheese War dominated my childhood. On one side of the war was County Creamery, the umbrella marketing group for the individual cooperatives processing the milk and making the cheese; the other side was my dad's Cheese & Dairy group, one of the cooperatives that used County Creamery's services. The Cheese War papered over my childhood with adult information. Although it was exciting to have a million-dollar contract signed on the roof of our 1955 Ford while we children sat inside, I knew it wasn't part of a typical childhood. I also knew I was part of something important; after all, the signing occurred after our father had arranged to meet a courier at South Prairie Store, about two miles from our farm, where he signed the paperwork after borrowing a pen from my sister Linda.

I observed the ins and outs of the Cheese War closely, proud of my family's role in the fight and resentful that it ran our lives. I wished the Cheese War would go away, but I knew we were right to fight it. I learned strategic thinking as I listened to the ever-evolving plans for how to address one crisis after another. I saw how people could be remarkably courageous and terribly human.

I admired the people who supported our side, and I knew which families of the children on my school bus were against us. It influenced my choice of where I sat when I climbed aboard. I would walk down the aisle, choosing a seat by noting who was occupying it and whether that child's family was an ally of mine. All of the adults knew where each other's loyalty lay, too. That knowledge sometimes affected my plans, such as when my parents said I could not join other Tillamook High School freshmen in decorating a homecoming parade float because the work was being done at the Fenks' barn. They were on the other side. "I'm glad you are friends with them," I quoted my mother saying when I wrote about it in my journal. "And I'm sorry, but I can't be seen driving in there." My mom knew that someone from the other side would recognize her or the car and that she might become the subject of gossip and speculation.

Petty actions pointed to the animosity between the dueling cooperatives. For example, young women from farms competed every year to be the Tillamook Dairy Princess. The winner went to the Oregon Dairy Princess contest and represented Tillamook County at events, including Tillamook's large June Dairy Month parade. County Creamery had a monopoly on the contest during the Cheese War. My father's group tried to be part of the event, with its board agreeing in May 1966 to contribute $125 "toward promoting the Dairy Princess contest."[1] At the June 15, 1966, meeting, though, the Cheese & Dairy board rescinded its monetary support because it "was not allowed to participate on the committee as previously agreed."[2] I was a budding feminist, and I did not want to be the Tillamook Dairy Princess. But I was keenly aware that the politics of the competition meant I wasn't going to be successful if I did compete.

While all of this was going on, I could have reached out to other children who were on our side: Janet Lucas or Dixie Sayles. But I didn't. I felt isolated, alone in my experience, with only my sisters to know what I was going through. At Tillamook High School, I did become friends with Nita Naegeli, the daughter of a farmer on the same side of the issue. I don't recall talking to her about the fight, however. We talked about school and clothes, homework and other students—the typical high school routine.

I was elected to noncontroversial positions like president of Future Teachers of America. But Nick Steiner, whose family supported our side, competed to be president of the Future Farmers of America, a major honor in a dairy town. The vote split along Cheese & Dairy v. County Creamery lines, like a referendum on the larger contest. He won, just as he won when he ran for president of the Tillamook Catholic High School student body. He recalls, though, that, "Kids in high school got into mischief about the dispute. Almost had fist fights with each other. Kids confronted each other in the hallway. Some were jerks about it."[3]

I tried to shield myself from such ugliness, in part by making my father into my hero. I saw that he persevered despite personal losses and the exhausting battles of the Cheese War. He was a leader. I wasn't old enough to understand that he had made mistakes, and he was requiring deep sacrifices by his family. What I knew was that my dad's laugh changed from a chuckle to a harsh bark. Night after night, he came in from milking the cows to eat dinner from a plate on his lap while he talked on the phone about that day's developments. I watched him and listened to him, and I wished his voice were gentler and he had time for me.

I clung to the fairy tale, that the dragon would be slayed and everyone would live happily ever after. Then we lost the Cheese War. I was shocked. I followed my parents' cues and kept my chin up in public—we losers had to be gracious in a setting where the wounds cut deep—but I grieved in private. For self-protection and perspective, I began to view events through a long lens, placing them in the great march of history rather than on the summit of my small world. I had learned on the farm that the best plans can fail because the prize cow dies or the weather doesn't deliver what is needed to grow the crops, and yet the world continues and I must keep trying. I knew that failing might not mean being wrong, a lesson solidified through defeat in the Cheese War.

A few years ago, my sister Linda asked me, "Remember when all of the Tillamook farmers were fighting? What exactly were they fighting about?" I gave a quick answer, which she thoughtfully rebutted. She said we should find the answer, but a cursory search revealed that there were multiple factors that contributed to the discord and people had their own perspectives, sometimes calcified or broken by time.

Linda and I began researching the Cheese War. We reviewed the tapes and transcripts of interviews I had conducted with my parents in 1989 and 1993. We read the newspaper articles our mother had saved. We talked to farmers who had been on our side. We read the available history in books such as County Creamery's commissioned story, *The Tillamook Way*; Tami Parr's *Pacific Northwest Cheese*; and Joseph E. Taylor III's *Persistent Callings*. We tracked down court cases in the Tillamook County Courthouse and the State of Oregon Archives. Even though much material had been winnowed out of the case files as they aged—what a trove those documents would have been—we were able to glean some new details. People checked their attics and garages, giving us additional original source material. We were stunned that minutes of meetings from that period still existed, and they added a lot of detail and facts to the story. Sometimes, we were surprised by the information we uncovered; sometimes, our memories were confirmed; always, we wished we could interview now-dead participants in the fight.

In this book, we share verified actions and events that occurred during that turbulent time. My sister and I use some of the experiences of our family and allies as a way to understand the experiences of the community and the Oregon dairy industry. Our goal is to tell the rest of the story, the one that has never been told. I continue to add material to the book's website, cheesewar.info, and to our Facebook page, Tillamook Cheese History.

Our information was further enriched by Jim Becker; Walt and Virginia Beeler; Helen Blaser; our sister, Cathy Froland; Joe Jenck and his mother, Andrea Jenck; Fib and Rita Johnston; the late Clem and Liz Hurliman; Dave and Carol Leuthold; Janet Lucas Walker and her late father, Vern Lucas; our brother, Steve Milne; Nick Steiner; and Mike, Pat, and Tom Tone.

I am very grateful to my brother-in-law, Rich Kirk, who read drafts of the book, edited photos, took our author photos, and seemed to enjoy the process. I am grateful to John David Kirk, my brother-in-law's brother and my friend, who scanned countless pages of minutes and created two maps for the book. I have great gratitude and love for my family: Eric, Leah, and Drew.

My deep thanks go, of course, to my late parents, George and Barbara Milne.

Linda made the book possible. Beyond creating the book's Field Notes—the first of which opens the book—she put her keen mind, writing and editing skills, and research capabilities to work on behalf of the book. And always, she encouraged me. Thank you, Linda.

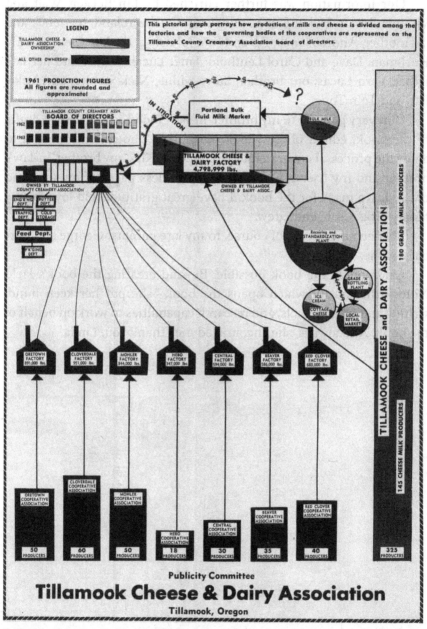

During the first lawsuit of the Cheese War, Cheese & Dairy produced an advertisement to explain the relationships and connections among seven small cheese factories, the large Cheese & Dairy factory, and County Creamery, the marketing group for Tillamook Cheese. *Headlight Herald*, April 28, 1963

KEY TO ORGANIZATIONS

Tillamook County Creamery Association = *County Creamery*

Countywide marketing cooperative organized to serve Tillamook County producer cooperatives. Its functions included marketing the cheese and milk, maintaining each factory's bookkeeping and recordkeeping, providing cold storage, and shipping the cheese. Since 1968, it has also produced the cheese and other dairy products as a restructured producer cooperative. County Creamery is also abbreviated as TCCA and T.C.C.A.

Tillamook Cheese Association = *TCA*

Producer cooperative composed of farmers who shipped milk to be used for cheese production; one of two predecessors of Cheese & Dairy. TCA merged with the Grade A Shippers Association in 1962 to form Cheese & Dairy.

Grade A Shippers Association = *GASA*

Producer cooperative composed of farmers who shipped fluid milk to be bottled for consumption; one of two predecessors of Cheese & Dairy. GASA merged with TCA in 1962 to form Cheese & Dairy.

Tillamook Cheese and Dairy Association = *Cheese & Dairy*

Producer cooperative formed in 1962 from Tillamook Cheese Association and Grade A Shippers Association. County Creamery bought Cheese & Dairy in 1968. Cheese & Dairy is also abbreviated as TC&DA, T.C.&D.A., and TCDA.

Tillamook Fluid Milk Shippers Association = *Shiveley Shippers*

Subset of Cheese & Dairy Grade A farmers who left the organization and formed a producer cooperative in 1963 that gained membership in County Creamery. It was also known as Shiveley Shippers because its first president was Gaylord Shiveley. Tillamook Fluid Milk Shippers Association is abbreviated as TFMSA.

FIELD NOTE 1

Treasure Hunt at the Museum

BY LINDA KIRK

In 1959, my fourth grade class visited the Tillamook County Pioneer Museum. That trip showed me the museum held treasures. First among them was a mossy, hollow stump like the one that sheltered Tillamook's first pioneer, Joe Champion, after he sailed into Tillamook Bay in 1851. Fixed in my memory is an image of thick, craggy bark encircling a cramped living space, and also a question I asked myself, "What was it like to live in a stump?"[1]

On a return trip in 2011 with my mother and my sister Marilyn, we set out on a new treasure hunt. We had an appointment with Ruby Fry-Matson, the museum's administrative assistant. We met her in the reference library several steps down from the main level. Ruby remembered the Cheese War from her days growing up on a dairy farm in south Tillamook County.

In the museum's files, Marilyn and I hoped to locate an interview that Beale Dixon gave in 1987. Dixon led the opposition cooperative, County Creamery, when our father led the Cheese & Dairy co-op. We were also looking for a biography of Warren McMinimee, attorney for County Creamery. Our target list included County Creamery newsletters, photographs of people we remembered from the Cheese War, and newspaper stories. Ruby said Tillamook County Library had back issues of the *Headlight-Herald*, Tillamook's weekly newspaper, on microfilm. We would go to the library on our next trip.

Ruby found a written transcript of an interview Beale Dixon gave Gerry Hysmith, a columnist for the *Headlight Herald*, eleven years after he retired as manager of County Creamery. The interview filled two cassette tapes. Transcribed, it ran fifty pages. While Ruby answered questions from Marilyn and Mom, I skimmed the transcript. Hysmith, an experienced interviewer, said she and Dixon were old friends. Dixon told Hysmith about visiting the Tillamook plant three years before he took the County Creamery manager job. Dixon said his first trip to Tillamook was in 1948 while he was managing a dairy cooperative in Battle Ground, Washington. He went to a meeting in Portland, where a Whatcom, Washington, co-op manager persuaded Dixon to walk with him through the new plant in Tillamook—even offering to borrow pajamas for Dixon, who hadn't expected to stay overnight, much less go to Tillamook. "It was quite amazing to me that I later came down here to be manager," Dixon said.[2]

While I read the transcript, Ruby retrieved a three-page biography of Warren McMinimee. The biography was unsigned but must have been written by Harry C. Elliott, who represented Tillamook in the Oregon House beginning in 1953, when McMinimee first served in the senate. This was an unpublished treasure we could not have found without the museum's files. Looking back on the year that he and Warren McMinimee were first elected, Elliott wrote, "Together we moved to Salem." Then this handwritten note about McMinimee's wife: "Louise did not go and Warren had a room in the house we rented." Elliott remembered that McMinimee's service as a three-term district attorney "was interrupted when he went into the Navy as Executive Officer of his ship. He was cited for bravery in the Battle of Iwo Jima."[3]

At the museum, we hoped to find County Creamery's annual reports and monthly newsletters from the 1960s. Those publications were not available, but we did find photographs of cheese factories that were no longer standing, along with a scrapbook that had a snapshot of a cheese factory tour guide. We found high school yearbook photographs of three Cheese War combatants: Otto Schild, Cheese & Dairy board member and later County Creamery's board president; Ferd Becker, Cheese & Dairy strategist; and Anita Jeanne Stewart Neilson, stenographer for County Creamery, who fed information to Cheese & Dairy.

At the end of the day, as I climbed the steps at the back of the museum, I carried photocopies collected on this trip. In our hunt, we had found treasures—treasures that gleamed like my childhood discovery of Joe Champion making his home in a spruce stump.

CHAPTER 1

An Important Vote

In Tillamook County, Oregon, the rain falls, the wind blows, and the cow manure stinks. The odor is tolerated; after all, it is a necessary piece of the farm system that brought fame and money to Tillamook.

Cows have always produced manure. In the 1960s, spreading it on the fields was the best way to get rid of it—put the waste to work fertilizing the pastureland that produced the grass that fed the cows that made the milk that created the cheese. The smelly cycle signified success in Tillamook. Farmers hauled the heavy manure from the barnyard pile when their pastures had dried enough to handle the weight of the loaded spreaders. Continual rain for the majority of the year meant the pastures were often too wet, and large manure piles grew behind the barns, waiting for the day when the ground was dry and the farmers had time. Then, they spread the manure. A lot of stinky manure.

The smell faded as the manure soaked into the soil, but inevitably, some residue washed into the many nearby rivers and creeks and tidal flats. The groundwater was fed by more than ninety inches of rain every year. Whether the rain came in a thunderstorm or, more typically, a steady mist, it kept falling from the gray, gray sky. It grew the grass and the trees, creating the jobs that kept Tillamook County going.

But oh, the wind. The county's tourism slogan was "Land of Cheese, Trees, and Ocean Breeze," although natives thought the breeze was more gusting than wafting, more constant than pleasant. Some local wits, focusing on the rain, altered the optimistic slogan to a more realistic quip of "Land of Cheese, Trees, and Mud Up to Your Knees."

For farmers, the pastures of grass compensated for the weather. The tender green shoots of spring were like candy to the cows, and then the grass of summer provided hay and silage. As soon as the early settlers discovered the river bottom land, they claimed it from the Indigenous Tillamooks and began clearing the trees from it. Yearly floods regularly deposited more of the rich soil, precious loam that was the most valuable inheritance farmers could provide for their children.

On the river bottom pastures, cows produced bountiful buckets of milk. Farmers knew how to get milk from their cows, and the local cheesemakers knew how to make cheese from the milk. A boy could grow up on a farm and know he would work the land or make the cheese as an adult. A farm girl would know she would probably marry a farmer or cheesemaker. Generations of families had come to assume that their way of life would not change, a view reinforced by Tillamook County's geographic isolation.

Hemmed in by the Pacific Ocean to the west and the Coast Range of mountains to the east, Tillamook residents had a feeling of "us" versus "the valley." Portland and Salem, located in the Willamette Valley beyond the Coast Range, were major Oregon population sites. By 1960, modern roadbuilding and transportation had vastly improved the ability of Tillamook County residents to reach the valley, but they were still required to navigate narrow roads, sharp curves, and bad weather. They had to watch out for Portlanders, Salemites, and other out-of-towners, none of whom seemed skilled at driving through mountains and on rural roads but wanted to reach Tillamook County's beaches when the weather was good.

In the 1950s, Tillamook gained more frequent contact with the larger world when television sets became affordable, but the reception was on-again, off-again. The weekly newspaper, the *Headlight Herald*, was thriving and was the main source of local news, supplemented by delivery of the daily Portland papers. KTIL, the local radio station, also provided news, but the station was mostly appreciated for playing polka music during the morning milkings in farmers' barns. The cows seemed to release more milk when they heard music, or perhaps the farmers, many of Swiss and German descent, simply enjoyed hearing polkas while doing the milking.

As Tillamook's cheesemaking fame grew, the farmers and other residents took pride in what they had created. They even gave their Tillamook High School sports teams an appropriate nickname—the Cheesemakers.

This Nestucca River farm near Hebo, in south Tillamook County, was a typical farm scene in 1963. Oregon State Archives, Oregon Highway Division, OHD 7285

Tillamook County's farmers had a good routine: milk the cows, do the chores, raise the family, go to church, see friends, grow the crops, and do it all again the next day and the next week and the next season and the next year.

And yet.

By the early 1960s, the cheese that had sustained the region was one of the driving forces that divided Tillamook County farmers into two camps. The split generated the Cheese War.

The war was led by two outsiders who had come to Tillamook County after World War II. The first was an ambitious business manager with an outgoing personality and a clever mind. Beale Dixon came to town to run the Tillamook dairy industry's umbrella cooperative, the Tillamook County Creamery Association. George Milne came to Tillamook to be a dairy farmer. To fulfill his dream, he was willing to work

George Milne (*left*); Beale Dixon (*right*). *Oregon Journal*, May 17, 1963

from four o'clock in the morning to nine o'clock every night on land no local farmer had wanted to buy. He wasn't related to anyone in the county, and his wife, Barbara, was citified. Milne just wanted to farm. But farming wouldn't be his sole priority when he couldn't ignore—and couldn't get corrected—the manipulation in the marketing and sale of his milk.

Dixon had great influence because County Creamery was a powerful player in Tillamook and in the larger dairy industry. All of the Tillamook farmers were patrons, or contracted members, of their own cooperatives, and those factories were members of County Creamery. In turn, County Creamery represented the individual factories to the outside world, sold their products, managed their bookkeeping, and acted as their purchasing agent. All of the factories elected representatives to the County Creamery board. In addition to managing County

Creamery, Dixon oversaw all of the cooperatives, including the largest, Cheese & Dairy, which processed drinking milk as well as made cheese. The cartons of milk carried the label "Tillamook Milk" and sold to area groceries. National and regional milk distributors, such as Carnation, Alpenrose, and Mayflower, bought the Grade A milk in bulk, made products with it or labeled it as their own, and placed it in urban stores. Tillamook's business model had worked for many years, built around the demand for cheese and milk.

Nationally, milk was touted as "a necessary, perfect food,"[1] with an emphasis on using cow milk in children's and adults' diets. From the industrial revolution forward, milk consumption spread throughout the so-called Northwestern Cow Belt of northern Europe, Great Britain, and North America[2] even though it "spoils easily, carries disease, and causes digestive trouble for many of its consumers."[3]

Milk for the kitchen table was in demand, and the more butterfat, the better. During World War II, the government had subsidized the price consumers paid for milk and provided dairy farmers with a guaranteed higher price.[4] The era after the war was a time of optimism and expansion for dairy farmers because they were being paid well for the products they produced, and their costs were reasonable. A farmer could work a part-time outside job while continuing to run a small dairy farm. Times were good, but they began to change in the 1950s.

Oregon's dairy farmers were caught in their industry's economic crosshairs. In a 1961 article, *The Oregonian* reported on increasing strife in the industry, which it attributed to "Too many people producing too much milk for a shrinking market." The article went on to list "milk strikes, milk wars, consumer boycotts, oversupply, undersupply, antitrust suits, supreme court decisions, tight controls, loose controls, no controls, price supports, price cutting, price fixing, price wars, cutthroat marketing, curbed competition, and wide open competition" as problems facing the industry.[5]

Farmers were used to coping with floods, hay crops that got rained on and ruined, cows that got milk fever and died overnight, and all of the other heartbreaks of dairy farming. They were used to working hard and then working harder. The usual responses weren't correcting their industry's woes, however. Tillamook farmers had local economic worries, too: County Creamery, their marketing cooperative, had difficulty

selling their cheese, and it lacked negotiating power with the distributors of its grocery store milk, also called fluid milk.

And then, several board members of Cheese & Dairy learned of
another possible reason why their financial situation was tenuous. A
front office employee at County Creamery alerted them that Beale
Dixon had made unsecured loans to Portland grocery stores.

Dixon loaned money to create a sales advantage with the distributors. They could secure grocery shelf space if the store manager was
receiving easy loans tied to the placements. The store loans were
attractive to the distributors because they were protected if the stores
defaulted on the loans. The distributors would want to continue buying
Tillamook milk, which was good for Dixon because he had too much
of it as a result of many farmers switching to Grade A to get the higher
payout it offered. At the same time, he hadn't been able to sell enough
cheese to easily pay cheese milk producers at the rate they were expecting. The issue came to a head in 1962 when the Cheese & Dairy board
discovered that Dixon had also given Carnation, one of the distributors,
a sweetheart deal for fluid milk, despite a board directive not to do so.

Milne, serving as president of Cheese & Dairy, led the board
majority's complaint against Dixon. Most of the board members were
younger, successful farmers who embraced change at a time when cul-
tural and societal change in the United States was beginning to gain
momentum. America's president, the relatively young John F. Kennedy,
had just launched the space race to compete with Russian advances in
rocketry and exploration. He declared that America would put a man
on the moon by the end of the decade, at once unthinkable and thrill-
ing. Change was rumbling through America, and people reacted with
interest or dismay.

In Tillamook, some farmers boldly believed they could effect change
in their corner of the dairy industry. They were opposed by other farmers, both cheese milk producers and Grade A producers, who believed
just as passionately in the status quo.

The Cheese & Dairy board majority decided to take their issues
to the full County Creamery board at the organization's 1962 annual
meeting. They wanted to fire Dixon for his loan program and for selling
their milk cheaply. To them, it was logical to reach beyond their board
because they wanted to remove Dixon as dealmaker, one of his chief

roles as manager of County Creamery. They did not trust him to negotiate sales contracts or make appropriate store loans. The Cheese &
Dairy board majority swung for the fences in trying to fire him from his
countywide job. If Dixon lost the top job, the riled-up board members
figured, he would probably resign his positions managing individual
cheese factories. If he didn't resign, they knew they had the votes to fire
him from Cheese & Dairy.

Annual meetings had long agendas, meaning the farmers left home
soon after the morning milking, skipping all of their usual chores and
tasks, and did not return until it was nearly time for the evening milking. Attending the annual meeting was a big break from the farming
routine, and it was important and interesting. Lunch was provided,
and the meeting included socializing as well as business. Most farmers
chose to attend and brought their spouses.

In the afternoon of the June 13, 1962, annual meeting, the County
Creamery board considered firing Dixon. Milne made the motion and
laid out the reasons why it should be done. Several board members spoke
in favor of the motion. Several other board members spoke against the
idea; either they thought the loan program was reaping enough benefit to ignore the details or they didn't consider Dixon's actions to be
egregious enough to fire him. A representative of Carnation, one of the
Portland distributors that had benefited from the questionable loans,
had driven two hours to Tillamook to speak on Dixon's behalf. Dixon
stood in the back of the room the entire time, listening along with the
board members and the farmers.

Milne had a good idea of how the County Creamery board members would vote. In an earlier Cheese & Dairy board meeting, a motion
had passed 9 to 1 in a secret ballot to recommend that County Creamery demand Dixon's resignation. The Cheese & Dairy representatives
were the largest bloc on County Creamery's board, and the sole Red
Clover Cheese Factory representative had promised to vote with them.
County Creamery's board included fourteen members, but the board
chair could not vote. Milne could tell that some of the remaining thirteen County Creamery board members would indeed vote against his
motion, but he had counted and recounted, and while the vote would
be close, he had the seven votes to send Dixon on his way.

The roll call began.

The first six votes went as predicted: all "ayes" for firing Dixon. Then it was Millard Bailey's turn to vote. He was a Cheese & Dairy representative to the County Creamery board. Milne counted him as another aye vote, but when Bailey's turn came, he said, "nay." The reaction to his surprise vote rippled through the audience. Bailey's unexpected vote tipped the balance. The motion failed. Beale Dixon would remain in his office in the Tillamook Cheese factory.

The meeting erupted into chaos. Farmers yelled at each other and the board members while the board chair banged his gavel and futilely called for order. The meeting was "gut-wrenching,"[6] according to Filbert "Fib" Johnston, a young farmer at the time and the son of Cheese & Dairy patron Glenn Johnston.

Years later, the vote at the annual meeting is remembered as the first public volley in the Cheese War. Cheese & Dairy board members who opposed Dixon were not going to back down, but what should they do next? On the other side, Dixon and County Creamery had barely survived a mutiny; how would they respond? The county's farmers had broken into two camps, symbolized by the small cheese factories scattered throughout Tillamook County and the large factory north of Tillamook.

CHAPTER 2

The Whys and Wheys of Dairies and Cheesemaking

Tillamook is a dairy Eden, a great place to grow pastures of grass that inspire cows to produce milk. In the early 1850s, David Wilson brought the first domesticated cows into the area.[1] As the herds grew, the farm wives made all the usual butter and cheese and buttermilk and cottage cheese from the milk, but they had lots left over. Wasting the milk was unthinkable, and the pioneers' minds turned to people living in cities. City dwellers needed dairy products, but Tillamook's isolated location made delivery difficult. Tillamook's farmers needed to find transportation to reach Portland—or possibly even San Francisco or Seattle.

The farmers began to turn the excess milk into butter, and rather than rely on pack trains going over barely passable mountain trails in those pre-railroad days, they sent it out on ships going to Portland or California. Relying on the Pacific Ocean had its drawbacks, however: leave the mouth of Tillamook Bay, then go north to the mouth of the Columbia River, and if successful in navigating those two treacherous bars, go inland on the Columbia and Willamette Rivers to Portland. Alternately, go over the Tillamook bar and sail south for days to San Francisco. The ships' delivery and return schedules were always in question, but despite all the unknowns, water transportation on "butter boats" was a way to turn milk into money.[2]

Butter wasn't as stable as cheese, though, and ice wasn't available to keep butter cool. Cheese would last longer on the arduous journey to market. In 1889, Merriman Foland and Bob Richards became Tillamook's first commercial cheesemakers. Although their early attempts were inedible, they kept trying, eventually establishing a small cheesemaking factory[3] that was much like the ones along America's East Coast, where individual farmers had started pooling their milk and delivering it to nearby factories.

Tillamook's cheesemakers used their own recipes, sometimes creating brick cheese—a softer, sharper cheese than cheddar or Swiss cheese—with varying results. In 1894, Harry Ogden and T. S. Townsend, who were also Tillamook cheesemakers, brought Peter McIntosh into the county. McIntosh, a Canadian, introduced a full-cream cheddar recipe and taught cheesemakers how to make the cheese.[4] Later, he said, "You could store your cheese and wait for the boat without any danger of losing out through your product spoiling, as butter might spoil."[5]

Cheddar cheese was commercially successful, leading Tillamook's farmers to build more small cheese factories, with three dozen of them strewn throughout the county by the start of the twentieth century. "All roads in the county seem to lead to cheese factories,"[6] an early observer noted of the buildings sited on the main north-south highway, tucked into narrow river valleys or plainly visible in wide open meadows. Some of the factories were privately owned; others were owned collectively by the nearby farmers, who organized them as cooperatives.

In 1909, ten of the cooperative factories formed a marketing group and named it Tillamook County Creamery Association. Its purpose was "to procure higher profits for its members."[7] One of County Creamery's first actions was to hire a local attorney, Carl Haberlach, to market its cheese. Soon, Fred Christensen was hired as the cheese inspector, and he persuaded, educated, and forced the member factories to make McIntosh's cheddar cheese.[8] The independent factories held out as long as they could, but the cooperative model appealed to most of the farmers.

Like all cheese at the time, Tillamook's cheese was sent to stores as large rounds that the clerks cut into smaller wedges for individual purchase. While the outer rind was stamped "Tillamook," customers could tell it wasn't always the same product. As Harold Schild, a later manager of County Creamery, explained in *The Tillamook Way*, County Creamery's commissioned history published in 2000, "customers knew that even though everyone made cheddar, some factories had a distinct flavor and storekeepers were accustomed to people saying, 'This cheese isn't the same as the last cheese I purchased. I want Mohler cheese and I don't want cheese out of Central.'"[9]

Alder Vale Creamery. Tacoma Public Library, D67477-47, Richards Studio collection

By 1915, twenty-five factories had tucked under the Tillamook County Creamery marketing umbrella, and it had reorganized as a cooperative responsible for inspecting, standardizing, and selling the cheese.[10] By 1918, Tillamook County had twenty-seven creameries.[11] County Creamery hired Guy Ford, a dairy inspector, to gain consistent quality for the milk and help to eliminate the taste differences among factories.[12] By 1929, the number of factories was down to nineteen, but those remaining factories sold nearly 6.8 million pounds of cheese in 1928—about 4.3 million more than in 1909—and it was valued at nearly $1.8 million,[13] or more than $29 million in today's dollars. In south Tillamook County, the six factories increased their production year after year. By 1940, Tillamook became Oregon's leading dairy county.[14]

At the factories, the farmers, or their older children entrusted with delivering the milk, could usually find a reason to linger to catch up on news or, if lucky, eat cheese curds. Farmers took pride in their factories. They were there every day when their cows were producing milk; farmers and their families could see what was going on in the buildings. Factories always needed extra labor in the summer when the volume of milk grew like the grass in the pastures, serving as a source of local employment for the sons of farmers. But it wasn't just a business arrangement. Area farmers felt an emotional connection, much like the feeling of community pride that people had for their local schools.

In the early years, cheese factories practically shut down in the winter. Farmers dried up their cows—stopped milking them—and then had them all freshen—give birth to calves and have full udders of milk—in the spring. That way, the farmers didn't have to buy as much hay in the winter and could use the abundant spring grass to feed their cows.

When the cows were producing milk in the spring and summer, the factories hummed. One woman, Marie Culberson, recalled growing up at the Maple Leaf factory near Tillamook. She and her sister stayed out of the way when full production was underway.[15] But on slower days, Marie might ride around the yard in a farmer's wagon while her dad, the cheesemaker, added the latest contribution to the vats. Marie and her sister, Helen, knew each farmer, just as the farmers knew them, their family, and every other farmer who shipped to that factory.

The farmers hauled their milk in round metal cans with handles on the sides. The cans had lids that fit tightly. Every morning and evening, the cows would be brought into the barn, given some hay and grain, and milked. During the evening milking, the buckets of milk were poured into the cans, and the lids might be set lightly in place—or the cans might be left open—so the milk would cool. After the morning milking, the lids would be pushed firmly into place, and the farmer would load the milk cans onto a wagon, hook up the team of horses, and leave for the factory.

Milk for cheese, the thinking went, didn't need to be pasteurized because heating the milk during the production process would kill any troublesome bacteria or pathogens. The cheese would be safe to eat, and indeed it was. Government did not monitor the quality of cheese milk, although regulators had required milk sold as a beverage to be pasteurized since the early 1900s. Those regulations were enacted after children in America's expanding cities contracted potentially fatal illnesses like tuberculosis, scarlet fever, and diphtheria after drinking contaminated or adulterated milk.[16] Farmers and their marketers dif-ferentiated between pasteurized drinking milk and straight-from-the-barn cheese milk by labeling the latter as Grade B milk, not available in stores for customers to drink.

At every factory, the head cheesemaker inspected the cheese milk for cleanliness and quality. Usually, the inspection consisted of lifting the lid on a random can and sniffing the milk to check if it had spoiled. The cheesemaker did a visual inspection, too, because dirt, rats, hay, and other foreign objects might be lurking at the bottoms of the cans. Some farmers had reputations as messy milkers or poor keepers of their barns and cows, and their milk cans would receive especially thorough inspections.

The milk was also tested for butterfat content, or the percentage of fat in the milk, which along with volume was the basis of pay to the farmer. Cheese factories used the Babcock test to determine the amount of milk fat quickly and accurately.[17] Developed by Stephen Babcock at the University of Wisconsin in 1890, the test measured the amount of butterfat as well as detected any adulteration, such as watered milk or additives. Babcock deliberately did not patent the test so everyone could use it.

Farmers milked butterfat-producing Jersey and Guernsey breeds of cows. In the 1960s, as consumers' desire for lower-fat products grew, many farmers switched their herds to Holsteins, which produce more milk with less butterfat. But in the cheese factories of the early twentieth century, an entire shipment of milk from a farmer would be accepted if the butterfat content was high enough and the milk inspec-tion didn't identify an obvious problem.

If the cheesemaker did miss any wayward items, cheese factory workers were the next quality control to find and remove them, but it was not a foolproof system. All of these variables meant that some-times, despite the milk being heated and a cheesemaker's best effort to compensate for noticeable problems, the cheese would mold or develop off flavors. One cheese would be of World's Fair quality; the next might explode and roll off the shelf or weep and never harden. Fred Christensen, the cheese inspector, worked tirelessly on these issues.

The cheesemaking process created curds that became the cheese. The cheesemaker drained off the whey, which farmers could take back to the farm as free food for their pigs and chickens. The cycle—delivering milk and hauling home whey—continued when farm trucks became prevalent in the 1940s and 1950s. The big difference was that farmers didn't have to dedicate as much time to getting their milk to the factory. A factory wasn't needed every few miles, so farmers began to close or consolidate their factories. Still, the factory system dominated Tillamook cheese production. Farmers liked the control they had in their own factories. Farmers talked about "my factory." Cheese milk producers also took pride in making possible the Tillamook cheese that allowed the local dairy industry to flourish.

Dairy farming attracted the attention of US Navy veteran George Milne. Milne was an excellent mechanic, with the desire to work on diesel engines since his teenage years. He joined the navy four months before Pearl Harbor, and his physical strength, good mind, and ability to work well with other servicemen made him a confident leader. But Milne was tested severely by his World War II naval service. He grew up in the service, growing physically by several inches and growing metaphorically when he became a noncommissioned officer and when he survived the sinking of his ship in a battle with Japanese forces at Guadalcanal in the South Pacific.

By the end of the war, Milne had risen through the ranks to be a chief machinist's mate. When the navy asked him to attend officer candidate school, however, he declined. While at war, he had decided he wanted to be a dairy farmer, building on his high school membership in Future Farmers of America, and the dream had kept him motivated. After returning to the upper Willamette Valley with his wife, Barbara, and running two small farms near his birthplace, he was able to buy a dairy farm in Tillamook.

The Milne family arrived in Tillamook on Armistice Day, November 11, 1947. George and Barbara named their farm Tillagem—a combination of Tillamook and George's initials. They bought registered Jersey cows because they produced a lot of butterfat and were gentle. "When we started our farm," George Milne recalled about the late 1940s, "the little factories paid straight on the butterfat basis. Each factory set its own price, but they paid about $1.20 per pound of butterfat. Several years later, the price dropped to 78¢ or 80¢ per pound. People complained about things being tight, and wondered if things were being run right, or whether the cheese was as good as it had been. Would the milk be worth more if it were used for something besides cheese production?"[18]

Farmer Hans Leuthold considered these questions and decided to go Grade A.[19] Farmers could be paid more for providing bottled milk, also called fluid or Grade A milk, which was sold as a beverage. Going Grade A wasn't an easy or inexpensive answer to their thin paychecks, however, and County Creamery did not encourage its farmers to go that route. Dairy farmers had to meet several criteria to be paid the Grade A rate: the farm had to produce milk year-round, bacteria counts had to be low, sanitation had to be maintained, and premises had to qualify and pass inspections.

"In the old days," recalls Dave Leuthold, Hans's son, Grade B cheese milk farmers "put lime wash on the barns and let the cobwebs take over." Hans laid cement floors and put plywood over the wall studs. "Quite fancy buildings, compared to cheese producers," Dave Leuthold says.[20] Milking year-round created more expenses for the farmer. The cows had to be fed extra hay in the winter, crops had to be grown and harvested—or bought—and stored, and the switch from seasonal milking might mean the farmer couldn't keep a side job for predictable income.

In Tillamook County, Grade A milk bypassed the local cheese factories. The milk was shipped to the cheese factory in Tillamook because it had the equipment to process and bottle milk. The Grade A farmers formed their own cooperative, the Grade A Shippers Association, and it functioned the way the cheese factory cooperatives did, including having its milk marketed by County Creamery and having representation on the County Creamery board of directors. Yet going Grade A wasn't a complete answer. The proverbial rat in the milk can was that "the margin between the Grade A and cheese milk prices was constantly shrinking," Milne said, "so it became less likely that a farmer would do it."[21]

The Grade A milk producers needed the price of milk to increase to cover their additional expenses, but their paychecks continued to falter because the Portland distributors who bought the milk paid as little as possible. The farmers were price takers, not price makers, and as Thomas Owens noted in his 1962 thesis about the Portland milk

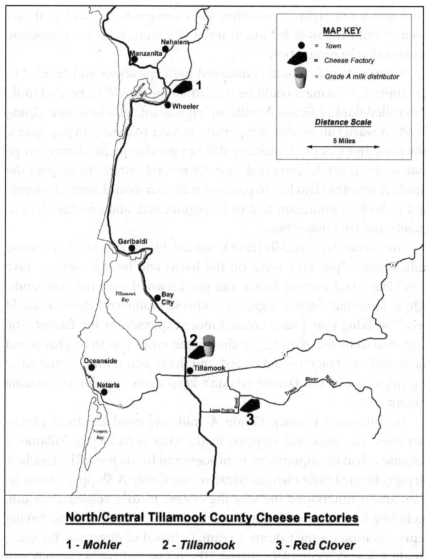

North/Central Tillamook County Cheese Factories

1 - Mohler   2 - Tillamook   3 - Red Clover

North and central Tillamook County cheese factories in the 1960s, by location and use.
Courtesy of John David Kirk

market, "For the most part then, distributor relationships in the market
for bulk milk are marked by coordination rather than rivalry. Rivalry of
a sort does, however, exist. This rivalry takes the form of attempts to
wring concessions in price or service from competing producer groups.
This is particularly effective when fluid supplies are plentiful relative to
demand since the alternative market (manufactured milk), is relatively

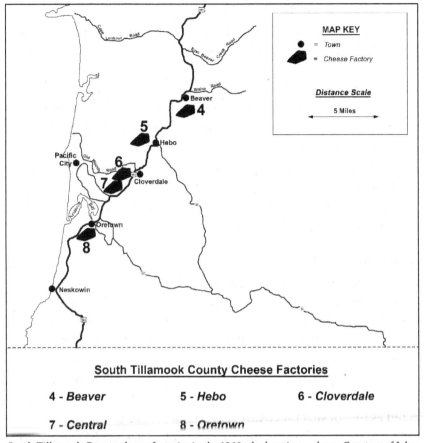

South Tillamook County cheese factories in the 1960s, by location and use. Courtesy of John David Kirk

unattractive pricewise."[22] Owens added, "Price changes in the Portland-Vancouver fluid market are initiated in an atmosphere that is redolent of a poker game. All the aspects are present including the opener, the bluff, the counter and the call or showdown."[23]

By 1958, Portland-area distributors had pleaded "nolo contendere"—avoiding an admission of guilt but accepting conviction—in federal court for conspiring to fix milk prices in the Portland area.[24] While Grade A producers were playing a losing hand against the distributors, cheese milk producers didn't have good cards, either. County Creamery set the cheese milk price lower than the price for Grade A milk. Manager Beale Dixon, trying to make both systems work, was in a tough spot right along with his farmers.

CRACKS IN THE STATUS QUO

As early as 1956, Dixon was pleading for the status quo when farmers wanted to charge more for their products:

> He felt that the timing for a price increase was bad. Everyone knows that the dairy farmer needs more money for his product, but price increases must come in an orderly manner and not through arbitrary methods or milk strikes . . . Going off in several directions and placing authority elsewhere weakens an organization of our type.
>
> "We have one of the world's finest Dairy organizations—let's think before we go off on tangents and tear it apart."[25]

The farmers who decided to go Grade A weren't thinking about changing an organization's way of functioning. These farmers were forward thinking—or desperate. They agreed to take on additional bank debt—borrowing against their cows or equipment or buildings—to meet Grade A regulations that might provide a long-term, larger pay day.

George Milne became a Grade A shipper. By 1958, he had been elected to the Grade A Shippers Association board. He was then elected as one of several GASA representatives to the County Creamery board. He was chosen for leadership roles, despite being a relative newcomer to the Tillamook farming community, in part because of his farming skills. He had developed a productive herd of registered Jersey cows. He was growing good pastures on heavy clay soil, across the aptly named Brickyard Road from a tile factory. Joe Jenck, son of dairy farmer Hooker Jenck, says his dad called Milne "the only real farmer in Tillamook" because "he knew how to grow things on not-too-good ground."[26]

In recognition of Milne's grass-growing ability, he won local and state awards, including second place in the 1955 Oregon Grassman of the Year contest. The *Albany Democrat-Herald* noted, "the 33 year old veteran . . . got two cuttings of silage, which is considered quite an accomplishment on this tight clay soil. In 1948, Milne's first year on this farm, herd production averaged 254 pounds of butterfat. In the past seven years, he has increased this to 397 pounds."[27]

THE WHYS AND WHEYS OF DAIRIES AND CHEESEMAKING

Being a good farmer under difficult conditions got a fellow noticed in Tillamook. The other farmers also saw Milne's ability to work hard and to keep going. They took note when Milne overcame a potentially career-ending accident.

On a Sunday morning, Milne was harvesting green chop—fresh-cut grass—in a hillside field out of sight of the neighbors. The rest of the family was in town, attending or teaching Sunday school, and expecting him to join them for church after he finished this chore. But the field chopper clogged. To clear the blockage, Milne disengaged the tractor's power takeoff. Because he was in a hurry, he didn't wait until the blades stopped turning before he opened a panel on the equipment. A piece of the machinery flew out of the opening, knocking out his front teeth. The impact threw him backward, and his right foot slipped under the chopper, where the blades were still rotating. His big toe was sliced off.

Milne did not lose consciousness. He pulled off his belt and tied a tourniquet around his leg, unhooked the field chopper, and used his wounded right foot to shift gears on the tractor. A neighbor took him to the hospital. The doctor who closed the wound on Milne's foot told him that he would never walk again, but Milne told the doctor, "I have to. I have to do the evening milking." He did that milking and walked the rest of his life without a limp.

Milne's toughness combined with his likability, ease in leading meetings, and relative youth helped him overcome the reticence of most of his peers about letting a first-generation farmer into the ranks of Tillamook farming leadership. He wasn't deeply rooted in Tillamook, but his star was on the rise in the growing Grade A world.

As Grade A gained shippers, it meant that fewer farmers were in the cheese milk business. The small-factory cheesemaking tradition— the heart of Tillamook's dairy industry—began to falter. The network of cheese factories was already showing signs of age. Building mainte- nance was becoming an issue. It was inefficient to make such relatively small batches of cheese and, even with consolidations, there were more factories than necessary. The quality of cheese still varied by cheesemaker as well as by cleanliness standards, setting up problems when County Creamery sold all of it under the Tillamook brand name.

The small factories were rapidly becoming symbols of an outdated economic model. In 1959, Dixon told the farmers at the annual meeting of the Grade A Shippers Association, "in our county association we still have too many small cheese operations . . . but . . . the problem of merging was one which the producers of those associations would have to solve for themselves."[28] The minutes reported that when a farmer asked for an explanation, Dixon noted that

> the wage rate problem, the small amount of milk per man hour worked, doubling of real and personal property taxes this year. He felt that elimination of duplicating expenses in the smaller plants would make it appear that the merging of the smaller operations would make money for their producers.[29]

Later, in the middle of the Cheese War, Dixon switched to supporting retention of the cheese factories. "The County Creamery board became weighted toward them," Barbara Milne explained. "The way to keep the majority of the County Creamery board, who were members of small factories, happy was to be sure the cheese side made enough money to give them good returns."[30]

By the 1960s, Beale Dixon became a juggler, doing his best to please the factories and the Grade A shippers, and to keep their finances looking healthy.

From Milking Pit to Ice Cream Counter

BY LINDA KIRK

The first time I milked a cow was in 1962, on the morning after the Columbus Day storm. Cyclone winds had knocked out electricity to much of western Oregon, including my parents' Tillamook farm. No electricity meant no milking machines. We would be milking by hand. At 12, I was tall enough to reach a cow's teats while standing in the milker's pit. The cows were elevated, a bit like actors on a stage. Dad told me to squeeze and pull. "You'll get the hang of it," he said. Sure enough. Milk streamed, not with every pull, but with most pulls. My job was to take some pressure off the cow's udder. My older sister, Cathy, carried full buckets outside and poured milk on the ground because no tanker truck would be coming to collect the unrefrigerated milk. My younger sister, Marilyn, hauled pails of warm water from the house to wash the cows' teats and udders. Mom helped us milk.

One cow I milked had blunt teats as narrow and short as a child's fingers. She milked out easily. Another cow had teats like overgrown carrots—long, wide, tapered, and orange. Her teats were stiff and warty. I squeezed and pulled. No milk. The cow shifted her back feet. I tried again. No milk. She didn't kick my hands, but she lifted her near back hoof. Dad took over.

When I was a child on the dairy farm, Dad was the milker. Our milk went to the big factory in Tillamook. I remember my mother stopping by the factory every week in 1960, when I was 10. It wasn't because she wanted to tour the factory—that was for tourists. It wasn't to buy ice cream cones—which weren't offered back then—or to sample the cheese cubes on toothpicks, although we sisters scooped up plenty of those. Nor was it to buy quarts of milk or pints of cream, because we had our own supply of milk and cream at home, fresh from our cows.

Every morning, after milking, my dad had two final chores. In steaming water, he sterilized the stainless-steel teat cups and rubber liners, and the strip bucket. Then he brought a stoppered metal pail of milk to the house. Mom poured the milk into gallon pickle jars she put in the refrigerator. By suppertime, one of us kids could ladle cream from the top of the milk.

Why did Mom go to the cheese factory every week? To save money. Like all members of Grade A Shippers Association, and later the Tillamook Cheese & Dairy Association, she got a discount at the cheese factory. Also, she went to the cheese factory to conduct her own farmer/owner quality control inspection. Was the sharp cheese truly sharp and not mislabeled medium cheese? Was the mild cheese creamy, not crumbly? Did the employees take time to be friendly but also work hard? Was the floor mopped—even in the corners? Was the lawn out front mowed?

At the factory, Mom usually bought one pound of old-fashioned butter—not sweet cream butter. She chose old-fashioned butter because it was cheaper and because it used whey butterfat, a cheese by-product that she knew was a glut on the market.

Next, Mom bought Tillamook cheese. She asked the woman behind the counter to cut about two pounds from the wheel of sharp cheese. Lowering the arm with the attached cleaver blade to cut a wedge that weighed precisely two pounds was no easy task. After a few months of cutting cheese, the salesperson learned to rotate the wooden base of the cutter just enough, then bring down the sharp blade with enough force—but not too much—to lop off a wedge close to the correct weight. Almost always, the employee would weigh the wedge and then ask something like, "Is two pounds and three ounces okay?" "That's fine," Mom would say. She never asked the employee to trim the wedge or cut a new one. Most trips, she also bought Monterey jack, especially if the sales room had her all-time favorite: Monterey jack with caraway seeds.

As items stacked up on the long counter, the employee noted them on a portable receipt dispenser. At the end of the transaction, she pulled the three-layer receipt from the machine and tore it along the perforations. The white copy went on a needle spindle with other producers' receipts. They would go to the main office, where the purchases would be deducted from farmers' milk checks. The pink copy went to Mom. The rectangle of blue carbon paper went into the trash can.

Always, Mom bought Tillamook ice cream. Buying ice cream meant that she had to make the cheese factory her last stop of the day. She needed to transport those boxes of ice cream twenty minutes before she could drop them in the chest freezer in her garage. Usually, she came home with something chocolatey. Often, she bought just plain chocolate ice cream. Sometimes, chocolate ripple, rocky road, and—my favorite—chocolate marshmallow ripple. For variety, she bought butter brickle or raspberry ripple. Rarely, strawberry. Never vanilla.

Eating chocolate marshmallow ripple ice cream at the supper table in our farmhouse in 1960, my world felt ordered, even static. I did not see conflict coming.

CHAPTER 3
Strange Bedfellows

Now a major Oregon tourist attraction, Tillamook's large cheese factory north of town was built in the late 1940s, when farmers from several area factories consolidated to make cheese manufacturing and milk processing more efficient. At the time, the Tillamook Factory was located at the south end of town. It was outdated and at capacity. Three centrally located cheese factories—Clover Leaf, Maple Leaf, and Holstein—were willing to consolidate if a larger factory were built that they could use, too. The board members of the combined factories named their new cooperative Tillamook Cheese Association (TCA).[1] County Creamery took the lead on construction of the new factory and, under the direction of General Manager George Lawson, built a $1.5-million plant several miles north of Tillamook in 1949.[2]

County Creamery moved its office from the Goff Building in downtown Tillamook, adding its office and a storage facility to the new factory. Tillamook Cheese Association and County Creamery shared

This photo, part of a full-page spread, told newspaper readers about the opening of Tillamook's new cheese factory. *The Oregonian*, October 30, 1949

the costs of the building, apportioning the utilities, repairs, and maintenance. In 1950, Lawson died suddenly, and in January 1951, Beale Dixon was hired to be County Creamery's next manager. He held the position for twenty-four years.

Dixon came to Tillamook with a background of banking in tiny Scotts Mills, Oregon, and then managing a Battle Ground, Washington, dairy cooperative. His banking career didn't turn out well; the bank ran aground. Dixon would explain the situation later to his biographer.

> And I graduated from high school in 1923. There was no work available for me, but a friend of the family got me a job working for a bank down at Scotts Mill [sic], Oregon, a little community east of Salem about 23 miles. And I became the assistant cashier. I was the bookkeeper. I was the typewriter man and everything in this little bank, which closed in the big depression of '31. Well, I should say the depression came all the way through from 1925 in that community.
>
> After working for the city banking department for a few months, and they didn't need me any longer, I went back to my hometown of Battle Ground to help my parents.[3]

Contemporary news accounts[4] reported that Dixon's time in Scotts Mills didn't unfold exactly that way. Scotts Mills did not have a city banking department. Beale's brother, J. O., or "Jack," ran the bank and brought Beale to town to work with him. The bank did close during the Depression, but the closure was at least partially a result of a bank customer discovering that his money had vanished, which led to further discoveries of money missing from customers' accounts. Beale prepared the monthly bookkeeping reports, and Jack approved them. Jack went to prison briefly for the banking irregularity; Beale and his wife, LaVerne, moved to Portland and then to Battle Ground, Dixon's hometown.

According to *The Tillamook Way*, Dixon drove a truck in Battle Ground and then worked in the warehouse of a cheese factory.[5] Eventually, he became its manager. When Dixon moved to Tillamook to be the general manager of County Creamery, most farmers felt he was a good match. Dixon was from a small town. He had experience running a dairy manufacturing plant. He was friendly. No, he wasn't local, but the farmers hadn't been able to find anyone local to run the cooperative.

Farmer Steve Steiner was one of the Tillamook residents who helped to move Dixon and his family from Battle Ground. Steve's son, Nick, says, "When County Creamery was recruiting for a new guy, the job was quite a step up for Beale. He wanted the job."[6] In contrast, Dixon said in his biographical interview that he turned down the first overture from County Creamery, accepting the position only after a second approach.

In Tillamook, Dixon and his family became part of the community. The children attended the local schools, and LaVerne became a well-respected piano teacher. In his spare time, Dixon played tennis. He was active in St. John's Episcopal Church, singing in the choir and volunteering to mow the lawn. *The Tillamook Way* described Dixon as having "a dominant personality and people reacted strongly to him." Pete Sutton, a later County Creamery manager, said in the history, "Dixon was a strong-willed person, and he saw things in black in [sic] white, good or bad. It was his nature."[7]

"Beale was the man of the time," Ed Yates, a former head cheesemaker, recalled in County Creamery's book. Dixon "got named some bad nicknames, like 'fluid-milk Beale,' because they had all this milk and he got Tillamook into the fluid-milk business."[8]

"Beale Dixon was fun to be around, bouncy," remembers Fib Johnston. Dixon told "a truth that had fingers of truth," Johnston says.[9] Marvin Pangborn, a farmer who later opposed Beale, told George Milne, "I just didn't like him, the way he talked. I just had a bad feeling about him from the start," according to Milne's recollection.[10] Hans Leuthold's son, farmer Dave Leuthold, also knew Dixon. Dave Leuthold recalls him as "a pleasant enough fellow" at a New Year's Eve party. "He could turn it on for the camera, make anyone think he was their friend."[11] Jim Becker, the son of Dixon opponent Ferd Becker, adds, "Beale was no dummy."[12]

Gradually, Dixon gained the trust of most of the farmers and community members. But somehow, a few people heard a rumor about Dixon's connection to a closed bank. A handwritten note by Barbara Milne, with an unknown date, says, "Dixon—Bank President—Scotts Mill [sic] (By Molalla) or Scottsvalley [sic]. Brother cashier. Bank went bottom up. Heard brother went to pen."[13] The rumor sat quietly, never tested or explored in a time before easy travel and inexpensive long-distance telephone calls.

According to County Creamery's own history, Dixon hit the ground running.[14] A September 14, 1962, article in the *Northwest Dairy News* quoted a source who said, "when Dixon took over his post more than eight years ago the association was in debt and even in danger of losing its bank credit."[15] Others in the community remembered the time line differently. Anita Neilson, County Creamery's stenographer, wrote in her scrapbook, "This statement is ridiculous. In 1950 we had just built our large plant—Tillamook Cheese Ass'n and Grade A Shippers. Later storage added. It was all planned that our facilities were to be financed on an 8 year revolving debenture plan. We never were at the point in danger of losing bank credit . . . at least not when Dixon came here."[16]

The new building put the two types of milk—Grade A drinking milk and Grade B cheese milk—under a single modern roof. As early as 1952, the TCA board of directors wanted to ensure that both groups were treated equally, talking about extending "every effort for continued improvement of the situation for both the shippers to the fluid milk market and to the cheese factories."[17] All of the cooperatives had representatives on County Creamery's board. By 1958, thanks to the volume of milk shipped by TCA and GASA members, those two large co-ops had a total of seven representatives. Each of the eight small factories had one representative.

Dixon felt successful in the early years of running County Creamery. Later, he told his biographer,

> I remember going to—you see, the manager of a creamery would make a report at each one of these cheese factory meetings shortly after the first of the year, along in February . . . And after I went the first couple of years, I began to get compliments from the members. And they would come to me after the meeting to shake my hand and say, "We never had information like this before." I think that had a lot to do with my success . . . I think I learned something in the bank. I think I learned how to talk to farmers.[18]

The farmers and cooperative board members were not always as malleable as Dixon preferred. The minutes of the May 9, 1955, GASA board meeting reveal Dixon scolding a board member for calling a producers' meeting, saying, "it was a mistake to . . . have outside people in where a controversial question is involved . . . Comments of management should not be made public."[19] Generally, though, Dixon didn't receive a lot of pushback from his farmers, in part because he provided positive news. The GASA minutes for February 21, 1957, reported:

> General Manager Dixon then gave his report. He stated that all divisions of the association were making good progress in every way. We sold more cheese last year than we produced. Cheese sales picture was reviewed. Selling expenses are down substantially due to a cut in advertising. We have no unsecured borrowing and only 20 cents per pound borrowed on cheese.[20]

Despite this rosy report, farmers had a few concerns. One was the reduction of the advertising budget, which wasn't going to help County Creamery sell more cheese. Another was the accuracy of the financial reports. On this point, GASA board member Ferd Becker's experience reading financial reports became critical.

FERD BECKER AND HANS LEUTHOLD

Becker was a former banker and brought that knowledge to his work on the board. Born in Germany in 1907, he moved to Russia as a small child when his parents joined a program to earn land by farming.[21] When Becker was 5 or 6, he was in the family's barn and heard horses coming fast. Becker scrambled into the hay mow and watched while a half-dozen Bolshevik soldiers chose fresh horses and rode away. Soon after, his family returned to Germany. Pete Becker, a tailor in Tillamook, helped his brother's family move there.[22]

After high school, Becker worked at a Tillamook bank, but he wanted to have his own farm and raise cattle. Before he turned 30, Becker bought a forty-five-acre farm on Ninth Street, on the edge of town.[23] By 1961, he had the top herd of registered Jerseys in Tillamook County.[24] In addition to forty-five cows, Becker had several dozen calves and four bulls—two herd bulls and two replacement bulls. When he found rare time to relax, Becker headed to the golf course or played the card game Pitch—high, low, jack, and game.[25]

Ferd Becker with one of his prize bulls. Courtesy of Jim Becker

At his farm in the 1960s, Becker stayed with what had worked for thirty years. He was one of the last Grade A shippers to install a refrigerated bulk tank.[26] He continued milking in his stanchion barn until he left farming around 1970, when his Parkinson's symptoms worsened.[27]

His son says that while Becker was active, "He went [to meetings] because he thought it was important for the farmers. He could speak for them better than a lot. They encouraged him to do that. He didn't mind antagonizing [management]."[28] Wearing striped bib overalls and his signature newsboy cap with a flattened, sloping crown,[29] Becker had the knowledge and temperament to lead inquiries and get answers.

When migraines forced Becker to give up his dairy board positions, he became an elder statesman, helping his farming peers develop strategies and build alliances. "He felt responsible," his son says. "He had helped to get it to this point, and he still wanted to help."[30] After the morning milking, Becker sometimes visited or talked on the phone to Vern Lucas, Glenn Johnston, or George Milne.[31] Becker typically floated a proposal or asked for information. He planned and looked for ways he could help. His meticulous files[32] helped him prepare several detailed letters to the Tillamook weekly newspaper,[33] and he sometimes volunteered to write minutes for co-op meetings.[34] Through the questions he asked and the answers he demanded, Ferd Becker helped his friends develop a strong Oregon dairy industry and thriving cooperatives.

GASA minutes from the 1950s show Becker questioning Dixon and others about their statements and actions. As a member of GASA's board, Becker noted that the County Creamery board had passed a motion "which gives the County Board power to override any action of the Grade A Shippers board or any of the factory boards."[35] He went on to say "that he didn't like to work under these conditions."[36] Hans Leuthold, another board member, asked if Becker wanted any action taken.

Leuthold's willingness to challenge the status quo was impressive, given his connections to the aristocracy of Tillamook farming. Leuthold was born in Portland to Swiss-German parents, but his mother was related to Tillamook's prominent Wyss family.

Leuthold didn't speak English as a young child, but he grew up loving to argue.[37] During the Cheese War, he had unlimited opportunities to argue about cooperative management and the decisions Beale Dixon made as manager. Leuthold had welcomed Dixon to Tillamook, but his friendly feeling for Dixon diminished over the years.

Leuthold milked registered Guernsey cattle—large, caramel-colored cows with white spots—on his McCormick Loop farm. He and his sons showed Guernseys locally and took cows to national events.[38] The Guernseys were accustomed to visitors during the evening milking at Wilsona Farms, and while Leuthold and his guests debated, the cows searched their concrete mangers with their tongues to capture any remaining morsels of grain. All the while, the talk and the milk flowed. While Leuthold did enjoy an argument, he also kept an open mind and was able to change course if persuaded. Barbara Milne said he "had intelligence, ability and was able to assimilate new ideas or shift positions."[39] Fib Johnston, Glenn Johnston's son, describes Leuthold as "solid, honest, like a father to me."[40]

Hans Leuthold (*left*); Otto Schild (*right*). *The Oregonian*, April 21, 1963

Leuthold was ready to support Becker at the GASA board meeting, but no further discussion is noted in the minutes, other than one director, Frank Jud, defending the resolution and saying "that if one of our directors couldn't work under those conditions he should resign."[41] That same day, Becker was chosen unanimously by the GASA farmers as their representative to County Creamery. He lost, though, to Otto Schild in the contest for GASA board president. Schild was from an old Tillamook family and inherited the family farm on rich Wilson River bottomland. He was tall with a ruddy complexion. He usually wore overalls. Barbara Milne remembered, "He called me 'Mrs. George.' He called all the women by their husbands' first names. He wasn't the kind of person you joked with."[42]

TILLAMOOK'S INTERNAL QUOTA

In 1954, Oregonians voted to end the state's World War II–era milk price controls.[43] In 1956, County Creamery established a quota for its Grade A farmers.[44] By design, the quota pool—the aggregate of all participants' milk—was open to any qualifying Tillamook farmer. Quota milk gave farmers a price advantage. As Otto Schild said in a meeting in 1958, "each 100 pounds of quota was worth nearly $500 last year over factory price . . . this fact encouraged the swing to Grade A from Factory."[45]

Under the system, milk checks for Grade A farmers reflected a blend of the higher quota milk price and a lower non-quota price for surplus milk. This blended price went up when quota milk weighted the average of the two types of milk.[46] The Tillamook quota system held risks. One worry was that farmers would produce more milk than distributors wanted, creating surplus milk. A second issue was that farmers would have to quit dairying if distributors set prices too low. In November 1957[47] and again in March 1958, the GASA board headed off any move to close its Grade A milk pool—the quota—to new members; the resolution was amended in November 1958 to say that the Grade A pool should be kept open "in order that as many producers as possible . . . can take advantage of the increased return for fluid milk."[48] In a nod to cheese milk producers, the board also recommended "that the price spread between the two grades of milk not be further increased until substantially all of our local fluid milk supply is being sold."[49]

ON STRIKE

In spring 1959, the manufacturing/drinking milk conundrum became a secondary issue because the farmers faced a strike at the large cheese factory. Seventeen County Creamery employees represented by the Teamster Union struck for higher wages. The Teamsters were a small crew, but they handled the fluid milk. Their contract negotiations, where they pushed for a pay increase of 34¢ per hour over a two-year period, had stalled for more than a year; County Creamery was offering them 10¢ more. Dixon noted that other departments had accepted 10¢ for the same period and called the Teamsters' demand "exorbitant."[50] In sympathy with the length of the negotiations and the lack of progress, other Teamsters in the cheesemaking, packaging, trucking, and feed departments walked off their jobs, too, leaving about 160 jobs vacant.[51]

Dixon convened the County Creamery board on a Sunday afternoon, April 30. "We were told, 'They've gone on strike. We need people to fill all these jobs,'" Milne remembered. So, board and association members did the Teamsters' work. Milne and board president Otto Schild drove a truck route. They delivered dairy products to area restaurants, working long hours to carry out the truck route and keep up with their farmwork. Milne recalled having to clean up after the morning milking, put on a white shirt, and then go to the creamery at about nine thirty in the morning. "I got done about four in the afternoon, went home and started working on the farm, then did the evening milking."[52]

The strike by Teamster Local 569 went on for sixty-nine days. Union members along the West Coast picketed retail outlets, asking consumers not to buy Tillamook products and asking other companies' warehouse employees not to handle the products. The strike affected cheese sales in eleven western states.[53]

The Teamster strikers received attention from Jimmy Hoffa, the national leader of the International Brotherhood of Teamsters, Chauffeurs, Warehousemen and Helpers of America. Hoffa "said he was 'keeping abreast of the progress in the strike'"[54] and had received updates from the Portland representative of the union. *The Oregonian* reported that the union was supporting the strikers financially.

At a special GASA meeting on June 23, 1959, to update the farmers about the strike, County Creamery's attorney, Warren McMinimee, compared the strike to a leaky dike, according to the meeting's minutes. "You have to keep moving here and there to plug the holes. The answer to our problems lies here in our own community. If just half of the 17 men actually on strike decide to throw the strike over we can end it here and now. Neighbors and friends should endeavor to talk the men into coming back to work."[55]

Indeed, *The Oregonian* ran a photo of Kermit Christensen, a Teamster member who had returned to work, saying he didn't think the union "was right."[56] The *Wall Street Journal* wrote a front-page article about the strike under the headline "Tillamook's Cheese Is Unfair, Teamsters Cry," and the article was read into the *Congressional Record* by California Representative Edgar W. Hiestand. The article highlighted the Teamsters' consumer boycott:

Oregon Teamster, [the] official union newspaper, calls the dispute with Tillamook Creamery Association an all-out economic war . . . In Medford Oreg. some farmers are already reported to be fighting boycott with boycott. They go into stores and, if Tillamook cheese is not being sold, they threaten to quit buying there . . . Bucking the Teamster demands is a band of determined and traditionally stubborn dairy farmers, men proudly boasting Swiss ancestry . . . The milk handlers get $2.19 to $2.24 an hour . . . the Teamsters contend, "Tillamook's milk handlers are the lowest paid for their category in Oregon."[57]

To settle the strike, Governor Mark Hatfield sought an injunction against the strikers through the National Labor Relations Board.[58] He also called in representatives from both sides to work with a federal mediator. "Hatfield read them the riot act," said Milne. "He told the County Creamery reps to get with it; get this strike settled. He got the strike settled."[59] Dixon wrote later in his annual report to County Creamery members, "the Union appealed to the Governor for assistance. In a conference with the Governor the Union reduced their demands to 11c [per hour] and the Board decided to accept."[60] Actually, news reports listed a settlement of 21¢ per hour, or a raise to $2.45 per hour—10¢ less than the strikers had initially requested. Each worker also received a $200 payment.[61]

Dixon took credit for settling the strike. His labor strategy had cost his farmers more than $200,000 in lost sales, or nearly $2 million today. Filling in for the union members had required the farmers to work two jobs, but Dixon told them in his Secretary's Report for the 1959-60 *Annual Report*,

The strike situation was developing a great deal of publicity, most of it favorable to us . . . The sixty-nine day strike ended with striking employees returning to their jobs July 8, 1959. It was a terrific effort on the part of all those who kept operations going during the strike . . .

There can be no question as to the great value to the Association through this experience.[62]

Almost a year later, Beale Dixon and his family were awakened at 2:30 in the morning by a bomb blast in their driveway. "The blast had dented the side of the car, ripped off chrome, broken windows and blown two hubcaps 20 feet away," according to the front-page story in the May 20, 1960, edition of *The Oregonian*. "A window of the Dixon house, about 25 feet from the car, was also blown out by the concussion. Dixon ruled out any possibility that the bombing may have been connected with former labor troubles at the plant. 'Our union situation here has been very fine since the settlement of last year's strike,' he said. 'I just have no idea who would be wanting to do such a thing, either to me or to any member of my family.' "[63]

Neither the perpetrator nor the reason for the bombing was ever discovered. But the pressure continued for Dixon to keep all of his stakeholders content. In his 1961-62 Secretary's Report, he said, "As soon as increased sales of fluid milk were assured, steps were taken to reduce the cost of selling cheese. . . . In the past, fluid milk prices have been allowed to increase even with overproduction . . . it is extremely important for us that prices for all milk be kept in a proper relationship, not to have fluid milk areas constantly increasing in both price and volume of production with the manufacturing milk producer's problem becoming more and more hopeless."[64]

The farmers recognized the difficulty of balancing production and pricing, and they looked for a solution.

CONSOLIDATION

More and more farmers were going Grade A and transferring their cheese factory milk to the fluid milk market. The impact became clear in the minutes of a Tillamook Cheese Association board meeting and special patron meeting on May 15, 1961, where Dixon reported that cheese "factory milk is now down from 1960 as over 50,000 lbs more milk is going into Portland every day from the Grade 'A.' This will have a bad effect on the factory making costs, but consideration of some of the other plants closing and having their milk come into TCA is now being talked of."[65]

Having one cooperative for both types of milk would be much more efficient. Both Grade A and cheese milk were being processed at Tillamook's big factory, and under the internal quota system, Grade A milk that wasn't sold to the distributors as drinking milk was being used to make cheese. Why not form one cooperative? As president of GASA, Milne worked with the board members of both Tillamook Cheese Association and Grade A Shippers Association to explore the idea. As part of the proposed agreement, the Grade A milk would be marketed by the new organization.

Dixon favored merging cheese and fluid milk production into one system. In a pre-1963 undated letter, he wrote to an official at the Oregon Department of Agriculture about a visit with a US Department of Agriculture official who had recommended "additional requirements on manufacturing milk in order to gradually raise the level of qualtity [sic] in the hope that it would help bring about one grade of milk . . . . I am wondering if Oregon could not be one of the leading states in adopting these recommendations."[66]

Grade B farmers felt threatened by these discussions, thinking correctly that it could mean the closure of their cheese factories. Meanwhile, the wariness between the producers of the two grades of milk led Dixon to plead with his farmers "for all patrons to work in harmoney [sic] with their Boards of Directors and the Management as only by harmoney [sic] can progress be made."[67]

In 1961, Milne got board members Leuthold and Schild interested in consolidation. TCA board members—Glen Ackley, Millard Bailey, Hooker Jenck, Ernest Josi, and John Landolt—agreed. The idea was growing in popularity, but even the plan's supporters understood that consolidation might be risky. Milne said later, "I remember thinking to myself—I probably expressed it a little, but not very often because you had to be careful where you said it—but I thought, gee, the ideal would be if we got all together, we could get the little factories to come in, too. Think how efficient it would be! They already had bulk milk tanks in the valley instead of handling these stupid cans. We wouldn't have to maintain all these separate little buildings, and have depreciation and help for the head cheesemakers and all that stuff, and the cheese trucks going back and forth."[68]

Discussions at the October 2, 1961, meeting of GASA's board provide an example of the debate. The minutes included reasons "for the fluid milk shippers needing to help the cheese factory":

1. Present milk going to Portland eliminates surplus "A" for the milk factory.
2. This lack of volume going through the cheese plant puts them in trouble.
3. T.C.A. with high overhead would not allow them to compete with the rest of the T.C.C.A. factories which would tend to reduce the surplus payout for fluid milk.
4. A merger would permit both organizations to do what was best for both grades of milk.
5. The T.C.A. membership favored progressing with the merger if the "A" patrons favored too. Hope to accomplish the merger by January 1, 1962.[69]

The meeting attendees also expressed concern about the impact of merging:

1. What effect would a merger have on labor. Answer was that there would be little change from the present.
2. How near are any of the smaller plants to closing? This is an unknown answer. It probably depends on what inducements the new organization might offer to some of the smaller plants to get them to close. It was pointed out that the Grade "A" patrons should not let the T.C.A. payout slip for even one year because the trend is towards consolidation. We are operating too many plants and dissipating too much money through duplication. Most smaller plants can be liquidated 100%. It was suggested that perhaps the new organization could guarantee the smaller plants 100% liquidation. Any losses that might be sustained would more than be offset by the increased volume of milk.[70]

"There was an awful lot of explaining to do to people," Milne remembered. "Well, frankly, it was a job of education. People would say, 'I can't believe that, or I can't accept that.' It never got to, 'Let's forget [it].' It was not a question of dissolving the association."[71]

Why would the leery members of the two cooperatives agree to the merger? According to Milne, "A cheese shipper would say, 'Now I belong to this, and someday I'll go Grade A and have a market.' And the Grade A shipper would say, 'We need these people because they have the factory for cheese and we get so little extra for Grade A milk.' "[72]

The majority of the members of both cooperatives voted to go ahead with one combined co-op, effective January 1962. The proposed name was Tillamook Dairymen's Association, but by the next meeting, it became Tillamook Cheese and Dairy Association (a blend of Tillamook Cheese and Grade A Dairy Association), or Cheese & Dairy or TCDA. Beale Dixon was named its general manager. The newly formed Cheese & Dairy was the county's largest cooperative. "Of the 325 dairymen joined in merger, about 180 are now Grade A milk producers,"[73] reported *Northwest Dairy News*.

Milne was elected president of Cheese & Dairy. The first meeting, on January 4, 1962, was full of organizational details, but the overall tone was one of optimism and good will.[74] Barbara Milne reflected on the merger later and said, "In a way, it was not smart. They only had the same goal when they used their milk to make cheese. Otherwise, they had different goals. Cheese shippers were not particularly enthusiastic about supporting Grade A farmers' effort to make more money."[75]

Years after the merger, a judge presiding over a Cheese War court case made a posttrial statement that took the same view:

I can understand why those people who started Grade A would think, "Well, why duplicate all this overhead; we will just see if we can't go into this big cheese cooperative and use their facilities." And that is a sensible thing to do, and it looked sensible. But the problem is that the bedfellows so established were fundamentally incompatible.[76]

FIELD NOTE 3

Farm Chores

BY LINDA KIRK

School was out for the summer. I said goodbye to Mrs. Wilkerson and the fourth grade, stuffed my school papers into a brown grocery bag, and rode the bus home on a clear, windy afternoon in 1960.

The next day, Dad had us three sisters feeding grain and milk to the calves morning and night. Feeding grain was easy. We scooped calf grain with old Folger's coffee cans and poured the pellets into the small wooden manger in each calf's pen. Feeding milk was more of a challenge. It took patience. In the milk house, we measured milk into suckle buckets. Then we hauled the buckets to the barn. Next came entering each calf's pen and poking the bucket's rubber nipple into the mouth of the calf. Most calves grabbed the nipple with their upper gums and lower teeth and sucked the bucket dry in strong pulsing pulls. Other calves—not many—gummed the nipple and then butted the bucket once, even twice, before settling down to rhythmic sucking.

Dad said feeding calves was not a paying job. The way he figured it, feeding calves was part of helping the family. Feeding calves was like getting the cows from the field or washing dishes. Other jobs, however, were paying jobs. He said he would pay us to shovel out calf pens when the manure and sawdust bedding stacked up. He would pay us to scrub the floors and walls in the milking parlor with stiff brushes dipped in bleach water. Also, he would pay us to pull tansy plants.

A penny a plant—that's what Dad offered my older sister, Cathy, and me to pull the tansy ragworts that had invaded our pastures. Alkaloids in tansies, a species native to Europe and Asia Minor, were killing Tillamook County dairy cows by destroying their liver cells. New plants could generate from root fragments or from seeds. Before the introduction of flea beetles, ragwort seed flies, and cinnabar moths, yellow-blooming tansies seemed invincible in coastal Oregon.[1]

Dad's a-penny-a-plant offer went something like this: "I want you to start in the fields closest to the road. Pull every tansy—tall or short. Be sure to pull out the roots. If the tansy has a root, I will pay you a penny. No root, no penny. Stuff the plants in a gunny sack and haul the sack loads to the driveway near the milking parlor. Pile the plants on the gravel where I can take a look at them."

We trudged out to the field, toting our gunny sacks. Some weeds were two feet tall, some almost three feet. Often it took a pull from the left and a pull from the right, and then a repeat pull from the left. At the end of the first day, we tallied our stack of tansies: five hundred plants—all with roots. We had earned $2.50 each. Not bad, but not highly profitable.

The next day, we headed out again. We had learned that some tansy plants grew with a single stem, but some had multiple stalks that shared one root system. We decided to separate these stalks while being careful to keep root hairs attached to each of them. Hadn't Dad said he would pay a penny a plant as long as it had a root? At the end of the day, we hauled our last loads to the driveway. We counted twenty-two hundred stalks—all with roots. At a penny per stalk, the total was $22. We were rich!

Dad looked at our pile of tansies. He saw root hairs extending from every stalk. He examined our tally sheet. Slowly, he pulled his wallet from his back pocket. He counted out $11 for Cathy, and $11 for me. Then he gave each of us a look—a long look. "From now on," he said, "I will pay you by the hour."

Over the next two months, the hours added up. When August brought the county fair, Cathy and I had folding money in our pockets. We could buy cotton candy, and we could ride the Tilt-a-Whirl. I remember I had enough tansy-pulling money to buy cookies at the Home Extension booth, where women sold homemade cookies at two for a quarter. The chocolate chip cookies sold out before noon, but oatmeal raisin cookies were always on offer.

Cathy and I saved most of our summer money to buy school clothes. We studied the fall/winter catalogs for Sears Roebuck and Montgomery Ward. When Mom took us to town, she almost always stopped at the library, J. C. Penney, Safeway, and the cheese factory. At J. C. Penney, we checked the racks upstairs for ready-made blouses and skirts. We checked the pattern books and bolts of fabric downstairs to see if we could do better by asking Mom to sew and helping her with cutting out, pressing, and hemming.

Fifth grade started. Mrs. Dawes taught my class. At home, Dad took over feeding the calves in the morning, but my sisters and I still fed them in the evening. My parents were talking about milk prices and the possible merger of two co-ops, but I was not paying attention. It would be two years before it was commonplace for a dozen farmers to gather in our living room and talk with loud voices. Two years before I had any idea of what a lawsuit was. Two years before I met an attorney. Two years before I entered a courtroom.

CHAPTER 4

Hard Times

George Milne was an award-winning dairy farmer, but the accolades didn't increase his bottom line. He struggled to pay his bills every month even though he had gone Grade A, built Tillamook County's second milking parlor, bought more cows to increase production, and grew lush fields of grass on clay soil. He was a success in the eyes of others, yet his success didn't help him overcome the economic reality of not earning enough to breathe easy about paying his bills. As Floyd Woodward, another farmer, said, "Seventy-five percent of the ranchers in Tillamook county are either working out, the wife is teaching school or they are dipping into Dad's pocketbook . . . it's a case of survival in our area."[1]

"Working out" was when one took a job off the farm to supplement income. Milne agreed to take over his rural area's school bus route after several drivers had been chased away by two teenage brothers who were bullying the other students and whoever happened to be driving the bus. Sure enough, on Milne's first morning of driving, the boys tried to intimidate other children. Milne pulled the bus to the side of the country road, walked to the back of the bus, and told the misbehaving boys in a firm, loud voice that they were not going to do that to anyone anymore. They looked at the rock-solid war veteran with his bulging farm muscles and steady glare. They decided not to test him, and there were no more incidents. But eventually Milne had to quit because the job took too much time away from the farm.

Barbara Milne worked for the 1960 US census, doing in-home follow-up visits while her children were in school. The money she earned was temporary, though. What George Milne really needed was a larger payment for his milk, but that decision was controlled by Carnation and Alpenrose and the other milk distributors.

"At that time," Milne explained later, "distributors for milk companies would call in a representative of each co-op and say, 'So-and-so up the Columbia is selling for less, so you'll have to match that.' The farmers were forced to compete against each other, and distributors gained from it. 'We're Mr. Big; we have to compete with Foremost or Standard Dairy—just have to have it a little cheaper. What can you fellows do?' They had us over the barrel all the time."[2] Milne recalled, "There were lots of complaints, but what could be done? Farmers squawked and hollered, 'We'll just have to hold the line.'"[3]

Milne could see disaster looming for himself, and he knew other dairy farmers felt the same way. They were working hard to earn a living doing what they loved and were good at, but the profit margin was too narrow. Would they have to give up dairy farming?

Milne took action. On March 21, 1961, Milne told the GASA board that he and several other board representatives had met with Junction City farmer Howard Gibson, who proposed a system to set statewide milk prices. According to the minutes of the meeting, though, "Mr. Dixon spoke once again on the things against this type of thinking and organization. The leadership of these groups comes from persons with no plant or cooperative ties, no responsibility to make a profit from surplus milk handled. These people have no investment in cooperatives in the form of allocations, etc."[4]

However, the majority of Tillamook farmers felt they faced a choice of continuing to lose money by competing with their peers outside of the area or cooperating with them for a possibly better future. After hearing opposing viewpoints from Milne and Dixon at the GASA board meeting of April 10, 1961, the board members declared their interest in a statewide system. The board passed a four-point policy that emphasized independent marketing of surplus milk and an open pool:

1. We would always be glad to meet with any group for the purpose of discussing suggestions on milk marketing that we feel might be an improvement.
2. We are committed to the principle of an open pool. All fluid sales should be shared equally in a market pool—not distributor pools. These pools should be open to all producers who wish to market fluid milk.

3. Surplus should be furnished by all producers in ratio to
    their share of sales in the pool.
4. We insist on marketing our own surplus inasmuch as we
    have spent fifty years in building up a solid market for same.[5]

Throughout the Pacific Northwest, farmers had problems with
surplus milk. In 1961, Puget Sound, Washington, farmers sold less than
half of their Grade A milk for $5.63 cwt (all payment was written as
"cwt," based on the hundredweight, or the price paid per one hundred
pounds of the commodity); the majority of the milk was surplus and
sold for $3.53 cwt. Washington's Yakima Valley farmers sold Grade A
milk for $4.25 cwt; about two hundred thousand pounds a day went
into surplus at $3.17 cwt.[6]

In Oregon, Mayflower announced that it would drastically cut its
price to dairy farmers. The minutes of the April 17, 1961, meeting of
the GASA board reported that "Secretary Ely briefed the board on the
recent price cut in the fluid milk market. He stated that the decline
was from $5.97 for fluid milk to $4.85 per cwt. We have no choice but
to go along with the decline and attempt to work our way out of the
situation."[7]

At $4.85 per cwt, farmers saw a $1.12 cut. Given that Oregon State
University placed the cost of production at $5.49 a hundred,[8] or 64¢ more
than Mayflower proposed to pay the farmers, the milk producers faced an
emergency.

The farmers chose to fight against having prices dictated to them.
When representatives of other Oregon cooperatives called a meeting,
Milne sent GASA representatives to attend. The farmers focused on the
state legislature, which met biannually. It was approaching the end of
its 1961 session; the farmers would have to act quickly to get any relief
through a new law.

They proposed a bill that would put the Oregon Department of
Agriculture in charge of setting prices paid to farmers for Grade A milk
sold to processors or distributors. The bill would continue distributor
pools, with an option to establish market pools. The department would
hold hearings and set a minimum price that processors would pay in
each region. The law would affect about 1,800 milk producers and 250
dealers. It would sunset on December 31, 1962.[9]

The farmers found immediate support for the legislation from Representative Kessler Cannon of Bend. He developed House Bill 1752, which Tillamook's representative, Ed Ridderbusch, also supported. During one of the hearings, held at night, about three hundred farmers from around the state traveled to Salem to enthusiastically express their support for the measure.

Dixon and Carnation Manager Hugh Gallagher testified at a hearing that the bill would be a fine idea. According to the record, Dixon, chairman of the Oregon Dairy Industry group, said that

> his group of about 32 people were in favor of this bill. In ans. to [sic] question he stated the problem being faced is one of production, rather than distribution and that the industry has been guilty of attempting to maintain too high a price. Without the help of this bill and a more realistic pricing of milk it cannot keep milk from out of state from coming into the pool . . . It will not restrict the number of people who can sell milk, but will go into effect as a distributor pool bill.[10]

Actually, the farmers were willing to negotiate a reasonable price: more than the losing proposition from Mayflower, and less than a sky-high price that would endanger their relationships with the distributors. Gallagher, an ODI member whose company was a rival to Mayflower, noted, according to the hearing transcript, "as a distributor in the milk industry he was wholeheartedly in favor of [the bill]. He feels the present situation is completely intolerable and something must be done."[11]

Despite concerns that the new law would create artificial price controls or raise the price of milk to the consumer, House Bill 1752 became the Producer Milk Stabilization Law. It was signed by Governor Mark Hatfield on May 23, 1961, having gone through the entire lawmaking exercise in about two weeks. The law charged the Oregon Department of Agriculture with determining the minimum price paid to a region's farmers, based on five criteria: production costs, consumer demand, the price of non–Grade A milk, the milk supply compared to milk consumption, and Grade A milk prices in adjacent states.

In addition to distributor pools, the law provided for market pools as an alternative. A market pool would include all the farmers and distributors in a region. Each farmer would be assigned a base consisting of the producer's daily average "sold during the four lowest months of each calendar year." If farmers created a market pool, the department would oversee a system that equalized payments to the farmers: "the department may determine amounts to be withheld from producers by a milk dealer and paid to the department for the benefit of producers selling milk to other milk dealers in the market area in which the market pool is established in order to equalize payments between producers."[12]

After passage of the bill, the Oregon Department of Agriculture held hearings to determine the minimum price for Grade A milk in each market. At least one person testified that payment should rise to $6.43. Reality set in, however, as Beale Dixon and others testified against that rate of pay. "The price must be conservative," Dixon said, "or somewhere along the line we may have a market pool or eventually a federal milk marketing order." He mentioned that prices in other states were $5.43 to $5.23 per hundred. "We should not set our price so high it will attract milk from these other areas."[13]

Dixon's warning against a market pool was a contrast to his statement two months earlier at a legislative hearing for the proposed law. In April, he had supported market pools, saying, "most state-wide distributors feel a milk marketing pool, permitted under the bill by referendum, eventually would have to replace the distributor pool if the industry's present problems are to be solved."[14] Dixon's verbal dance about market pools confused the issue, but the farmers' fear of cheaper, outside milk flooding the system had an impact on the type of pool they chose. In the eighteen months of the temporary law, only one region—the one including Tillamook and Portland—petitioned the department to ask its farmers to consider using a market pool rather than a distributor pool. Farmers voted 584-464 against the move, however.[15] It turned out that while many farmers were ready to embrace a new model in marketing their milk, even more preferred the familiar model of selling to a distributor.

While the final rate varied across the state, the price in Tillamook's market area became $5.80, which was much better than Mayflower's offer of $4.85, which had jumpstarted the legislation.

LOANS AND CONSEQUENCES

Although the national consumption of cheddar cheese had grown from 5.1 pounds per capita in 1953 to 6.1 in 1962,[16] sales of Tillamook's cheese had fallen 10 percent between 1950 and 1962, while the population of its primary market—the three West Coast states—had grown 47 percent. Tillamook's unsold cheese inventory increased 96 percent. Meanwhile, the cost of selling the cheese rose 375 percent,[17] as Cheese & Dairy noted in a series of newspaper ads aimed at its cooperative's patrons as well as County Creamery farmers.

Some of the Tillamook farmers blamed Beale Dixon for the problems. He was in charge of sales, and he knew he needed better results or he would lose the farmers' loyalty. His anemic product sales weren't generating enough money, and he had a glut of Grade A milk. Perhaps he could kill two birds with one stone. He went to Alpenrose, a family-owned dairy and distributor in Portland that already bought Tillamook's milk and relabeled it as its own, then sold it in Portland-area grocery stores. He came away with a plan, which he explained at the June 6, 1960, meeting of the GASA board.

> Mr. Dixon went thoroughly into the problem of selling more bulk milk in the Portland area. He stated that somehow we had to sell more fluid milk and to maintain an open pool in order to sustain milk production in Tillamook County. He asked the board just how far they think he should go in making various overtures to prospective customers. It was the general feeling of the board that we should be ready and willing to spend up to several hundred thousand dollars in credit grants or loans in order to get a sizeable milk order.[18]

Dixon had adopted an "if you can't beat them, join them" philosophy, and with the board's approval, he found a willing partner in Alpenrose Dairy. The Portland-based dairy was trying to grow its market share while competing against deep-pocketed Mayflower and Carnation. The new partnership meant Alpenrose would use its existing distribution system to sell more milk, and Tillamook would supply milk and cash for store loans. As Dixon told the board in March 1961, "we are borrowing approximately $200,000 on the amount of cheese that would be

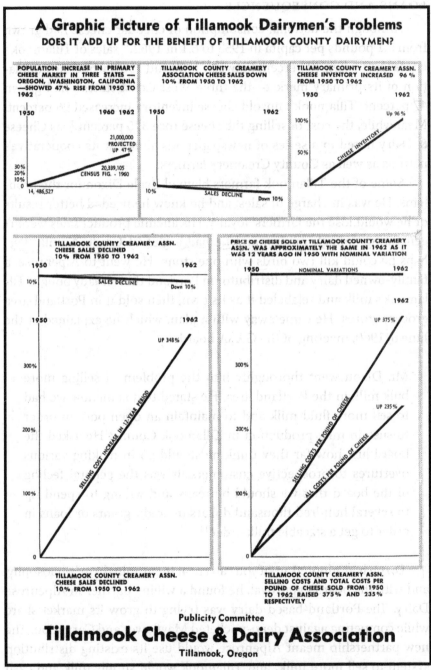

A Graphic Picture of Tillamook Dairymen's Problems
DOES IT ADD UP FOR THE BENEFIT OF TILLAMOOK COUNTY DAIRYMEN?

POPULATION INCREASE IN PRIMARY CHEESE MARKET IN THREE STATES — OREGON, WASHINGTON, CALIFORNIA —SHOWED 47% RISE FROM 1950 TO 1962

1950   1960 1962

21,000,000 PROJECTED UP 47%

30%
20%
10%
0

14,486,527

20,339,105 CENSUS FIG. - 1960

TILLAMOOK COUNTY CREAMERY ASSOCIATION CHEESE SALES DOWN 10% FROM 1950 TO 1962

1950   1962

0
10%

SALES DECLINE   Down 10%

TILLAMOOK COUNTY CREAMERY ASSN. CHEESE INVENTORY INCREASED 96% FROM 1950 TO 1962

1950   1962

100%

Up 96%

50%

CHEESE INVENTORY

0

TILLAMOOK COUNTY CREAMERY ASSN. CHEESE SALES DECLINED 10% FROM 1950 TO 1962

1950   1962

10%

SALES DECLINE   Down 10%

1950   1962

UP 348%

300%

200%

100%

SELLING COST INCREASE IN 12-YEAR PERIOD

0

TILLAMOOK COUNTY CREAMERY ASSN. CHEESE SALES DECLINED 10% FROM 1950 TO 1962

PRICE OF CHEESE SOLD BY TILLAMOOK COUNTY CREAMERY ASSN. WAS APPROXIMATELY THE SAME IN 1962 AS IT WAS 12 YEARS AGO IN 1950 WITH NOMINAL VARIATION

1950   NOMINAL VARIATIONS   1962

1962

UP 375%

300%

UP 235%

200%

SELLING COSTS PER POUND OF CHEESE

100%

ALL COSTS PER POUND OF CHEESE

0

TILLAMOOK COUNTY CREAMERY ASSN. SELLING COSTS AND TOTAL COSTS PER POUND OF CHEESE SOLD FROM 1950 TO 1962 RAISED 375% AND 235% RESPECTIVELY

Publicity Committee
Tillamook Cheese & Dairy Association
Tillamook, Oregon

Cheese & Dairy's publicity committee bought an ad in the Tillamook newspaper to inform farmers about Tillamook Cheese's shrinking market share, falling revenue, and rising costs. *Shopping Smiles*, May 5, 1963

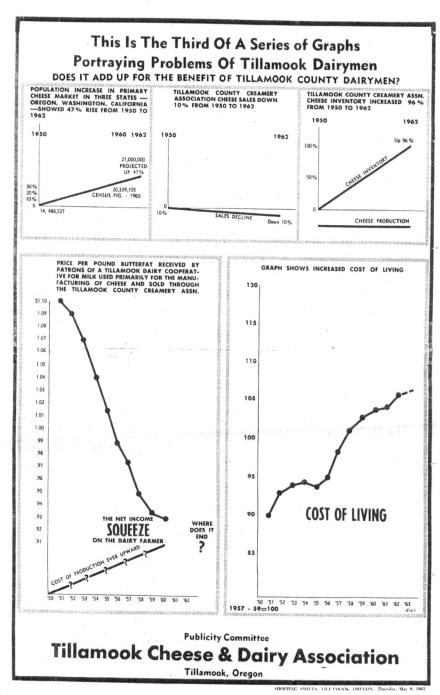

In this ad, Cheese & Dairy demonstrated the collision course of the cost of living and the price the farmer was receiving. Charts showed lower sales and higher production costs. *Shopping Smiles*, May 9, 1963

produced by 20,000 pounds of milk each day over a nine-month period, which is the average age of our cheese in storage. Therefore it is reasonable to assume that we could afford to lend $200,000."[19]

The proposed loan program would work for County Creamery, Alpenrose, and the stores. It would enable Dixon to dispose of excess Grade A milk without having to tell the TCDA board that he couldn't sell it or that the board would need to institute new rules to avoid producing so much milk. In turn, Alpenrose would be able to offer loans of Tillamook's money to entice stores to stock Alpenrose products at no risk or cost to the distributor. The stores, operating on thin profit margins, would welcome the loans. Further, "there was no written agreement of any kind between the Creamery Assn. and Alpenrose"[20] or any significant collateral. Alpenrose immediately accepted the deal.

Loans were not new in the grocery or restaurant industries. After Oregon's Depression-era Milk Control Act was axed by voters in the 1950s, competition for grocery shelf space became heated. For years, equipment loans and discounts to stores had been part of how milk distributors gained shelf space. In the Portland market alone, "The discount and loan practices are said to amount to $4 million annually," the *Capital Press* reported on January 20, 1961. "A survey . . . disclosed that the actual payers of discount deals are the milk producers."[21]

The system could have been scrapped in favor of producers selling directly to stores without including loans. But producers would incur huge costs to set up their own distribution systems, cutting into their cash flow and savings; stores might not be interested in stocking loan-free milk products, eliminating a way to dispose of excess milk; and existing distributors would compete to retain the stores' loyalty. Perhaps distributors could have eliminated the underhanded loans, creating a level playing field for all providers of milk for stores, but they wanted to retain their advantage. The Oregon dairy farmers' emergency milk pricing bill of 1961 had included fair trade language to end the loan system, but it wasn't in the House of Representatives' final version.[22]

Curly's Dairy, a Salem business that distributed milk products to area groceries and restaurants, sued Mayflower in 1961, accusing it of requiring businesses to buy all or most of their dairy products from Mayflower. Judge John F. Kilkenny's January 1962 verdict noted that Curly's offered loans, too, "and that such financing is welcomed by grocery stores and other outlets interested in the sale of dairy products."[23] Kilkenny ruled in favor of Mayflower.

In 1962, Howard Gibson of Junction City told a legislative committee, "one reason distributors can't solve their problem is the volume kickbacks and rebates and the financing business in lending money to grocers."[24] Yet Dixon had faith in loans, perhaps from his banking experience, and the GASA board was used to making small loans to stores and restaurants, using the businesses' equipment as collateral and declining to make unsecured loans.[25] One loan recipient was Roy Espe, a restaurateur in Lincoln City, a town just south of Tillamook County.

In February 1959, Dixon recommended that the cooperative make another loan to Espe—this time, unsecured. No board member bothered to make a motion; rather, "the consensus was that it was against our policy to make direct unsecured loans of any type."[26] A month later, at the March 9, 1959, board meeting, "Mr. Dixon brought up the topic again, saying that the loan had been made and that 'it was evident that our relationship with the customer was in jeopardy.'"[27] Ferd Becker protested, according to the minutes. "He stated that his last knowledge of the transaction was that if it couldn't have unanimous agreement of the board that it would not be made."[28]

Mr. Dixon responded that "he felt that since prior loans had been made to Mr. Espe by the dairy and that since security for the loan had been found that it was essential that the loan be made in order to preserve the good will of the customer." Because of the negative reaction to his move, Dixon offered to assume the loan himself, and board member Otto Schild joined him. The minutes did not note if they actually did assume responsibility.

In early 1961, GASA's loans to Alpenrose felt similar to the cooperative's previous efforts to stimulate sales, and so the board authorized sending $200,000 to the distributor to offer to its retail accounts. "The notes, none of them recorded, were then reassigned to [County Creamery]," according to *Northwest Dairy News*.[29] Otto Schild told a reporter with the industry paper that the "loans returned about 7.5% interest compared to the 5.5% rate County Creamery paid to borrow the money." In addition, County Creamery gave Alpenrose 3 percent of the fluid milk sales income as a direct payment to the Portland distributor's ad agency.[30] Although Dixon and Schild said in the interview that the loan program wasn't implemented exactly that way, they didn't specify how it differed. As noted later by some farmers, "Should any of the stores default, the association, and not Alpenrose, would be left holding the bag."[31]

After Tillamook began offering the small loans to stores, GASA's fluid milk sales to Alpenrose "passed the 40,000 pound mark by April 1961."[32] Schild told the reporter that the incidence of loss was low.[33] Dixon and his wife were awarded a trip to New Zealand by the grateful GASA board,[34] and the board approved Dixon's concept of a formal lending program through their cooperative. The board put him in charge of the program but prudently required that all potential loans be reviewed and approved by First National Bank of Oregon.[35] The board's action was similar to its earlier decisions to make loans if collateral could be found.

Likewise, the newly formed Cheese & Dairy took time during its first organizational meeting in 1962, as the fourth item of business, to authorize Dixon to make loans to "merchants who purchase milk from the wholesalers supplied by this cooperative."[36] Like the authorization given by GASA, Cheese & Dairy's included a provision that all loans would be supervised by First National Bank. At the next board meeting, Dixon "discussed the setting up of a $25,000 reserve to cover possible losses on loans in Portland stores." The board passed a motion to create the reserve.[37]

Dixon arranged for one loan of about $40,000 that was managed by the bank. That amount was much greater than the $5,000 to $10,000 loans that GASA and Cheese & Dairy had authorized in the past. In early 1962, Dixon made a new pitch to Cheese & Dairy:

> Mr. Dixon thought that funds necessary for financing of loans in Portland should now be borrowed directly by the T.C.&D.A. Mr. Leuthold moved and Mr. Waldron seconded a motion to authorize the Secretary to borrow from the First National Bank per an agreement to be drawn by the bank. Carried.[38]

The board thought the required bank oversight was in place for these store loans, which made it comfortable continuing the loan program begun under GASA, except Dixon did not continue to make loans through the bank. To Dixon's way of thinking, he needed to offer more expansive loans, and offer them in quantities that the bank might not approve, given its requirements for safety and security. His solution was to ignore that part of the board's directive. Cheese & Dairy was now going into debt to make potentially risky loans.

Unbeknownst to the Cheese & Dairy board, Dixon continued sending unsecured money to Alpenrose accounts and added Carnation to the loan program. The distributors were loyal purchasers of Tillamook's excess milk because Tillamook's grocery store loans got the distributors' products onto the shelves. Tillamook's milk sales were looking good, but the loans were not approved by the bank, and Cheese & Dairy was the only organization on the hook for any loan defaults.

In his biographical interview years later, Dixon focused on the sales, starting with the initial sale to Alpenrose, but not on the loans themselves.

> Well, I guess I must have worked for at least three years trying to sell more milk in Portland when the break came. And I hope I'm right in saying that in 1962 we got an order from the Alpenrose Dairy in Portland to send them a 40,000 pound load of milk. They liked it. By fall of that year, we were selling them 75,000 pounds a day. And I, without taking time to do some figuring, I think it would be safe to say that we were obtaining $200,000 more a month for our producers, selling that milk at grade A than we were able to get for cheese at that time. Another good result of it was that we had less milk going into cheese, and our inventory was coming down into a more manageable situation. And we were able to raise our price on cheese. It was a marvelous thing for Tillamook County.[39]

The additional sales were stimulated by the loan program. Dixon risked loan defaults from the grocers; however, Dixon knew that Cheese & Dairy would be stuck with any losses—not the distributors and not County Creamery. And indeed loan defaults began to occur. A County Creamery office employee alerted a Cheese & Dairy supporter to what was going on.

(*Left*) Anita Neilson. Courtesy of 1937 Kilchis yearbook, Tillamook High School, Tillamook, Oregon; (*right*) Glenn Johnston. Courtesy of the Johnston family

TAKING A RISK

Anita Jeanne Stewart Neilson didn't like the duplicity she was witnessing. She was a lifelong resident of the area who with her husband, Bob, farmed on Eckloff Road. She was a stenographer at County Creamery's office in Tillamook. She took minutes at the board meetings, including GASA meetings.

She and her husband shipped their milk to GASA, and then Cheese & Dairy, while she was employed by County Creamery. Such duality was not uncommon in the insular Tillamook dairy industry. In her job, she overheard conversations and saw documents that she knew contradicted what Beale Dixon was saying in board meetings and to the patrons. She felt compelled to risk her job to get information to Cheese & Dairy directors.

At the end of one workday, Neilson sneaked documents out of the County Creamery office. That night, she went down the road to talk to her neighbor Glenn Johnston. He was always in his stanchion barn at that time of night, milking his cows and perhaps creating a poem.

"He loved to talk, he was always a student," his son, Fib, says. "He was writing all the time and it would come out as a poem."[40] An example of Glenn Johnston's writing was captured in a letter to the editor of the *Headlight Herald*, published on February 10, 1963:

The Marching Milkers

When reading all those articles
About this STATE MILK MESS,
I'll bet a lot of city folk
Will scratch their heads unless
It's true that though we fight
And rant and rave and cuss
It looks as if the whole darn State
Was out of step 'cept us.[41]

Johnston, who sang beautifully, was often a soloist in the Tillamook Catholic Church's choir. He wrote a fight song for Cheese & Dairy. The song is lost now, unfortunately, but it was heard at least once, at a Cheese & Dairy board meeting.[42]

Ferd Becker's son, Jim, remembers Johnston as "Honest as the day is long. A gem. Personable."[43] Throughout the years of the Cheese War, Glenn was very loyal to the cause. He aligned with Cheese & Dairy and didn't quit. He served on Cheese & Dairy's board, including as its secretary.

In Johnston's barn, Anita Neilson handed her neighbor some documents to read. By the light in the barn, with the cows chewing grain and flicking their tails, Johnston read about loan deals that had not gone through bank approval. Fib later recalled that his dad "blew green smoke" over what he read. Neilson took the documents back to the County Creamery office, and Johnston shared the information with his good friend, Dale "Doc" Sayles.

Sayles was an innovative veterinarian who had his quirks. Farmers relied on him to figure out their cows' breeding problems; as Nick Steiner says, "He made Tillamook farmers money by getting cows bred back earlier or figuring out how to get them pregnant."[44] He offered a cow health service, visiting farms monthly to do blood tests, manage fertility problems, and spot potential health issues. He would hand-write the records at night after each visit, putting them in wooden boxes that he built in his shop and kept at each farm. Doc and the other vet in town, Roy Peterson, sometimes traded work shifts.

Doc liked to research cow medicines and modern veterinary techniques, which is one reason he wanted to have his own herd. He got his wish in about 1960, when Nick Steiner's father, Steve, sold a small acreage and forty-five cows to his good friend, a deal hammered out at Steiner's dining table. Steiner moved across Highway 101 to his larger acreage. Doc never bought a tractor; he used one of Steiner's. When he was making house calls, he piled his vet supplies into the back seat and trunk of his 1958 Ford Fairlane.[45] If he ran out of sugar for his coffee, he raided the dextrose in his supplies, adding six teaspoons to his cup.[46] He had trouble sleeping, so he would sometimes nap during the day in the alley of Steiner's barn, "lying in the bed of Steiner's pickup, boots sticking out,"[47] according to Nick, who remembers Doc as one of his heroes.[48]

Doc Sayles and Glenn Johnston discussed what they should do with Anita's information. They decided to share it with selected Cheese & Dairy board members. Anita continued to ferry information, so some Cheese & Dairy board members knew that Dixon was lying to them and to the general membership about the loans. It made those board members determined to question, observe, and act. The majority of the Cheese & Dairy board, joined by the Red Clover board, drew a line in the sand and said "no more"—no more business done the way Beale Dixon did it. They were ready to fire him.

CHAPTER 5

Too Much Milk, Too Much Dixon

When farmers stopped accepting Dixon's decisions, it sometimes put them at odds with their neighbors, relatives, and friends. The upstarts called themselves rebels because they were going against the norm. They were probably unaware of a popular song at the time, "He's a Rebel," sung by the Crystals and played during KTIL radio's nightly two-hour pop music show, but the rebel nickname excited some of their children because the Cheese War evoked the same kind of individualism and romanticism they heard in the song.

The men were united by their common cause, but they did not fit one mold. Vern Lucas was quieter than Glenn Johnston. Bass Tone was more plain-spoken than Hans Leuthold, who was a polished public speaker. Tone's brother-in-law, Clem Hurliman, was so proud of his Swiss heritage that he added a painting of a Swiss flag to the end gable of his home. Joe Beeler inherited his family's farm, as did many farmers of that generation. Hooker Jenck was friendly to everyone. Ferd Becker was cerebral. George Milne was the new guy who became their leader.

Ferd Becker and George Milne had become acquainted at Jersey Cattle Club meetings. Becker's son, Jim, says, "He and Mom would talk about George. His name came up all the time—what strategy, what was going on. [Ferd and George] would talk on the phone or Ferd would go to the [Milne] farm and talk. If he had something to say, he would say it; George would be more polite."[1]

Milne wore black-framed glasses under a twill baseball cap, often with a pipe angled from his mouth. He didn't have to cope with the opinions or opposition of relatives because none of them lived nearby and none of them were farmers. Nick Steiner, Steve's son, recalls, "Whatever the topic, [George] had read all the papers and evidence; he and Doc Sayles were the two brainiacs. George had a reputation for really being honest. A reputation of being really bright . . . he spoke like he had an education."[2]

"People trusted George," Barbara Milne said later. "They knew he was sincere. They didn't think he was in it for glory or power."[3] Fib Johnston remembers that Milne "had integrity. He would be fair. He was the board president because others wanted to make motions and be free to move around. He lived extremely close to his convictions. A hard man to crack. That gave him respect so he was reelected."[4]

The group of farmers was close-knit. Rita Johnston, Glenn's daughter-in-law and Fib's wife, says about the group she observed in action, "They were brothers."[5] They trusted each other, and they relied on each other for ideas and advice and help. They had a camaraderie, a covenant, that carried them through doubt and loss and hardship.

It wasn't that these farmers wanted a fight. But "they couldn't compromise their integrity," Rita Johnston says.[6] Joe Jenck, Hooker's son, says, "We fought because what we fought for was right. The other side knew they were wrong. No one could say Cheese & Dairy farmers were not honest."[7] Fib Johnston says, "They never buttered the truth."[8] In Rita Johnston's view, they were not "smooth-tongued people."[9]

Joe Jenck remembers it this way: "All of the guys were considered a little radical. They were progressive. They thought, 'We can't sit still.' They took a risk to get a reward. The others wanted things kept the same." He pictures his dad, Hooker, saying, "I'm not backing up."[10] Joe says his dad "knew that change will come, so either embrace it or you will die."[11]

The bottom line for these farmers? "They were big men, with big hearts," says Fib Johnston. "They were smart men. When they had to get into the soup, they did it."[12] The farmers wanted to see their mission through to completion, so they sacrificed. They didn't farm exactly the way they wanted to, and they didn't make as much money as they needed to, and they weren't there for their families as often as they should have been.

Some of the men's families were ostracized because of their stand. Some of their close relatives, even their brothers farming the same property, disagreed with them. But in their minds, it was all worth it because they were pursuing a larger goal. They were saving the Tillamook dairy industry. They were righting wrongs. It made a bond between them. They couldn't let the other guys down. The farmers "had fights" among themselves, says Fib Johnston, "but they would come together in consensus" because "they already agreed on principles."[13] Many Tillamook dairy farmers, including Bob Blaser, Harley Christensen, James and Robert Durrer, Ken Jenck (Hooker's older brother), and Floyd Woodward were determined to push forward. They banded together to change their foreseeable future.

They began to tackle the issues that had inspired them to stop conforming. They learned that Dixon tried to get rid of more of the surplus milk by accepting Carnation's offer of a heavily discounted price. The distributor would receive a price break of almost $11,000 a month, or nearly $101,000 today. The farmers didn't want to lose that much money every month, and Dixon's unauthorized deal further eroded his relationship with Grade A farmers. Dixon mentioned the Carnation deal at the May 15, 1962, Cheese & Dairy board meeting, noting, "We are confronted with a problem at Carnation in which they have been offered milk at $5.15 per cwt and we are to decide if we want the business at that price."[14]

A handwritten addition to the May 15 minutes, approved at the June 5, 1962, board meeting, said, "Asked Dixon if any decision [at] Carnation on this item. Dixon replied, 'Not as yet.'"[15] The additional note would become important. The mid-May meeting continued with directors questioning Dixon:

> Why if so much surplus was available in Seattle and elsewhere in Washington it didn't come into the Portland market?
> Why does Tillamook constantly take the lead to lower fluid price?[16]

Ultimately, the directors passed a motion that Milne, not Dixon, should attend a state hearing scheduled by the new Milk Audit and Stabilization Division of the Oregon Department of Agriculture and testify that Tillamook wanted a $5.80 milk price.

When the board held a June 5, 1962, special meeting, it approved the mid-May minutes with the handwritten addition. The board also quizzed Dixon about a statement he had made at the May 29 board meeting "that the members [sic] motion to hold the price at $5.80 didn't mean anything. Mr. Dixon replied that the T.C.C.A. board would have to pass on this motion."[17] Dixon seemed to want County Creamery to be the final authority on the selling price even though the state Department of Agriculture would make the decision.

At the June 5 meeting, Dixon was asked more questions about the $5.15 Carnation deal. It turned out that three Oregon cooperatives had already agreed to sell their milk to Carnation for the lower price and Dixon had committed Cheese & Dairy to join them. The board voted to revoke Dixon's deal, despite Otto Schild speaking against the motion.[18] Over the next several meetings, Schild repeatedly protested Cheese & Dairy actions based on a perceived lack of decorum or respect for the system and Beale Dixon:

> Mr. Schild felt that the presence of patrons at this meeting to witness the castigation of Mr. Dixon was in poor taste.[19]

and

> Mr. Schild noted that he felt that the board should set up policies, get reports, but not try to manage the operation. Cooperatives are only strong when they have good strong management.[20]

To some of the Cheese & Dairy board members, it seemed that the corollary of strong management would be a passive board. The majority of the board refused that role. Meanwhile, despite repeated requests since April, no report had been given to the board about the price when Grade A quota and Grade A surplus were mixed. At the June 5 board meeting, Milne told Dixon and Bob Ely to "prepare a detailed breakdown of the March payout at once."[21]

YOU'RE FIRED

The Carnation deal was the last straw for the Cheese & Dairy board majority. The only inducement it needed to fire Dixon was the growing conviction that he could not be trusted to carry out the policies of either the Cheese & Dairy or County Creamery boards. The board made a strategic error, though. Rather than immediately fire Dixon from the Cheese & Dairy board or wait until a County Creamery board meeting to directly present a motion to fire him, the Cheese & Dairy board passed a motion at the end of the June 5 meeting. Hans Leuthold said,

> In the very best interests of the producer members of our association, in order to promote harmony and efficiency, which is now lacking in our organization, I move that the Tillamook Cheese and Dairy Association recommend to the T.C.C.A. board at the next regular meeting on Wednesday, June 13, 1962 that the T.C.C.A. board demand the resignation of their general manager, Mr. H.S. Dixon effective immediately June 13, 1962.[22]

Arnold Waldron seconded. Hans Leuthold is quoted in the minutes saying, "This was nothing personal that he liked Mr. Dixon fine."[23] Using a secret ballot, the board members passed the motion 9-1. The lone "no" voter wasn't recorded in the minutes. Several directors commented "that this had been building up for some time and that they had lost confidence in the manager. Mr. Milne stated that this is not a matter of personalities, but a matter of what is good for the association."[24]

The Cheese & Dairy board majority thought it was acting appropriately. By "recommending" that another board "demand" Dixon's resignation, however, the board punted its responsibility. The rebels were inexperienced managers who assumed that a different board, with different experiences with Dixon and no direct risk from the loan program or the Carnation deal, would agree to enact Cheese & Dairy's proposal. The two-step process gave Dixon time to work on getting enough votes to thwart the motion before the general meeting of Tillamook County Creamery Association. Still, Cheese & Dairy almost succeeded in removing him.

George Milne presented the motion at the County Creamery general meeting on June 13, 1962. Dixon recalled later,

> The board of directors called a meeting of all of the associations in the county. It was held up at the high school cafeteria, and by a fairly close vote, they voted down the idea of asking me for my resignation. I'd like to say, too, that somehow or other, I think dating back to about 1935, I seem to have lost my fear of losing

my job. And I think that was a strengthening thing for me. At that point I would have been perfectly happy if they had voted me out. Well perhaps not perfectly happy, because I would have had a sense of failure and not accomplishing what I thought I ought to accomplish. But I had no fear financially, let me put it that way. And I had a very supportive family so that I didn't have any problems there.[25]

Millard Bailey's vote created the 7-6 victory for Dixon. Bailey, from south Tillamook County, had changed his vote after the Cheese & Dairy meeting where he had voted in favor. Fib Johnston said later that Bailey "had made a bed for himself in what he thought was a more comfortable political situation, and he was accepted into their group."[26] Bailey himself said, "Beale Dixon was a great guy and he held us above water; he was a strong individual."[27]

Dixon retained his position with County Creamery, but the Cheese & Dairy board voted the following week to remove him from his management position with their cooperative. Joe Beeler made the motion, and the board members voted 8-3 to fire Dixon from their organization.[28] Otto Schild, Millard Bailey, and Karl Zweifel voted to retain Dixon. Next, Red Clover voted to remove Dixon as its manager, too.

With Dixon banished from the Cheese & Dairy board room, the board needed to hire a new manager. Cheese & Dairy's bylaws didn't provide any guidance beyond copying the language in County Creamery's bylaws that said, "The Board of Directors may appoint and remove at its pleasure a manager and other officials, agents, and employees, prescribe their duties, and fix their compensation."[29] The Cheese & Dairy directors were busy farmers who didn't have any experience hiring a manager; that person had always been provided by County Creamery. The board didn't conduct a search for a manager, choosing instead to trust a familiar face. Their hiring decision would turn out to be a mistake.

Bob Ely moved over from County Creamery to manage Cheese & Dairy. Ely had worked for County Creamery since 1948, according to *The Tillamook Way*. He was described as "good with figures,"[30] but he had no managerial experience. Unbeknownst to the Cheese & Dairy board, Ely was "getting advice from Dixon," as George Milne later described it,[31] which meant that County Creamery's interests were in the mix of any decision Ely made. Ely said later, "[I] was right in the middle. I looked to Beale Dixon as my supervisor, and I was working for him. The Cheese and Dairy guys weren't working for him. I thought that Beale, although not perfect, was far more right than this rebel group."[32]

At a special meeting on July 26, 1962, the Cheese & Dairy board decided to appoint a finance committee to hire a certified public accountant to review bookkeeping and financial statements.[33] It also passed a resolution that said, in part, "that the Tillamook County Creamery Association be and it is hereby restricted from making any further agreements or loans involving the Alpenrose Dairy Inc. without the consent and approval of the Board of Directors of the Tillamook Cheese and Dairy Association."[34]

More and more, Cheese & Dairy was distancing itself from County Creamery and Beale Dixon. The Cheese & Dairy board wrote to its members on August 2, 1962:

Unfortunately, the Board has been forced to pass resolutions to protect our right to control Tillamook Cheese and Dairy Association money used in making loans. We firmly believe in a strong County Association, but must safeguard the rights of the producer-members of our own Tillamook Cheese and Dairy Association. We have every hope that these matters can be worked out satisfactorily.[35]

At its August 13, 1962, meeting, the Cheese & Dairy board discussed a marketing agreement proposed by County Creamery. George Milne had asked Cheese & Dairy's attorney for an opinion and reported that the lawyer said that it was improper to include language in the agreement that Cheese & Dairy would "operate under direction of and with the assistance of the Board of Directors of T.C.C.A."[36] Such an arrangement would override the authority of Cheese & Dairy's board and put one cooperative in charge of the other. Split votes had become common on the Cheese & Dairy board, with Millard Bailey, Otto Schild, and Karl Zweifel unified against motions that censured Beale Dixon or created more independence for the cooperative, and the board voted with its usual 8-3 split not to accept the marketing agreement.

Then, Otto Schild and Millard Bailey moved and seconded, respectively, to withdraw loan agreements with Alpenrose and Carnation. Such an action would help the Cheese & Dairy board majority rest easier, but most of the board members voted to wait until the legal question was settled about who had been given the authority to make those loans. If Cheese & Dairy voided the faulty loans, it would be claiming responsibility, something the majority of the board did not want to claim at all.

WARREN MCMINIMEE

Warren A. McMinimee, County Creamery's lawyer, had probably written the marketing agreement that favored County Creamery and suggested the motion that would have left Cheese & Dairy responsible for grocery store loans.

McMinimee was Beale Dixon's not-so-secret weapon. The lawyer was influential in Tillamook County, where he had been district attorney for three terms beginning in 1936. He became a state senator, representing Tillamook and Lincoln Counties. He was named both Junior and Senior First Citizen of Tillamook, having served on government, service, professional, and business boards. McMinimee was the first chair of the Tillamook YMCA and was the Grand Master of Masons in Oregon.[37] When he died, he was vice chair of the Oregon Department of Transportation's Parks and Recreation Advisory Committee.[38]

As a private practice lawyer, McMinimee loved to find loopholes that were "not quite illegal," says Jim Becker, the son of Cheese & Dairy farmer Ferd Becker. Jim says the lawyer was "Not an honest man. Ferd did not like him *at all*." Jim recalls that McMinimee "wasn't above pulling something."[39] Fib Johnston describes McMinimee as both "a generous man" and "vicious as a lawyer."[40]

Nick Steiner, farmer Steve Steiner's son, recalls McMinimee's courtroom demeanor. "[He] looked like he was wearing the same suit he wore in college. He'd have cigar ash on the suit jacket's lapel. He'd walk into court with his briefcase open with papers spilling out."[41] But his disheveled appearance hid a sharp intellect, and it was McMinimee's mind that rewarded him with clients. In some cases, he was hired as a defensive move, retained for a divorce before the other spouse hired

(*Left*) Warren McMinimee as a young lawyer. With permission of the Tillamook County Pioneer Museum; (*right*) Donald "Hooker" Jenck with a Belgian horse. Courtesy of the Jenck family.

him, for example. To pay for McMinimee's expertise, explains Dave Leuthold, son of Cheese & Dairy farmer Hans Leuthold, "He got the milk check assignment. That's how you paid your legal bill."[42] By 1941, McMinimee "had already attained such a reputation as a hard-fisted attorney,"[43] according to a newsletter article announcing he had been named Tillamook's Junior First Citizen. Over the years, his reputation was reinforced by the way he handled incidents such as Hooker Jenck's encounter with a Tillamook police officer.

Jenck farmed in south Tillamook County before buying a farm west of Tillamook. He got his nickname, Hooker, as a child when he was encouraged to use a pitchfork and "hook'er" into loose hay to move it into the barn.[44]

Jenck and his wife, Andrea, came back from their honeymoon just in time for the Columbus Day Storm of 1962. On October 12, monster winds hit the Pacific Northwest. The Oregon Coast always saw its share of winter storms, but this one started big and got bigger—a serious enough storm that schools took the unusual step of sending students home early. No one knows the actual peak wind speed because the wind blew harder than the weather instruments were designed to record. As the typhoon intensified, some of George Milne's thousand-pound Jersey cows were blown across the barnyard, through a wooden fence, and onto Brickyard Road. They survived. Sadly, as recounted in *A Deadly Wind*, John Dodge's book about the Columbus Day Storm, Steve Steiner and Jenck and other farmers lost parts of their herds because the cows were crushed when the barns collapsed on them.[45]

But before the Columbus Day storm and before marrying Andrea, Jenck was asleep in his car in town after a night of drinking. According to his son, Jenck had to talk fast when a police officer who was new to Tillamook tapped on his car window the next morning, ready to take him to jail because sleeping in a car was against the law. Jenck persuaded the officer to take him to McMinimee's house instead. At seven o'clock, McMinimee opened his front door to see Jenck and the officer. After the cop explained the situation, McMinimee grabbed Jenck, pulled him inside, and closed the door on the officer. After much banging on the door by the rookie cop, McMinimee opened it again. The officer demanded Jenck, but McMinimee coolly replied that his client had been with him all day. Jenck did not go to jail.[46]

In another story, farmer Joe Beeler wanted to buy the land next to his farm. The widow who owned it was interested in selling, but her son wanted $14,000 for a barn. Joe's son, Walt, says that Joe went to McMinimee for legal advice. After Joe left the law office, McMinimee called the widow, claimed that Joe did not want to buy the farm, and offered to buy it himself—and did. He rented it to Joe. But when the Cheese War began, he kicked Joe, a Cheese & Dairy shipper, off the land and rented it to Otto Schild, a County Creamery loyalist.[47]

THE FIRST LEGAL BATTLE

Cheese & Dairy recognized McMinimee's capabilities and fought back by hiring out-of-town lawyers with their own reputations for braininess and craftiness. Cheese & Dairy's lawyer, James Goodwin from Oregon City, near Portland, filed a request for a declaratory judgment against County Creamery in October 1962.[48] A declaratory judgment is "a binding judgment from a court defining the legal relationship between parties and their rights in a matter before the court."[49] Triggered by McMinimee's proposed amendment to the marketing contract, Cheese & Dairy sought guidance on County Creamery's and Cheese & Dairy's roles and responsibilities. Milne told the local paper, "this is not a suit for damages. It is merely an action taken to have the circuit court decide by law the rights of the two cooperatives. It is a constructive step taken for the welfare of everyone concerned. In this way questions that have arisen between the two associations will be settled and they can once again work together in harmony for the good of all the dairymen in the county."[50]

In reaction, Otto Schild found it "regrettable a certain group of dairy products producers have chosen to bring court action against the Tillamook County creamery association [sic] and air our internal troubles in court. In the nearly fifty years of Tillamook County Creamery association [sic] history, it has never been involved in court with its own members. The court action could well be the dissolution of our marketing program and could well jeopardize Tillamook's well established reputation, trade name and market."[51]

Tillamook County Circuit Court Judge J. S. Bohannon recused himself, and the case was assigned to his Clapsop County counterpart, Avery Combs. Meanwhile, an auditor hired by Cheese & Dairy made an ominous discovery. At a special Cheese & Dairy member meeting on September 5, 1962, Vern Lucas reported that twenty-three of the forty loans did not have loss-payable insurance clauses to cover any gaps in repayments by the grocery stores; only the one loan for $40,000 had been made through First National Bank, and one $30,000 loan of Cheese & Dairy funds had been made through County Creamery.[52]

Dixon had loaned about $370,000 of Cheese & Dairy's money—more than $3.4 million in today's money—and was ready to make an additional $140,000 in loans to stores that stocked Alpenrose milk.[53] Dixon was generating cash flow that offset his lack of cheese sales and took care of most of the excess Grade A milk, but he had put Cheese & Dairy in danger of losing its patrons' money if the stores didn't repay the loans.

The Cheese & Dairy board majority wanted to stop County Creamery from making unsecured loans to grocers with Cheese & Dairy's money. And so it passed a motion saying that County Creamery was forbidden to make loans without the consent and approval of Cheese & Dairy, and that the organization would seek a legal review of all agreements between itself and County Creamery.[54]

County Creamery's official defense of the loan program didn't mention the irregular loans. In *Tillamook Cheese News*, a County Creamery

publication, Dixon wrote the lead column, titled "The True Facts," saying in part,

> The loans have been checked recently by competent authority
> and have been found in good condition with no losses evident so
> far. Adequate reserves have been set up to cover possible losses.
> Much criticism has been recently made of this program, severely
> endangering a loss of sales which could cost our producers the
> loss of our market, which has increased returns to our producers
> at a rate of over $300,000.00 during the past year.[55]

The newsletter included copies of distributors' supportive letters,
with the managers of Alpenrose and Carnation writing that they wanted
to do business with County Creamery, not any other group, along with
a letter from McMinimee, declaring that the original marketing contract between County Creamery and Cheese & Dairy was valid.

The distributors' letters would have been easy to get, given that
Alpenrose and Carnation were keen to continue their advantageous
relationships with County Creamery. And McMinimee's letter focused
on a nonissue—the validity of the marketing contract, which did not
mention loans[56]—but did not address the legality of County Creamery
using Cheese & Dairy's money to make unauthorized loans.

Dixon's loan program and Cheese & Dairy's risk exposure created
deep concern that he had made decisions that could harm the organization. Perhaps Dixon needed more supervision, not less—but first, the
board majority needed to protect itself against a recall.

FIELD NOTE 4
Books and Pipes
BY LINDA KIRK

Tillamook County Library's wonderful rolling institution, the bookmobile, kept my 12-year-old brain alert during the summer of 1962, while the job of moving irrigation pipes helped the pastures grow and got the farm chores done as Cheese War controversies simmered in the background. The bookmobile's route included a stop in our driveway on Brickyard Road. On Thursdays, neighbors came from all around, toting books to return. To us three sisters, it felt as if we were hosting a neighborhood party. The bookmobile looked like a repainted bread truck without the double doors in back. When kids and adults crowded in, the floor rocked and the bookshelves jiggled, making it hard to read titles. I liked adventure stories and books about horses and dogs. I took my time with each selection. Unless Mom took us to the library in town in the meantime, this stack of books would have to last until the bookmobile returned.

Although our family routine was to read in the living room after supper, my parents made it clear that reading was secondary to farming during the day. For Dad, though, reading was also secondary to Tillamook Cheese & Dairy and County Creamery meetings. On meeting nights, Dad rushed through supper, drove to town, and came home late. That summer, as meetings piled up, Mom said she would change the irrigation, with my help, while my sisters would continue feeding calves.

In a field near the house, we confronted long pipes, wet and heavy. Unlatching the coupling, Mom raised the end of the pipe to drain the water, and then I lifted the other end. Keeping even, we carried the forty-foot-long pipe to the next setting and attached it. That first day, we managed okay until we came to one of the electric barbed-wire fences. Dad installed this fencing to ensure that escape-minded cows with thick, hairy hides got a discouraging jolt. The single wire was low to the ground—less than thirty inches high. Mom and I considered how to get past the fence. First, we lifted the pipe over and dropped it. My crossing strategy was to put one hand on a cedar fencepost, straddle the wire, and then hoist over my other leg. Mom, who wore a shirt-waist housedress, had a different strategy. We were easy to see from the houses lining the county road. Mom wanted to step across the fence without tearing her skirt, getting a shock, or entertaining the neighbors. She gathered the front and back skirt fabric with both hands, making impromptu culottes. Holding the cloth in place above her knees, she lifted one barn boot over the electric fence, and then the other.

When changing the irrigation became almost automatic, I could think about the books I was reading. I had borrowed *Old Yeller* from the bookmobile, along with five or six horse books and *We Were There with Lewis and Clark*. From the cover, I thought *Old Yeller* was a boy book, so I read the other books first. But when I started reading about Travis and his family's big dog, I didn't want to stop. On the last Wednesday in August, when Mom called me to change the irrigation, I was reading. My mind was in Texas, where wild boars slashed Old Yeller's belly and gave Travis a "hog cut" leg that swelled to the "size of a butter churn."[1]

That night, I read the final pages of *Old Yeller*. The next day, as we lined up for the last bookmobile visit of the summer, rain dripped off our jackets. If this rain turned into a soaker, Dad would shut down the irrigation pump, and with no need to move pipes, Mom might have time to make regular trips to the library in town and we sisters might have more time to read during the day, at least until school started again. Rain would not, however, give Dad more time to read. Instead, he would attend co-op meetings and fight the Cheese War.

CHAPTER 6

Bitter Discussions

The summer of 1962 included the launch of a recall effort against the eight rebellious Cheese & Dairy directors: Joe Beeler, Glenn Johnston, John Landolt, Hans Leuthold, Vern Lucas, George Milne, Ralph Redberg, and Arnold Waldron. The recall was led by the three remaining Cheese & Dairy board members: Millard Bailey, Otto Schild, and Karl Zweifel.

Cheese & Dairy's bylaws stated that a director could be considered for removal from office provided that written reasons, plus the director's answers, appeared with the meeting notice, and at least twenty members requested the removal of the director. More than the required number of Cheese & Dairy farmers signed the recall petition against the eight directors. George Milne recalled later, "The petition was worded real peculiar."[1]

Barbara Milne said, "Yelta Vanderzee came to our house after we saw his name on the petition, and he said, 'I think it's just terrible that some people are talking about recalling you. What can I do to help?' I looked at him and I said, 'But Yelta, you signed a petition asking for the recall.' And he said, 'Oh no, I didn't. The only petition I signed was one asking for a meeting so we could all get together and talk about it because I thought if we talked about it, people would understand.'"[2]

At the August 27, 1962, Cheese & Dairy membership meeting, "Mr. Pangborn moved that a vote of confidence be given by the membership . . . Voice vote carried unanimously."[3] Then, Ferd Becker moved "that the membership demand the resignation of Mssrs. Schild, Zweifel and Bailey and the removal of Messrs. Schild and Bailey from the status of delegates to the T.C.C.A. board."[4] By secret ballot, the motion carried, 114 to 67. When Milne "gave the three directors the opportunity to hand in their resignations,"[5] however, they refused.

Next, a three-page letter from the directors leading the recall was distributed to Cheese & Dairy producers on August 31, 1962. The letter attempted to respond to criticism about the loans by claiming that the directors facing recall were trying to ruin County Creamery.[6] Several days later, the eight targeted board members distributed their rebuttal to the recall effort in the form of a letter that "was mimeographed and circulated at our own expense."[7] The two-column format listed each of the twenty-five points made by the three who sought their recall and countered with responses from the men facing removal. Some of the accusations and responses are included in the table on the following pages.

Two meetings occurred on September 5. First came a special afternoon meeting about the unauthorized loans. Cheese & Dairy's accounting firm was concerned that the $100,000 and $30,000 loans to Alpenrose were endangering Cheese & Dairy's tax-exempt status:

> You have, to our present knowledge, one such loan arrangement, that involving Super-Valu Food Stores, Inc., Longview, Washington in the original amount of $50,000.00 at November 7, 1961, with a present balance of $43,733.33. The other loans seem to be handled under some other authority for the loan pattern does not fit the method that is described in [the January 4, 1962 board] resolution . . . Since you, as board members, have the possibility of personal liability resulting from your actions, you may do well to carefully consider the elements of this financing program . . . There would appear to be a rather serious matter of tax consequences that could jeopardize your tax exempt cooperative status.[8]

At the meeting, the board voted to stop making loans until its legal and tax statuses were clarified. In addition, the Cheese & Dairy board, no longer relying on motions phrased as requests, passed a resolution that removed Millard Bailey and Otto Schild as their representatives on the County Creamery board, with Joe Beeler and Ralph Redberg named as their replacements. Bailey and Schild remained on the Cheese & Dairy board.[9]

After the meeting, Barbara Milne was talking to a group of farmers' wives and saw Otto Schild. After her encounter with Schild, an

Statements from Three Board Members Seeking a Recall	Responses from Eight Board Members Facing a Recall
The eight directors have broken their agreements with Tillamook County Creamery Association and what does this do to you?	We eight directors have not broken any agreement, although it is not clear to what they refer here.
It takes the marketing of your fluid milk out of the county [sic] Creamery Association and puts it in the hands of some outsider over whom you have no control.	The marketing of fluid milk has never been in the hands of the Tillamook County Creamery Association. Tillamook Cheese & Dairy Association has full control of the marketing of Grade "A" milk now, not any "outsider."
Without fluid milk being marketed through the County Association your cost of operation and overhead will go up and payout price to everyone will go down.	How could this be? The Grade "A" milk is handled in a completely separate pool with costs of marketing and profits divided among the pool members.
Loans All arrangements made with the distributors, including loans, were authorized and approved by the boards of Grade A Shippers Association and Tillamook County Creamery Association.	Any producer can check the minutes of his association and find that the loans were made by management in a manner different from the authorization given by the boards. The loans were to be handled through the First National Bank and only one out of more than forty actually was!
Our loans are good, and we will go into every one of them any time you wish.	The loans were handled without the service of a bank appraiser or loan officer. The reassignments from Alpenrose to us have not been recorded. The insurance coverage on many loans was very lax.
We have never had better relations with our distributors than we had before this trouble started.	Certainly. Why shouldn't they like us when we agreed to everything they asked?
They refuse to admit that fluid milk is a dairy product.	On the advice of expert legal counsel, we say that the marketing of fluid milk is not covered by the marketing contract between Tillamook Cheese & Dairy and the Tillamook County Creamery Association.
See Article 11, Section 1—definition of dairy products. "The term 'dairy products' as used herein shall include cheese, fluid milk or cream for human consumption in fluid form, as well as other recognized dairy products."	This wording is in the Tillamook County Creamery Association bylaws under Article 11—Membership, and only defines dairy products in connection with who can be a member of the Tillamook County Creamery Association.

Statements from Three Board Members Seeking a Recall	Responses from Eight Board Members Facing a Recall
They have broken their marketing contracts with Tillamook County Creamery Association as its sole marketing agency by signing contracts with outsiders, endangering loss of sales and loss of our distributors on whom we must depend.	Tillamook Cheese & Dairy Association have not broken their marketing contract. The Tillamook County Creamery Association is the sole marketing agency for our manufactured products. The Voluntary Stabilization Plan covers only Grade "A" milk and cannot cause any loss of sales by the Tillamook County Creamery Association.
It's Your Business We have spent hundreds of thousands of dollars to build and keep a good name and reputation for Tillamook Dairy products and the people who produced them, to the place where they are recognized nationally.	This must refer to Tillamook Cheese since Tillamook brand milk isn't known nationally.
Now, these directors are destroying and tearing it down by making the degrading statements about our products and unbecoming conduct that is damaging the reputation and financial stability of Tillamook County Creamery Association.	We dare criticize the quality of some of the cheese being marketed because, we want to safeguard the reputation of our cheese and assure the financial stability of the Tillamook County Creamery Association.[12]

unknown writer added a typed comment at the top of a copy of the recall letter:

> Before at least twelve witnesses . . . Otto Schild was asked by Mrs. George Milne just who had written the three page article which was circulated by Otto Schild and others. She stated to him that she thought he was too smart to write and sign such an article. After repeating the question several times he admitted he did not write the article, that . . . McMinimee had, and he and the other [two] directors had approved the article and signed it.[10]

The second meeting of the day was the recall meeting, held at Fairview Grange Hall. The room was packed with farmers and their families. Tensions were high. According to Barbara Milne, "That was the time some person told the sheriff that there might be a chance people would try to prevent George from coming to the meeting because he was such a good president and the meeting wouldn't go as well if someone else led it. So they actually sent a deputy to our house. As I recall, they wanted us to go in the sheriff's car, but we refused and went in our own, with the deputy following us. Nothing happened."[11]

The meeting had nothing to do with Dixon, who had been fired as Cheese & Dairy's general manager. "But there he was with Bob Ely, standing on the steps of the grange, shaking everybody's hands as they came in the building," George Milne remembered. "He even had County Creamery office staff there."[12]

Ely made the meeting arrangements at the grange. Milne recalled, "I didn't notice at first, but he set up the microphone at the end of the table, next to the three directors who were bringing the charges. I didn't use it; I just used a loud voice."[13]

At the beginning of the meeting, Dixon's supporters said that Milne should let someone else lead the meeting because it was about a recall that included him. Citing the bylaws, Milne ruled the motion to be out of order. Later in the meeting, the minutes noted that Mr. Taplin, a representative of Mohler Factory, stated, "when chair made speeches he should turn over gavel . . . Chair stated that Mr. Taplin's point was not well taken."[14]

Dixon's supporters demanded several times that the former Cheese and Dairy manager be allowed to speak: "Mr. Schild stated Mr. Dixon had right to answer. Mr. Milne disallowed Mr. Dixon to speak." And later, "Mr. Bud Gienger again asked for Mr. Dixon to be heard."[15] The $5.15 deal with Carnation was discussed again. The disagreement on how to proceed led Glenn Johnston to say that "milk [is] not splitting [the] association, but one man is: Beale Dixon." Bud Gienger countered that "Dixon [is a] really good man."[16]

At the end of the long meeting, the farmers voted on recalling the eight directors. Milne appointed five men, representing both sides of the issue, to count the ballots. The eight board members retained their positions, 126–114.

The Cheese War continued. Increasingly, Milne opposed Schild, who remained on the Cheese & Dairy board. During one board meeting, the minutes noted, "Mr. Milne and Mr. Schild had a very bitter discussion."[17]

THE QUOTA LAW

After the success of crafting the 1961 state milk law, which was set to expire at the end of 1962, Tillamook's dairy farmers wanted to continue working with other Oregon farmers to draft an even better law to present to the 1963 legislature.

Milne, who had become secretary of the Oregon Farm Bureau Federation's ad hoc voluntary stabilization committee, began meeting regularly with the statewide coalition, along with Glenn Johnston, Hans Leuthold, Vern Lucas, and Ralph Redberg. If Oregon farmers could present another united front, they might get legislation that would end the painful non-negotiations with distributors. They wanted the Oregon Department of Agriculture to set the milk price with their input. Milne knew that if he could predict his income more reliably, he'd be able to manage his expenses and income, rather than get a nasty surprise when the results of the so-called negotiations with distributors were announced.

The farmers modeled their proposed law after the Willamette Plan, which was serving Eugene-area farmers successfully. Under the proposal, each farmer would receive a base, or quota, in a system managed by the Oregon Department of Agriculture. The proposed system would commit milk distributors to paying a guaranteed rate for the year's quota production, whether the Oregon farm was in Grants Pass or Hood River or Tillamook. Farm income would be much more predictable. The quota system would shift the determiner of a farmer's income from the distributors to the farmers themselves.

The quota pool would accept all eligible dairy farmers. The law defined quota as "a producer's portion of the total sales of Class 1 milk in a market area plus 15 percent."[18] The first year, the amount of the quota for each farmer would be based on the farmer's Grade A milk production from January through April 1963, the monthly average of Grade A milk sales in the farmer's milk marketing area, and the farmer's monthly percentage of the Grade A milk produced by all farmers in the market area, plus 15 percent.[19]

A farmer could increase his quota in the next year, either by buying more cows or generating more production from his current herd, but the amount over the previous year's production would be paid at a lesser rate, rather than the baseline quota rate. The farmer could increase the portion of his milk that qualified for the higher baseline price by buying cows with quota from a farmer who was quitting the business or cutting back. A newcomer could get into the dairy business by buying a herd with assigned quota. Alternately, a new farmer or a farmer upgrading his facilities to Grade A could establish a dairy, sell his Grade A milk as manufacturing milk for 180 days, and then receive quota less 30 percent for six months.[20] The quota proposal addressed surplus milk, too, saying that any milk produced above and beyond the amount in a farmer's quota wouldn't be part of the quota calculation; it could be sold for the best price offered.

A lot of details needed to be worked out, but if Oregon farmers weren't pitted against each other and could predict the size of their milk checks, they could make plans based on their expected yearly income. The farmers' proposal was called the milk stabilization law, or the quota law. The open pool meant the quota system would be available in the future to farmers who qualified to sell Grade A milk.

George Milne saw the quota law as the way to survive as a farmer. He wanted the law enough to lead extra meetings of Tillamook farmers to explain how the system would work and to gain their support, which was vital because they were a large bloc of the state's milk producers. Milne realized that Tillamook farmers should receive uniform, timely information about the proposed quota law, but the goal was difficult to achieve through occasional meetings, letters to the editor of the local paper, and informal discussions at the feed store. He decided to write an overview of the law, put it under a title of *Board Information*, and send it to the patrons. A note at the bottom of the message declared, "This letter was mimeographed and circulated at our own expense." *Board Information* messages became a routine way to keep shippers informed. Later, Hans Leuthold chaired the Publicity Committee and was assisted by Glenn Johnston, Vern Lucas, George Milne, and Dale "Doc" Sayles. When Cheese & Dairy separated from County Creamery, the messages continued, with the cooperative's managers, not individual farmers, responsible for developing and sending the newsletters at the co-op's expense.

The Cheese & Dairy board also sent its farmers important information about a backup plan, should the quota bill not pass. Five major Oregon milk producer groups—Mt. Angel, Lower Columbia, Farmers Cooperative Creamery of McMinnville, Carnation-Damascus, and

Cheese & Dairy—sent statements to the distributors, informing them that future price negotiations would be coordinated among all five farmer groups. Even if the quota effort failed, the distributors would lose their power to dictate bulk milk sale prices.[21]

THE MEETING OF THE OREGON DAIRYMEN'S ASSOCIATION

Milne became one of the statewide leaders of the farmers who were seeking a quota law. The farmers would need the political clout of the Oregon dairy industry, and that meant an endorsement by the Oregon Dairymen's Association. Even though the ODA represented farmers, it was heavily influenced by the agriculture professors at Oregon State University and the milk distributors who placed the farmers' milk in the stores. Oregon State University taught future farmers, conducted agricultural research, and provided the extension service that assisted farmers. The agricultural community, from farmers to distributors, paid attention to OSU's opinions. OSU's advice about the quota proposal was, according to George Milne, "Don't rock the boat."[22]

At the January 1963 annual ODA meeting, representatives of the Oregon Dairy Industry, consisting of distributors and producers, met before the general ODA meeting. ODI had supported the 1961 legislation and had developed a law for consideration at the meeting, but the final language was a surprise to the farmers. ODI proposed a decision-making committee of "three producers, two handlers not cooperatives, one processing cooperative member, and one non-processing [bulk only] cooperative member."[23] Four industry representatives could thwart anything the three producer members proposed.

"The industry would still rule," Milne remembered. "We didn't know what to do about it. We met with a group of 40 or 50 dairy farmers. I got to thinking that if you just change the wording to have a certain number of the representatives be bona fide dairymen who earn a majority of their living milking cows, why, it would eliminate most of those industry guys. The farmers agreed and we cooked up an idea.

"In the Oregon Dairymen's Association meeting, I said, 'It looks like the committee's done a fine job, with one exception: I propose that we adopt this with three-fourths of all the representatives being people who earn a living milking cows.' A guy from just south of Eugene immediately jumped up and seconded the motion.

"It had a kicker in it, but they had to vote on it. We had the other guys primed for the motion, and they all voted for it."[24]

The farmers started congratulating each other and slapping one another on the back. Frank Rood, a dairy farmer from Coos County, was president of ODA. Milne said, "He got red in the face and the guys from the college were mad. The rug had been greased and it had gone right out from under them."[25] In reaction, Rood recessed the meeting. He huddled with the other ODA leaders. When they reconvened, something occurred that wasn't planned for and could have ended the proposal's momentum: Rood announced that after a break for lunch, George Milne would lead the general membership's discussion of the committee's proposal.

Milne stared at the president with the same look he had given the two teenage bullies on his school bus. He could picture the officials thinking, "See what you can do, you hick."[26] He nodded once, telling the president that he accepted. The meeting was recessed for one hour.

Instead of a relaxed lunch spent celebrating with the other farmers, Milne needed to figure out how to save his proposal. He was comfortable leading meetings, thanks to his work with other dairy groups and to the classroom practice with *Robert's Rules of Order* that he had received as a Future Farmers of America student in high school. He could run this meeting. He strategized while chewing on a sandwich. Then he smoked his pipe and refined his plan.

After lunch, he reconvened the ODA meeting. He called on various farmers and professors to explain the issues and concerns. He made sure everyone was heard. He appointed a committee that included opponents of the proposal, and they discussed the issue late into the night. The next day, Rood again led the meeting. Farmers voted to approve the provisions developed by the committee. They elected Milne as the leader of the seven-member committee of producers.

Milne said that after the successful meeting, "A guy from the Roseburg area came up to me and said, 'You'll have to watch out when you fly that high.' Off the top of my head, I said I didn't see anything wrong with flying high as long as you keep your feet on the ground."[27]

Milne worked actively to create a milk stabilization bill. He was willing to give up farming time to drive to Salem or Portland for meetings.

Sometimes, Milne's cows had to wait to be milked. And for a man whose livelihood meant eating his meals at home and being near the house all day every day, Milne spent a lot of time on the road, eating restaurant meals and sleeping in hotels. His sacrifices would be worth it if the bill passed. True, he was working for all Oregon dairy farmers—but he was also working for his own farming future.

SELLING THE QUOTA IN TILLAMOOK

Dixon opposed the proposed law, although he had supported the 1961 law. The 1963 legislation, however, focused on producers, and the state would be setting the price of milk. The law would limit Dixon's deal-making ability; even though he could offer lower prices to distributors, it would be unsustainable because the farmers would continue to be paid at the guaranteed rate. And the statewide quota would replace Tillamook's internal quota system.

Dixon might have said he wanted cheese milk included in the bill or that the law would be ineffective. Instead, he said that the law would end Tillamook's autonomy and affect the price paid to producers:

> The agreement to join a "Voluntary Stabilization Plan" would mean that we would share our present sales with outsiders. This would prevent the increasing of our sales through our own efforts, to increase returns to more of our producers.[28]

His other argument was that the quota law would result in closed pools and that they were bad for farmers. In an article in an industry newspaper, Dixon is quoted as saying, "a great deal of pressure is being exerted on certain Tillamook producers by some Wilamette [sic] valley producers who want them to close the Tillamook pool and not permit more shippers to come on the market as long as there is an abundance of milk."[29] The same article reported, "Veteran dairyman Hans Leuthold, one of the 14 TCCA board of directors members, told your *Northwest Dairy News* field editor that he and at least 124 A-grade producers and some cheese producers are not concerned with a valley milk pool as charged by Dixon, but 'just want to get together with the rest of the producers in the state to agree on a stabilized price that is fair to both the producers and distributors.' "[30]

Despite Dixon's opposition, the statewide dairy farmers' coalition made progress. According to the *Headlight Herald*,

> Milne declared that representatives of about 900 of 1600 milk producers in the Portland-Salem-Eugene areas, southwest Washington and southern Oregon are very close to agreement on a voluntary stabilization program.
>
> George Milne, president of Tillamook Cheese and Dairy Assn., who has been active in seeking a voluntary milk price stabilization program among milk producers, said Friday: "If dairymen of the state do not get the milk industry stabilized, the economy of Tillamook county [sic] will be very seriously affected. What the dairyman doesn't get, he can't spend."
>
> Marvin Pangborn said: "It will be really rough on all dairy farmers if a milk price war comes along."
>
> Glenn Johnston said: "Dairy farmers have had two years to do something about this situation. Maybe they will now."
>
> Hans Leuthold said: "The dairy farmer cannot afford any price cut for his milk."[31]

Dixon's opposition continued, but as Milne asked, "Why should we fight the men who produce milk in other areas when we can all gain so much by working together to promote our product and increase sales?"[32] Dixon's repeated claim about a closed pool has become part of the quota story. Even when Dixon discussed it in a 1987 interview, he insisted that the state guaranteed to the producers that they would be given a quota. "And when enough producers came on the market to supply the market, then they wouldn't allow any more producers to come in. They would have a closed pool. This was their way of, you might say, inducing the farmers to come in to this grade A market."[33]

Dixon's concern about a closed pool was a red herring. Yet he continued to beat the drum about closed pools, asking in the February 1963 issue of County Creamery's newsletter, "Will the fluid milk market be closed for additional producers and the expansion of present quotas be prevented by joining into an agreement to accept the type of closed pools in effect elsewhere in the state?"[34]

The County Creamery board of directors signed a letter to the editor of the Tillamook *Headlight Herald* on January 27, 1963, that emphasized the "closed pool" falsehood: "The 'Willamette Pool' or 'Eugene Plan,' which is being proposed as a model for other producer pools in Oregon is substantially a closed pool."[35] Milne countered by writing in the *Headlight Herald* on February 3, 1963, "The person writing the creamery association letter must not have studied either the Willamette plan, which is now operating successfully, or the proposed milk stabilization law, which is patterned after it. The Willamette plan is not a closed pool. The proposed state law does not call for a closed pool."[36] He noted that under Tillamook's open but unsustainable internal quota system, "The dairyman invests more money, works harder, and receives less for his efforts."[37] Later, Milne said, "We had to work closely with the legislators to get the law passed, and that's the only way it got passed: Anyone could join."[38]

At last, the bill came before the 1963 legislature. Milne brought his family, even taking the rare step of letting his children skip school for the day so they could watch the vote from the visitors' gallery in the House of Representatives in the state capitol building. The quota bill was debated at length. One Republican lawmaker, Representative Shirley Field, a Portland attorney and 1960 candidate for state treasurer, held up a carton of milk, and said, echoing a fear when the 1961 Producer Milk Stabilization Law passed, that if the bill became law, the housewife would pay more at the grocery store.[39]

Finally, each legislator voted. As expected, Field voted against the bill, but she was in the minority. The bill, including the quota system with its open pool, became Oregon law.

At last, the farmers had a formula to better predict their income. Even if the economy was bad for dairy farmers, they could make the best of it with the quota system. The *Capital Press* declared that "passage of the new Milk Stabilization Act by the Legislature probably had more of an immediate impact on the agricultural economy of the state than any of the 1963 laws handed the Oregon Department of Agriculture to administer."[40]

George Milne and the other farmers had successfully shifted the balance of power in the Oregon dairy industry. Now, he thought, he could get back to his farm and the Cheese War.

CHAPTER 7

Bad Bookkeeping

Cheese & Dairy's board majority had a big issue: the manager, Bob Ely, was loyal to Dixon. The board noted that Ely had failed to produce the cooperative's essential financial information. In addition, when questioned at a January 1963 board meeting, Ely "admitted to being in attendance at meetings attended by Mr. McMinnimee [sic]."[1]

In March, Ely was allowed to resign from his position. The Cheese & Dairy board told its members:

> At a meeting on March 20, 1963, the board of directors of Cheese and Dairy Association asked Bob Ely for his resignation and hired Ed Burke to replace him as Manager of our organization. This was done because Ely would not take direction from the board. He remained in the office for a week and then received a full month's severance [sic] pay.[2]

Burke, a longtime County Creamery staffer who was the plant manager, resigned from that organization to take the managerial position at Cheese & Dairy.[3] By letting Ely resign, Cheese & Dairy attempted to keep the peace with County Creamery and the dairy community. The *Headlight Herald*'s story of March 24, 1963, said, "Members of the board expressed appreciation of Ely's long service, honesty and integrity."[4]

Dixon wrote to County Creamery members on March 29, 1963, acting as if he still had a role in Cheese & Dairy, "We are sorry to have Bob removed from this position, as he is the only one in our organization fully familiar with the work of that office, and he has been faithful to his job."[5] Ely continued to work for County Creamery until mid-1963, when he moved to Salem to be the milk pool supervisor with the Oregon Department of Agriculture.

LOSING MONEY

Meanwhile, County Creamery's board sent a letter to all patrons, complaining that Cheese & Dairy had published the names of loan recipients. "It is most unfortunate that these names were made public, as our customers expect this information to be held as confidential as possible. We want our producers to have complete information in regard to their cooperative, and nothing but harm can come to our sales efforts and to our producers by needlessly spreading information that does no one any good."[6]

The Cheese & Dairy board turned its attention to an underpayment by County Creamery for cheese delivered. Cheese & Dairy's Publicity Committee reported to producers in a *Board Information* message that blocks of cheese weighing a half pound more than the contracted 20.25 pounds were being accepted by County Creamery, but the payment for them was being calculated as if they were the lesser, correct weight. And when samples were weighed, every one was heavier than the contracted weight, which meant County Creamery had not paid for the true weight of any of the Cheese & Dairy 20.25-pound blocks of cheese nor notified the co-op of the overage. The rebel group told its patrons, "On our annual make of approximately 112,000 twenty pound squares in 1962, this 1/2 pound per square would equal 56,000 pounds of cheese. . . . Tillamook Cheese and Dairy is the only factory that makes twenty pound squares."[7]

The other factories were not subjected to strict pay-per-contracted-weight rules for overweight blocks of cheese. In fact, Cheese & Dairy explained, "Tillamook County Creamery Association pays the factories for them on their full weight."[8] Cheese & Dairy immediately tightened its production process to avoid losing more money to County Creamery.

There was another discovery. From April 1961 through March 1962, County Creamery had charged Cheese & Dairy too much for its share of water usage in the building occupied by both cooperatives. The common usage by different entities meant that costs like utility charges should be divided proportionally, but according to Cheese & Dairy, "It would appear from the information obtained from Mr. Dixon and the Tillamook County Creamery Association records that we were required to furnish more than our fair share of capital by an amount of $55,837.67 on this one item."[9] In 2022 dollars, the extra charges totaled more than $508,700.

County Creamery's managerial systems were used to administer the joint-use allocations; indeed, they were used for everything from billing to determining the number of factory representatives on the County Creamery board. But County Creamery's records made it difficult to track fiscal irregularities, and Beale Dixon wasn't alerting Cheese & Dairy to his actions. For example, depreciation was difficult to track, even though farmers understood the concept. They were aware of depreciation because they could survive day-to-day on income that was sheltered from taxation by depreciation.

Barbara Milne explained. "On the books, we didn't make any money a lot of years. But on income tax, we could take off depreciation and save taxes. Every year, five percent of the cost of our barn was a savings to us because it was an expense."[10]

Many of the line items in County Creamery's accounting records were intertwined with Cheese & Dairy because the two co-ops shared a building and equipment, and County Creamery had expenses and income from marketing the farmers' products. It was difficult for a layperson to determine whether costs had been allocated correctly. The balance sheet was discussed at every annual meeting. Barbara Milne said, "After the yearly audit, the auditor would come to the board and talk about ratios—the percentage of electricity charges to County Creamery and Cheese & Dairy, for example. The books were commingled. Storage expenses were allocated to Cheese & Dairy up to a certain point, but then became County Creamery's expense. We saw credit figures, costs, income, payments to shippers—and everything balanced at the bottom."[11]

The balance sheet looked official. But Barbara Milne kept asking her husband about County Creamery's depreciation. "I couldn't figure out the depreciation method," George Milne recalled, "and the CPA was always evasive."[12] Barbara Milne said, "Besides the operating costs, Dixon would also get depreciation on the factory areas, such as cold storage. If anything was left over, County Creamery allocated an amount back to the shippers."[13] According to George Milne, "Cheese & Dairy should have gotten credit for its share of depreciation." He went on, "But because the buildings were together, things were lumped together. We didn't get any credit; indeed, we got charged twice. County Creamery made more profit that way, and it looked good by allocating money they'd withheld for association fees. County Creamery was getting depreciation on top of depreciation."[14]

Cheese & Dairy told its members that "losses in the Grade A operations that were pointed out earlier by the auditors have already been partially corrected. These problems will need the continued attention of the Board. The Directors have been alerted to the fact that we must have accounting for the product as well as for the dollars."[15]

Cheese & Dairy's detective work continued. And, sadly, it bore fruit. At a special meeting on August 19, 1963, of the Cheese & Dairy and Red Clover boards, a CPA told the directors that inconsistent values had been placed on the cheese inventory. In addition, notes and contracts did not have proper documentation, improper values had been assigned to accounts, and internal controls were inadequate because the agreements were missing.[16]

VERN LUCAS

In the same meeting, Vern Lucas pointed out another bookkeeping maneuver that favored County Creamery at the expense of Cheese & Dairy. Lucas, a Tillamook native who grew up on a farm, understood accounting because, like Ferd Becker, he had been a banker. Lucas married Lorraine Wyss, who was part of an old Tillamook family. He took over the Wyss farm when they married.

George Milne counted Lucas as a close friend. Milne said, "We traded work. We put up silage together. Vern had the hay baler, we had the silage equipment."[17] Barbara Milne said, "I remember driving a tractor and baler, and hooked behind that was a flatbed wagon. Vern would stand on the wagon and stack the bales as they came off the baler. And if I didn't notice where I was going and avoid potholes in the field, why, Vern would be doing a bit of a dance on the back of the wagon!"[18] Milne said, "We didn't have much money and it was a way to get going. We did that for years."[19]

In 1962, the Lucas barn burned down. The family rebuilt, adding innovative individual stalls for the cows to rest in.

"He was a nice guy," Milne said. "He had a stubborn streak; he'd get on an idea and it could be difficult to move him off it."[20] Fib Johnston, Glenn's son, remembers that Lucas was "painfully honest, and would do anything to stay honest."[21] Steve Steiner's son, Nick, recalls Lucas as "clean cut, fastidious."[22] In meetings, Lucas repeatedly reminded the other farmers about the big picture while retaining a good grasp of details. For a while, he led the sales and marketing function for Cheese & Dairy. Lucas was president when the organization ended, and he negotiated the closing of the cooperative.

At the August 19, 1963, special meeting of the boards of Cheese & Dairy and Red Clover, Lucas had news. Thanks to the alert head cheesemaker, Fritz Baumgartner, Lucas was able to tell the board that "The total B Grade charged to T. C. & D. A. since January is 33,150 pounds. Fritz is here and he has had only 3,000 pounds."[23] Shockingly, County Creamery had paid Cheese & Dairy the lower Grade B rate for about thirty thousand pounds of top-quality cheese.

Dixon's recollection of the financial statements of those years differed greatly from Cheese & Dairy's experience. He told his biographer, "I had to be sure that the expenses were properly split on certain operations. That investment responsibility was properly designated. I got a fine compliment from our auditors that they have never seen such a well balanced or detailed manner of doing that. And yet we got, when we got into trouble, we got all kinds of accusations that we were unfair."[24]

Even in the 1950s, however, the Tillamook Cheese Association board had chided Dixon and asked for better bookkeeping:

> most of the cheese inventory counts were not in balance with the book figures. After considerable discussion of the inventory count, Mr. Dixon was asked to get various Head [sic] concerned with this problem together to work for monthly counts that would be in balance.[25]

Beale Dixon was an experienced bookkeeper. Repeatedly, though, his bookkeeping was in error or led to auditors' questions when those experts weren't being paid by County Creamery. The rebel farmers were continually reinforced in their opinion that Dixon shouldn't be managing their finances.

Although Dixon used County Creamery's 1962 annual report, produced in early 1963, to urge all of the farmers to market their products "through one strong marketing Association,"[26] his co-op members split on their reactions to the Cheese War. The boards of nearly all of the small cheese factories supported Dixon. They may have thought Dixon would champion their cheese production; they may have decided to stay the course despite Dixon's struggle to sell their cheese; they may have been resistant to change; they may have feared that their way of farming would have to change; they may have believed the upstarts were wrong. They stayed loyal to County Creamery.

The lone small factory to defy Dixon and County Creamery was Red Clover Creamery Association. It was a typical small cheese factory, a wood frame building painted a soft yellow with finned cylindrical vents rising from the roof and sited a few feet from a river. Inside, four vats were ready to receive milk and turn it into cheese. But Red Clover was atypical among the small factories because its board members were outraged by Dixon's lies and opaque bookkeeping. Red Clover board member Bert Quick said that he wanted "an accounting system that anyone could understand."[27] Red Clover board members saw County Creamery's actions as unethical. Finally, the members wanted their small factory to remain open, and the board didn't trust Dixon to keep it that way.

Red Clover had a stable supply of milk and steady leadership. It was close enough to Tillamook to have easy access to County Creamery staff, the feed store, and the big factory—but it was far enough away to justify not consolidating with the big factory north of town.

BASS TONE

Red Clover's board included Bob Blaser, Bert Quick, and Basil "Bass" Tone, who was Red Clover's representative on the County Creamery board. Tone grew up in Tillamook County. He started working in cheese factories when he was a teen, according to his sons. He began by making the wooden boxes used to ship the cheese. After learning cheesemaking at the Beaver factory, he moved to the original Tillamook cheese factory. He won awards for his aged cheddar.[28] Tone was a farmer, too. When his wife, Margaret, developed heart problems, he quit cheesemaking to farm full-time at Pleasant Valley. His barn, featuring dowels instead of nails, had been built by Adolph Schild, an early Swiss settler and uncle to Otto Schild.

Bass Tone on his farm, holding his twin sons, Pat and Mike. Courtesy of the Tone family

Tone wore blue-and-white striped overalls. A diabetic who made moonshine, he played the card game Pitch with Hans Leuthold, Doc Sayles, and Steve Steiner. Barbara Milne said, "He was very sincere, charismatic, good-looking; you just looked at him and liked him."[29]

The Tone twins, Pat and Mike, recall their dad stopping his flatbed truck at other farms to collect milk cans to add to his own, all to be delivered to Red Clover. He would muscle the full cans from the farmers' roadside wooden platforms, lifting them onto the truck bed, then moving down the road to the next Red Clover shipper.

When the Cheese War started, Tone was one of the cheese milk producers who sided with the rebels. He decided that the Cheese & Dairy / Red Clover side was right, and he didn't change his mind. He said, "I am not afraid to go it alone any day of the week . . . If I am down to the last man, I would still go it alone."[30] Tone played a key role in the Cheese War through his leadership at Red Clover, his insistence on high standards for Cheese & Dairy's cheese when he served as its inspector, and his skill as a sales ambassador to grocery store representatives. Red Clover benefited, and so did Cheese & Dairy.

STACKING THE COUNTY CREAMERY BOARD

The Cheese & Dairy / Red Clover alliance must have looked solid to Dixon. He concentrated on stopping Cheese & Dairy, knowing that he needed to discourage that significant bloc of opposition before more farmers joined it. He wanted to shrink Cheese & Dairy's influence on the County Creamery board, so he began to push to reduce the number of board representatives from Cheese & Dairy. Historically, the number of representatives from each cooperative had been based on its production.[31] Under that system, Cheese & Dairy was entitled to eight representatives on the County Creamery board.

In January 1963, County Creamery instituted a cap of no more than four board members, or 40 percent of production, from each cooperative. Formerly, Dixon had wanted to close the small factories; now he wanted—needed—them to stay open so their votes would counteract Cheese & Dairy's remaining votes. The change had been hatched at private meetings attended by handpicked County Creamery board members plus Beale Dixon and Warren McMinimee, according to Dixon's later court testimony.[32]

The new era started when the motion to put a ceiling on the number of representatives per factory passed, even with the "no" votes of the Cheese & Dairy and Red Clover representatives. As noted in the June 28, 1963, issue of *Northwest Dairy News*, "This action was taken [in January], despite protests by [Cheese & Dairy] that their production—over half the county's milk supply—entitles them to 8 directors."[33]

In a letter to the editor of the *Headlight Herald*, Ferd Becker summarized the change by asking, "Do you want to be controlled that way? Is this democratic?"[34]

County Creamery's board members from the small factories—minus Red Clover—doubled down on their support of Dixon and his policies. The reconstituted County Creamery board approved making further unsecured loans to Portland area stores, using Cheese & Dairy's money: Cheese & Dairy's *Board Information* told its members, "The total amount of $32,834.00 loaned [in January] includes an additional loan to a storekeeper who already had a loan from Cheese and Dairy Association."[35] In today's dollars, the unsecured loan was worth nearly $297,000. Barbara Milne said about the loans, "We researched all that junk, and we found out that they actually took things like a commercial mop bucket as collateral against a loan."[36]

Dixon gave pay raises to himself and his department heads, as noted in the *Headlight Herald*[37] and Cheese & Dairy's *Board Information* messages,[38] but Millard Bailey recalled in *The Tillamook Way*, "I don't know how many thousands of dollars of a paycut [sic] he took every year because he thought that if the farmers were going to suffer, he'd suffer right with them."[39] Cheese & Dairy representatives complained at a County Creamery annual meeting that Dixon handed out raises "without consulting or even informing the board."[40]

Because County Creamery was immune to any loan defaults that Cheese & Dairy producers might suffer, TCCA supporters weren't motivated to provide the same level of oversight that Grade A shippers were implementing. Dixon continued to prop up the failing areas of the cooperative through his bookkeeping and his loan-based sales. The weak spot in his plan was that all of the dairy farmers were going backward financially. Bulk tanks and milking parlors weren't saving Grade A shippers. Cheese milk producers weren't exactly rolling in clover because cheese sales weren't keeping pace with their peers across the country. In an ad, Cheese & Dairy highlighted the problem:

> Nationally, per capita consumption of cheese has increased from 7.7 lbs. per person in 1957 to 9.1 lbs. today (American Dairy Association statistics) . . . *there is no reason why the sale of the finest cheese in the world should remain static*."[41]

Everyone was hurting.

Once Again to the Courthouse

BY LINDA KIRK

One topic, the declaratory judgment suit, dominated suppertime conversation at our house in the spring of 1963. When Dad took a break from farm chores, he answered telephone calls from the Cheese & Dairy attorneys, fellow board members, and co-op members. In the evening, finished with milking, he talked to Mom after she put meatloaf and mashed potatoes on the supper table, and we served ourselves. Mom wondered if the Cheese & Dairy attorney, James Goodwin, was on track to be ready to try the case. Dad listed evidence Goodwin might introduce. Mom wanted to know if Dad would have to testify. He thought an affidavit would be enough. They knew the Tillamook circuit court judge had declined to hear the case. What kind of person was the visiting judge, Avery Combs? Dad told Mom rumors about which witnesses would testify for County Creamery.

After months of overhearing these discussions about legal maneuvers, I wanted to be in the courtroom on May 20, the first day of the trial. My parents seemed surprised but had no objection. Mom wrote a note to the school bus driver permitting me to ride from my junior high on Stillwell to the courthouse near the post office. More than two stories tall, the 1933 Art Deco courthouse sat alone on a wide lawn. It had two identical entrances, one on each end of the building, where recessed columns framed double doors. Yellow ochre bricks covered the exterior.[1]

People didn't run into the courthouse to get out of the rain. It was too forbidding, and the bricks on the steps were too steep and slippery. The courthouse was a no-nonsense structure—a place for serious people to make serious decisions. Inside the courthouse, high ceilings, wood paneled walls, limestone wainscoting and marble floors said,

"This is a government building." At the same time, the building welcomed everyone—while expecting loggers to trade their caulk boots for
soft-soled Romeos and dairy farmers to leave their barn boots at home.

On the first day of the trial, I felt more excited than nervous as I
climbed the steps at the south entrance, my arm weighed down by my
seventh grade history textbook. The building was intimidating, but also
slightly familiar. I had a friend whose mother worked on the top floor.
I remembered walking through the building, with Bonnie Hanrahan
leading the way, when we visited her mother in the 4-H office. On this
visit, at the top of the red brick stairs, I entered the courtroom lobby.
Ahead were doors marked "Circuit Court." I pulled open one of the
doors and stepped inside. At first, I could not find my mother, although
the benches were mostly empty. Then I saw the back of her head, and I
took a seat beside her.

Mom was writing notes. She shook her head to let me know she
couldn't talk. I was fine with that. I wanted to listen. Judge Avery Combs
sat in the front of the wood-paneled room. He said very little. I remember that an attorney spoke, but I could not follow his points. A witness
finished, and another one took his place. Their voices were low. Beside
me, Mom wrote quickly. She filled a page in her notebook and started a
new page. I could not tell what she was thinking. That was okay. I could
be patient. My parents would talk it over at supper.

At the meal that evening, and at many meals that followed, Cheese
War issues took center stage. That changed five years later, in 1968,
when Cheese & Dairy folded. For the next ten years, talking about the
Cheese War was intermittent. Still later, when the pain of losing the
Cheese War faded, Mom sometimes described testimony from one of
the lawsuits. Then I would remember that first time I entered a courtroom, back when I was twelve.

About five decades after I sat with my mother in the courtroom,
I returned to the courthouse on a morning that threatened rain. My
sister Marilyn and I had traveled to Tillamook to locate records from
the declaratory judgment court case. A clerk came to the reception
window that opened on the hall. We said we were searching for court
records from the 1960s where Tillamook Cheese & Dairy was the
plaintiff or the defendant. Soon we had files spread out over a long
table in the hall. Marilyn and I skimmed pages. If any document looked

as though it could help us understand the proceedings, we marked it for copying. By noon, colored tabs waved from dozens of pages. The staffer said the photocopies would be ready to pick up at two o'clock that afternoon. We paid the copy fee and headed to Marilyn's car. Time for lunch.

That afternoon, finished at the courthouse, we drove forty-five minutes south to Pacific City, where we ordered dory-caught fish at Sporty's. After supper, Marilyn and I holed up in our older sister's beach house and read the court documents. As we read, names of judges from the past appeared: J. S. Bohannon, Avery Combs, and Albert R. Musick. Attorneys came into view. On our side of the Cheese War, James Goodwin, Edwin Peterson, Glenn Jack, and Bruce Hall. On the other, Warren McMinimee and Douglas Kaufman.

Warren McMinimee was a name I heard at the supper table throughout the Cheese War. Attorneys on the Cheese & Dairy side changed, depending on the type of case. In contrast, when County Creamery did battle in court, the attorney most likely to be in the courtroom was one man: Warren McMinimee. His law partner, Douglas Kaufman, handled routine matters, but when a case in Circuit Court counted, Warren McMinimee took the floor. He must have been at the defendant's table when I visited the courtroom, but I did not notice him. My attention went to the courthouse, my mother's notetaking, and my expectation of learning more when I sat down to supper.

CHAPTER 8

Strife Builds

> There is strife in this isolated valley.
> —*The Oregonian*, April 21, 1963

By 1963, America was awakening from its long post–World War II self-satisfaction. Teens were listening to the Beatles, women were beginning to seek equality, African Americans were demanding civil rights, and everyone was beginning to hear about a small Asian country named South Vietnam. Tillamook residents were aware of the national turmoil, but they were most keenly focused on their own strife.

Throughout January and February 1963, farmers wrote letters to the *Headlight Herald* about the economics of dairy farming. Joe Beeler said, "We have taken many price cuts in the last few years while our expenses climb steadily."[1] Dale "Doc" Sayles wrote, "Many [farmers] are operating at a margin of profit which barely allows for the necessities of life."[2] Cheese milk producer Bert Quick, who shipped to Red Clover, pointed out the farmers' quagmire:

> In January 1953, butterfat was $1.11 per pound compared to the present price of 86 cents. . . . To the average farmer this makes a difference of making a fair profit or going out of business.
>
> While the making costs of cheese have risen slightly since 1950, selling and administrative costs for selling approximately the same amount of cheese have risen drastically. Selling costs in 1950 were below $80,000. This past year they were $276,244.00. Quite a difference.
>
> At the present time it is a process of elimination, with the big farmers getting bigger and the small farmers being completely eliminated.[3]

Then the board focused on a local grocery, Food Fair. In a *Board Information* message, Cheese & Dairy's board majority explained that Food Fair had removed Tillamook milk from its dairy case even though the store had taken out an equipment loan from Cheese & Dairy and still owed $7,700, or nearly $70,000 in today's dollars.[4]

When the news spread, "Some of the farmers' wives would go down to the store and fill their carts full of groceries," George Milne recalled. "Then they'd say, 'We can't find any Tillamook milk.' And the clerks would say they didn't have any, so the women would say, 'Oh, you don't have any? You can keep your groceries.' And the clerks were busy all day putting things back on the shelves."[5] The women may have borrowed a page from the playbook of southern Oregon members of the Oregon Farm Bureau during the 1959 Teamster strike.[6]

"We didn't tell them to do that. But you can't blame the owner for getting so mad," Milne said.[7] In May 1963, Food Fair's owners filed a $100,000 lawsuit against George Milne, Hans Leuthold, Dave Leuthold, Vern Lucas, Joe Beeler, and Glenn Johnston, charging them with conspiracy. Joe Beeler's mother had passed the family farm on to him, and "she told him to turn all the assets over to his sons—quick!" recalled Barbara Milne.[8] Joe didn't panic, and the lawsuit faded away, but it was an early example of the enthusiasm of the upstarts, including their families, for their cause, as well as one of many examples of turning to the courts to resolve conflicts.

GRANNY GOOSE

It was still early 1963 when Hooker Jenck received a letter from his sister in California. She wrote about family news and then mentioned that a snack food company, Granny Goose, was using newspaper ads to promote an aerosol cheese spread: grab a cracker, invert the can, press the tip, and out comes fluffy yellow goo. The ads bragged that the spread was made with Tillamook's cheese.

Jenck hadn't heard about Tillamook's cheese being used this way, and he wondered if other farmers were aware of it. Shippers were glad Dixon had made a sale, but they were insulted by the use of their high-quality cheese in a low-value product, and the Cheese & Dairy board was gravely concerned about not having been told about the sale. They were also concerned about the potential harm to the reputation of their cheese.

Jenck brought it up at the February 16, 1963, annual meeting of Cheese & Dairy, according to the minutes:

> [He] read a news article from a California paper noting that Tillamook Cheese was being put up in aerated cans for a spread. He asked if any of the board members knew about this. (None of them did.) Why did they have to find out through a newspaper instead of through the board members. Why doesn't the board know.[9]

Dixon admitted to the farmers that cheese had been sold to Granny Goose. "He noted that they were purchasing the cheese at the full price. He noted that this was no different than sales to other processors. We have sold them 40,000 pounds of squares to date."[10] Later in the meeting, Jenck returned to the topic. He "was not satisfied with canned cheese answers. Would like to be at the board meeting when they are discussed."[11]

Jenck's inquiry may have been a setup—a way to be sure the Cheese & Dairy board members and shippers were aware of the Granny Goose sale and that the information got into the meeting's minutes. Thanks to Jenck's questions, Dixon had admitted to the sale. He had not acknowledged authorizing the use of Tillamook's name without board approval or knowledge, however. Cheese & Dairy board members began to wonder if they had been given the full story.

George Milne and Hans Leuthold went to the County Creamery offices one night after they finished milking. Because they were board members, they were allowed into the office after hours. Milne said, "We looked through the files. We got files about going to Granny Goose with a deal to use Tillamook Cheese in pasteurized cans. Dixon hadn't told the board about it. There was a letter; the deal to use Tillamook's name was in the works."[12]

Milne and Leuthold waited until the next Cheese & Dairy board meeting to confront Dixon about authorizing the use of Tillamook's brand. "We asked about the Granny Goose deal and Dixon said, 'Oh, no.'"

Milne continued, "So Hans and I got up and went back to the files and ripped out the whole file drawer with the Granny Goose file and dropped it on the table. We just shoved it at him.

"They had a beautiful polished conference table. All Dixon could say was, 'They scratched the table! They scratched the table!' We pointed at the file and yelled at him, 'Look at the file! Read it!' Well, it finally got read."[13]

The board members were now fully aware of the Granny Goose sale and the approval to use Tillamook's name, and Dixon knew the majority was against it. He stopped pursuing further sales to that outlet.

TILLAMOOK FLUID MILK SHIPPERS ASSOCIATION

Millard Bailey, Otto Schild, and Karl Zweifel, the three Cheese & Dairy directors who supported County Creamery and had led the recall attempt, continued to serve on the Cheese & Dairy board despite a majority vote requesting that they resign. Their presence led to some heated discussions. At a special Cheese & Dairy board meeting on April 25, 1963, Schild mentioned that County Creamery might establish its own Grade A shipper group to receive fluid milk. Schild said the plan was to sell the group's milk to County Creamery—"take shippers from the T.C&D.A."[14] The idea surprised most of the board members and they were immediately concerned. Glenn Johnston responded, "It would split the T.C.&D.A. organization." For Bailey, Schild, and Zweifel, conflict with County Creamery was anathema, and they were willing to gamble on the demise of Cheese & Dairy if a new County Creamery Grade A group could be formed that would be loyal to the marketing organization.

Less than a month later, the Tillamook Fluid Milk Shippers Association formed and broke away from Cheese & Dairy. Schild, Zweifel, and fifty-seven other producers of the Tillamook Fluid Milk Shippers Association supported County Creamery. The Grade A group was also known as the Shiveley Shippers, named for Gaylord Shiveley, a former Cheese & Dairy farmer and president of the new group.[15] TFMSA members wanted County Creamery to be the marketing agent for their milk.

When Otto Schild and Karl Zweifel went with the new group, they could not continue as Cheese & Dairy board members. Hooker Jenck and Floyd Woodward were appointed to fill the vacancies. Millard Bailey, a cheese milk producer, remained on the board.[16]

With tensions at an all-time high, Ferd Becker received a letter on April 19, 1963, that threatened his life for his support of Cheese & Dairy. The *Headlight Herald* wrote about the letter:

> Ferdinand Becker, 1113 Ninth St., Tillamook, who operates a dairy farm locally, this week offered a reward of $500 to anyone who supplies information which results in the arrest and conviction of the person who mailed a threatening letter to him on April 19. . . . The letter to Becker, who is a member of the Tillamook Cheese & Dairy Assn. which is now involved in a controversy with the Tillamook County Creamery Assn., read as follows:
>
> "I have become convinced that you are out to break the ass'n. You are to quit and desist from meddling in all affairs pertaining to the Tillamook County Creamery Assn. and also the TCDA if you don't I shall burn your farm buildings and if that don't stop you I shall get my scope sighted deer rifle and pick you off. I can usually hit a deer at 400 yards on the first shot. The future of our county depends on this. If you don't think I mean business just try me. After you comes Lucas, Leuthold & Milne in that order."[17]

The sheriff investigated, and sent the envelope and letter to the Federal Bureau of Investigation for analysis. The culprit was never caught. Ferd's son, Jim, recalls, "He figured it was someone from down [in] south [Tillamook County]. It irritated him more that [the writer] didn't have the guts to sign it."[18]

The other men singled out in the letter downplayed the threat. Milne, with gallows humor intact, wondered why he was fourth on the list of targets. At about the same time, his oldest daughter answered the home telephone and heard an adult man say, "I'm going to get your family." George and Barbara Milne categorized it as a crank call. It wasn't as easy to dismiss their mailbox being knocked off its post, the only one of the cluster of rural neighborhood mailboxes to suffer damage. But George Milne reinstalled it, and no more damage occurred.

Then, someone put a note under the windshield wiper of Milne's car while it was parked in town. The note said, "I'm going to get your daughter." Immediately, Milne went to the sheriff as well as the publisher of the newspaper. He said later that he told the publisher to print the note if something happened.[19] Milne told his wife, but not his daughters, about the threat. The Milnes gambled that nothing would occur, and it didn't.

THE DECLARATORY JUDGMENT

The gap between Cheese & Dairy and County Creamery had grown even wider since the request for a declaratory judgment had been filed seven months earlier. Now the rebels faced deteriorating relationships with relatives and friends. They were also dealing with losing Cheese & Dairy shippers to TFMSA, stopping Dixon from burdening Cheese & Dairy with the responsibility for loans and straightening out the bookkeeping.

The declaratory judgment would answer many questions: Did Grade A milk have to be marketed through County Creamery? How should the facilities at the large Tillamook factory be divided? Could the original formula for determining the number of representatives from each cooperative to the County Creamery board be changed? Were the Shiveley Shippers admitted to County Creamery improperly? Should County Creamery have to consult with a member cooperative before loaning that group's funds? And, as George Milne said in an article in *Northwest Dairy News*, "The question is whether or not a cooperative has the right to run its own business without submitting to the jurisdiction of another cooperative."[20] A declaratory judgment might confirm and even expand Cheese & Dairy's autonomy.

In an article about the case, *The Oregonian* asked, "Why did the powerful member cooperative try to unseat the pint-sized but equally powerful Dixon from the managerial position at the creamery and ask him to resign as secretary manager of the lesser post? . . . Why, after all these years, has the member cooperative decided it was time to have its position in the 'family' clarified in a court of law?"[21] The reporter tried to find answers, talking to several key leaders on both sides. Hans Leuthold blamed Dixon; Otto Schild blamed Milne.[22] Dixon's perspective, as he wrote in his 1962 annual report, was:

This situation has greatly hurt the effectiveness of the County Association. It has caused the loss of valued employees, hurt relations with our customers, and could split up the marketing of dairy products through the one County Association. . . . It is my opinion that the future growth of the dairy industry in Tillamook area depends upon the outcome of this issue. All dairymen should continue to market all their production through one strong marketing Association with equal consideration for both fluid and manufacturing milk markets, in order to protect and keep what has taken over fifty years to build.[23]

Otto Schild chimed in on the issue of one strong marketing group. He didn't mind leaving the management of the cooperative to one person rather than the board. Or, as he explained it, "I want a good man to run the whole works . . . One good Manager in every good business."[24]

Cheese & Dairy's new manager, Ed Burke, alerted the board to a financial crisis resulting from the large number of shippers who had left the cooperative: Cheese & Dairy needed to calculate who owed what, how its bills would be paid, and how it would adapt to a reduced volume of milk. One of the first actions the board took was to stop milk check advances for April's milk. It was a bombshell for Cheese & Dairy's loyal patrons. Many farm families relied on the advances, but as Cheese & Dairy's *Board Information* for May 6, 1963, told its remaining farmers, it had "to protect the funds until the full liability of those who are leaving the organization is determined."[25] The lack of an April advance was a hardship. Advances resumed the following month, but Cheese & Dairy shippers would experience a delayed milk check later in the year and partial payments several times in the years to come.

MILK TANKER BLOCKADE

While the Cheese & Dairy board was trying to resolve its financial issues, County Creamery was shipping a mixture of Cheese & Dairy's milk and Shively Shippers' milk to fulfill its contracts with Carnation, Alpenrose, and Lucerne. Cheese & Dairy's lawyers warned that commingling the milk of the two cooperatives might weaken Cheese & Dairy's position in the coming declaratory judgment lawsuit. If County

On May 9, 1963, idled tankers were blocked from leaving the dock of Tillamook's cheese factory. *Headlight Herald*, May 12, 1963

Creamery were allowed to combine its sources of milk, Cheese & Dairy could lose its claim to be the unique marketer of its milk.

After hearing their attorneys' opinion, some of the Cheese & Dairy farmers set up a blockade at the Tillamook factory. The *Headlight Herald* reported:

> Since Thursday morning the six big tankers which customarily haul thousands of gallons of Tillamook county [sic] milk in daily trips over the hills to Portland have been parked at the local milk processing plant loading dock. Dairy farmer members of Tillamook Cheese and Dairy Assn. are enforcing a blockade on Portland milk shipments by keeping heavy farm trucks parked in front of the tanker-trailers. The farmers say the blockade will be enforced until a judgment is rendered by Circuit Court Judge Avery Coombs [sic] in an injunction action to be heard in Tillamook next Monday, May 13.[26]

Suddenly, County Creamery was in a tight spot. As reported later in *The Oregonian*, the blockade forced County Creamery to buy milk from around the state because it couldn't supply the Portland market solely from Shiveley Shippers' milk.[27]

George Milne remembered monitoring the cheese factory's driveway with Vern Lucas. One trucker got past them, so they chased after him as he drove east on the Wilson River Highway toward Portland. They honked the horn on Vern's truck and waved their arms out the windows.

Finally, the trucker stopped. He told them that he had to haul the milk because he needed to make some money. They let him go.[28] Meanwhile, the Cheese & Dairy board passed several motions to stop any payments or benefits of membership accruing to the Shiveley Shippers farmers.[29]

Cheese & Dairy's lawyers proposed to Judge Combs that the five-day blockade would end if doing so would not affect the declaratory judgment case. Cheese & Dairy wanted to be certain that the judge would not consider the commingling of milk sources as a precedent for how future production should be marketed. County Creamery's lawyer, Warren A. McMinimee, agreed to the proposal, and the driveway was cleared.[30] The judge scolded both groups for letting matters deteriorate to the point that the court got involved. Cheese & Dairy wrote to its members on May 15, 1963, "Dear Patrons, We are informing you according to the ruling of the court. There will be no more monkey business."[31] The larger news was that the Shiveley Shippers had been accepted by the judge as another party to the lawsuit.[32]

The court hearing began. Warren McMinimee represented County Creamery. When he tangled with his Cheese War opponents, he learned that his quick mind could be matched in the courtroom by Cheese & Dairy farmers who relied on their own intelligence and, of course, the truth. George Milne explained the experience of testifying, "The first few times in the witness stand, you have a lot of butterflies. After that, you know what's coming. You try to do like taking a test in school: You try to note every angle, everything you can think of so you'll handle whatever comes up. You have to know your facts." While milking the cows or driving the tractor in the field, Milne would think about his answers to lawyers' possible questions.[33]

CLEM HURLIMAN

Clem Hurliman also testified before Judge Combs. He was a County Creamery representative from Central Creamery in south Tillamook County who was one of eight children of the Clemens and Catherine Hurliman clan, Swiss settlers who had farmed in the Pacific City–Woods area since 1914. Other Hurliman relatives lived in Tillamook County, too, so the Clemens Hurliman family was called the Woods Hurlimans to distinguish them from the others.

The Hurliman family had deep roots in St. Joseph's Catholic Church in Cloverdale. Clem's father helped to build the church, Clem was the first person to be baptized at the church, and Hurliman descendants still attend the church. Clem married Liz Blaser from Tillamook and moved onto a farm on Meda Loop. They and their seven children were the Meda Hurlimans, and Clem farmed there the rest of his life.

For the extended Hurliman clan, the Cheese War led to lifelong familial splits. Clem Hurliman acted on his conscience, but his relatives felt betrayed because, after he became loyal to Cheese & Dairy, he continued to attend secret County Creamery meetings. Then he reported on the meetings to his Cheese & Dairy friends. As a result, the rebels knew what was going on in their opponent's meetings and could plan accordingly. Both sides were holding hush-hush informal meetings with their key supporters to figure out their next moves, and Cheese & Dairy was helped by its spy, Clem Hurliman.

Hurliman's courtroom testimony surprised most listeners. According to Hurliman, "the [County Creamery] meetings were held at the Arnold Walker home, at the YMCA in Tillamook and at Dixon's home."[34] When asked about the meetings, Dixon testified, "They weren't official meetings and I did not call them. The opposition group was holding many meetings. It was the feeling of some of our group they should be meeting, too."[35]

In the courtroom, Hurliman gave his testimony in an "aw shucks" kind of way. Barbara Milne remembered him as "a very engaging man with a smile that would make anyone smile. He was a down-home guy with a dry sense of humor."[36] Private notes of Hurliman's testimony[37] record him being asked by McMinimee, "Where was this meeting?" Hurliman replied, "Towards the river and that way [points west]." The lawyer asked him about a May 4, 1963, meeting at Beale Dixon's home. "Do you know why you were there?" Clem replied, "That is what I am trying to figure out."[38] The Headlight Herald wrote that Hurliman drew laughter from the courtroom audience when he testified about trying to remember all the off-the-record County Creamery meetings: "You can laugh if you want to, but we attended so many meetings that when you try to cipher them all out . . ."[39]

Hurliman was Bass Tone's brother-in-law, and they discussed the County Creamery meetings. Tone then spread the word among Red

Clover and Cheese & Dairy loyalists. But when Hurliman was asked in court by County Creamery's lawyer, "Were you secretly meeting with Bass Tone?" Hurliman said, according to Barbara Milne's recollection, "Well, of course I went to Tone's house. My mother is living there. Bass's wife is my sister. I went to see my mother. It's all right if I go to see my mother, isn't it?" Barbara Milne said, "McMinimee kept walking into things like that. He looked like a fool."[40]

After his testimony, Hurliman and a brother who farmed in north Tillamook County were loyal to Cheese & Dairy; the other brothers and cousins lived in the same area as Clem, but they stayed with County Creamery. Hurliman and his south Tillamook County relatives continued to worship together under the same small roof at their Catholic Church, but he and one cousin never spoke again. Liz Hurliman later recalled, "We have bench #3 at the Cloverdale Catholic Church. There were the Woods Hurlimans and the Meda Hurlimans. We sit on separate sides of church always."[41] When Hurliman died fifty-five years later, his wife worried that no one would attend the funeral. Instead, the church was full. The cousin, however, did not attend.

Thinking back to the trial, Barbara Milne remembered Hans Leuthold's testimony. "[He] was on the witness stand and McMinimee accused him of having secret meetings in his barn. And Leuthold said, 'Well, I can't help it if people drop in and stand around while I'm trying to milk.' That wasn't the point at all; of *course* it was a secret meeting. But he shut the lawyer up."[42]

On the last day of the trial, Dixon testified that "the Creamery Assn. hold more than $300,000 in notes taken over by them from Alpenrose Dairy of Portland without recourse, and that the Creamery group has an oral agreement with Alpenrose not to record these instruments, which represent money originally loaned by Alpenrose to their customers."[43]

In today's dollars, the unrecorded notes would total more than $2.7 million.

THE VERDICT

On July 2, 1963, Judge Combs issued his ruling in the declaratory judgment lawsuit. He said that Cheese & Dairy could market its Grade A milk through any entity it chose, must approve of any loans made with its funds, and should have its previous number of representatives on the County Creamery board restored. He declined to be more specific about who owned what, telling the parties to rely on the property deeds. The judge said that the Shiveley Shippers were admitted improperly to County Creamery. An article in the *Oregon Journal* explained,

> The Tillamook County Creamery Association is not a holding company and may not dictate the policies and management of the Tillamook Cheese & Dairy Association. TCCA may not control TC&DA's activities except the rights given it in specific contracts.[44]

Judge Combs added that Cheese & Dairy must honor its current marketing agreement with County Creamery until it expired as well as pay its proportional share—half—of Beale Dixon's salary. The judge ended by saying, "this is a matter which should never have been allowed to progress to the point where a court determination was required. . . . I urge all parties involved to give serious thought to the best interests of the industry in this county rather than to their own individual wishes and to attempt to settle the differences which now divide you."[45]

The rebellious farmers celebrated. Cheese & Dairy told its members it wanted to be "fair and impartial in working out the complete solution to our problems. However, we have every intention of standing firmly for the rights of our members in dealing with the Tillamook County Creamery Association."[46]

Having prevailed on most of the issues, Cheese & Dairy considered its next move. Joined by Red Clover Creamery, Cheese & Dairy announced the pending termination of its marketing agreement with County Creamery. The two organizations were fed up with their relationship with County Creamery and were ready to act on provisions in the contract to end it. The Cheese & Dairy *Board Information* for August 13, 1963, included this message:

MARKETING AGREEMENT WITH TCCA.

We are sending you a copy of the legal notice terminating the marketing agreements between Cheese & Dairy and TCCA. This step has been taken to clear the way for negotiations for a new marketing contract betwaen [sic] the two organizations which should have been written when Cheese & Dairy was first formed.

Red Clover Creamery Association has filed a similar notice of termination with TCCA.

Some of the reasons for this action by Cheese & Dairy are:

Loss of Cheese & Dairy's voting representation on TCCA board of directors.

Unfair charges made by TCCA manager to Cheese & Dairy for supplies and services. These charges have recently been increased again.

Lack of a written agreement covering the joint-use facilities that is a requirement in Cheese & Dairy bylaws.

Inadaquate [sic] and irregular bookkeeping records in TCCA.

Interference by TCCA between Cheese & Dairy and its members.

Refusal of TCCA to accept the judge's opinion in the lawsuit, thus prolonging the difficulties.

Insistance [sic] of TCCA on making loans, giving discounts and advertising allowances, etc. on Grade A bulk milk against the wishes of Cheese & Dairy.

Disregard by TCCA directors of their responsibilities under the bylaws.

Taking over by the TCCA manager of the rights and duties of the board of directors. (Example—Mr. Dixon recently gave pay raises to department heads and to himself without consulting or even informing the Board.)

The directors of Cheese & Dairy are obligated to protect the interests of our producers and will continue to work for more money in the milk check. Although we are prepared to independently manage our cooperative, it is our desire to reach this goal by negotiating a new marketing agreement with TCCA.[47]

COUNTING VOTES

On August 14, the day after the *Board Information* went to farmers, Cheese & Dairy and Red Clover representatives to the County Creamery board experienced a meeting full of fraudulent vote counting by John R. Craven Jr., County Creamery's board president.

Craven has been variously described as a preacher's kid, a good guy, and a shill for Dixon. He was a south Tillamook County native who shipped his milk to Oretown Creamery. His father had started Meda Creamery, near Clem and Liz Hurliman's farm, with his brother-in-law, Rome Dunn. Craven served on the County Creamery board for nearly three decades, and he had several stints as board president, including during the Cheese War.

Joe Jenck says his father Hooker "always had respect for Craven. They were one of the few that actually stayed friends through [the Cheese War]. But just because my dad respected him doesn't mean he hadn't had enough of him."[48]

"The factories needed a leader standing up for them," says Dave Leuthold, a son of Hans Leuthold, "because they were only producing cheese. Hans said John Craven was fair—narrow-minded and one-sided, but not one to stab you in the back."[49] Except he did.

The meeting began as yet another day of wrangling between County Creamery's supporters and opponents. McMinimee also attended as County Creamery's counsel. As the fifteen board members, including all eight of the judge-mandated Cheese & Dairy representatives, entered the room, the Cheese & Dairy and Red Clover allies had several items on their agenda. Because of the six-week-old ruling in the declaratory judgment case, the rebels were cautiously optimistic that they could get a few key items passed at the meeting. If so, they could avoid deploying their ultimate option: sever ties with County Creamery.

Throughout the meeting, however, both Cheese & Dairy and Red Clover's actions were thwarted by board president John Craven, who deliberately ruled that majority vote totals failed and minority vote totals succeeded "because chair did not recognize four T.C.& D.A. representatives."[50]

His actions came despite Judge Combs's ruling requiring proportional representation from the cooperative members of County Creamery. Craven must have known that McMinimee had pointed out to Judge Combs that Cheese & Dairy's attorneys had not amended their initial filing for a declaratory judgment to include two issues: whether the Tillamook Fluid Milk Shippers Association could be accepted into County Creamery membership, and whether County Creamery's slashing of the number of Cheese & Dairy representatives on its board should be voided. Because Cheese & Dairy's filing was flawed, McMinimee and Craven could gamble that the judge would soon rule in favor of County Creamery, and the men would not be punished for disobeying the judge's currently binding ruling.

Cheese & Dairy and Red Clover representatives to County Creamery's board didn't have this information and were puzzled by the vote counts during the meeting. Ferd Becker took informal minutes that were signed by nine witnesses and entered as an exhibit in a later lawsuit. According to the informal minutes, the coalition of Cheese & Dairy and Red Clover tried to take thirteen actions, with Craven declaring "pass" or "fail" based on his own vote count:

1. The board voted, 6 in favor and 9 against, on a motion to table corrections to the minutes of the July 12 County Creamery meeting. Although the motion failed, Craven declared that the motion carried. The board members were surprised by this turn of events.

2. As planned, George Milne moved to table the motion from a previous County Creamery meeting to accept the Shiveley Shippers for membership. If the Shiveley Shippers were accepted, their representative, Gaylord Shiveley, would have a vote. Craven ruled Milne out of order, prompting Glenn Johnston to ask Craven if he was using Warren McMinimee's authority or the judge's. Craven turned to McMinimee for guidance. Judge Combs had ruled that the Shiveley Shippers were improperly admitted to the County Creamery co-op. McMinimee read aloud from *Robert's Rules of Order*, focusing on a section that said that tabling a previous motion would take precedence over a current motion. Craven had to call for a vote on the tabling motion. When the tabling vote was held, nine hands went up in favor of the motion. Six hands went up against it. Milne's motion passed. But John Craven ruled that the motion had lost.

George Milne and other like-minded farmers protested Craven's decision, but he ruled again that the motion had lost. Because of the incorrect vote count, the Shiveley Shippers were admitted, and Gaylord Shiveley took a seat at the table despite the judge's ruling. Now there were sixteen County Creamery board members, although Craven was only acknowledging twelve.

3. After lunch, Ralph Redberg, a Cheese & Dairy shipper, continued with the challengers' agenda. He moved to discharge McMinimee and retain local attorney George Winslow Sr., a motion seconded by Bass Tone. With Shiveley at the table, the vote was 9 in favor and 7 against. The motion passed, but once again, Craven declared that it had instead lost. It was clear that Craven was going to ignore the increasing protests of the Cheese & Dairy and Red Clover representatives who knew, like everyone else at the table, that his vote tallies were not based on the court's ruling on the correct number of Cheese & Dairy representatives.

4. The board considered an appeal of the declaratory judgment verdict. Bob Rulifson, the Cloverdale Cheese Factory representative and a County Creamery loyalist, moved to appeal, meaning that the plaintiffs, whose representatives were seated at the same table, were being asked to vote to put themselves through another court battle. The vote was 9 against the motion and 7 in favor; it failed. John Craven, however, ruled that it carried.

5. Ralph Redberg, a Cheese & Dairy representative, then moved that "all expenses of an appeal be borne by those other than TC&DA and Red Clover."[51] No second to the motion was recorded in the informal minutes, but the vote was 9 for it and 7 against. Craven's declared outcome isn't noted in the informal minutes.

6. Hans Leuthold moved, seconded by George Milne, that County Creamery expel Cheese & Dairy and Red Clover effective immediately and without penalty. He added that a roll call should be taken. President Craven then asked McMinimee's opinion of the motion, and the attorney "advised his group to vote NO."[52] While the outcome isn't noted in the informal minutes, it must have failed or been declared so by Craven because a new motion was made on the subject.

7. Hans Leuthold moved that County Creamery cancel its marketing agreements with Cheese & Dairy and Red Clover, effective that day. George Milne seconded the motion. It passed, 9 to 6. The lower vote total was probably because one board member left the meeting, but it isn't clear in the informal minutes. In any case, Craven declared that the motion had lost. County Creamery did not want to release Cheese & Dairy and Red Clover.

8. Next, George Milne moved that Craven, Rulifson, and Beale Dixon personally pay all expenses connected to the County Creamery purchase

of a cream separator during the May tanker blockade, rather than charge Cheese & Dairy for it. Ralph Redberg seconded the motion. Again, the vote was 9 to 6; Craven declared that the motion had failed, not passed.

9. The Central Cheese Factory representative moved that TCCA buy the separator. Cheese & Dairy and Red Clover directors opposed the motion; the final vote was 6-9, with Craven ruling that the motion had passed.

10. Hans Leuthold moved to adjourn. The motion passed 9-6; Craven said the motion failed.

11. After a housekeeping item passed with an accurate vote count, the Mohler Cheese Factory representative moved that TCCA should handle cheese made by Cheese & Dairy, but if County Creamery didn't receive the cheese, no funds would be advanced. The vote was 6-9 against the motion; Craven said it had passed.

12. Milne moved that Cheese & Dairy buy the equities of County Creamery or, alternately, that County Creamery buy the equities of Cheese & Dairy. While discussing the motion, the board learned from McMinimee that he had discussed the idea with Cheese & Dairy's attorney and Milne on August 6. It did not seem that his client, County Creamery, was aware of the proposal. The board voted 9-6 for the motion, but Craven said it had failed.

13. Lucas made a motion that Dixon be discharged as County Creamery's manager. The board voted 9-6 for the motion. Craven declared that it had failed.[53]

With that vote, the County Creamery board fired Beale Dixon one year after the infamous annual meeting where the board had retained him by one vote. Dixon would have been out of a job if Craven had recognized all of the Cheese & Dairy representatives and counted the votes correctly. Craven and those board members who supported him saved Dixon's job.

Craven's actions intensified and prolonged the cheese industry feud. Ken Jenck, Hooker's brother, told patrons at special joint meeting of Cheese & Dairy and Red Clover on August 19, "I have never seen such a disgusting sight as the last T.C.C.A. Board Meeting and Craven."[54]

The next year, Craven told *The Oregonian* "that hostilities at times reached a point where he thought it was 'almost impossible' to hold meetings."[55] Another Portland paper reported that Craven described "stormy meetings ridden with cursing, shouting and even fistfights."[56] A rumor went around Tillamook that Craven's garage had been blown up with dynamite, but no contemporary coverage mentioned it.

THE SPLIT

Four days after Craven miscounted the votes, Judge Combs rescinded two of his decisions in the declaratory judgment—that the Shiveley Shippers could not be accepted for membership in County Creamery and that the number of Cheese & Dairy's representatives to the County Creamery board could not be slashed—because the decisions "had not been properly before the court for determination in the original court action, and ordered that his previous rulings be withdrawn."[57] McMinimee and Craven were not punished for their actions at the board meeting.

The boards of Cheese & Dairy and Red Clover decided to pursue termination of their marketing agreements with County Creamery when the contracts concluded in October 1963, and if the membership agreed, they would no longer have any representation on the County Creamery board, making the judge's reversal a moot point. Shiveley Shippers would continue to be part of County Creamery, however.

On August 19, the Cheese & Dairy board met in the afternoon in Vern Lucas's basement and in the early evening at Hans Leuthold's home. While at Leuthold's, the board passed a motion, "Because Mr. Millard Bailey has acted in a manner contrary to the By-Laws of the T. C. & D. A. and the Cooperative Laws of the State of Oregon, I move his share of stock be cancelled."[58] At last, Bailey was removed from his leadership role—and the organization.

After the two daytime meetings, Cheese & Dairy and Red Clover held a special joint meeting at Fairview Grange for their patrons. Among the questions from farmers was one from C. R. Neilson, husband of County Creamery stenographer Anita Neilson, who asked, "Aren't we still responsible for about 70% of these loans if they go bad?" The answer: "Yes we are."[59]

Cheese & Dairy's attorney told the rebels that County Creamery owed Cheese & Dairy more than $1.5 million, or more than $13.5 million today. The Cheese & Dairy farmers were stunned and horrified.[60]

The two boards asked patrons for their preferences on next steps. The members discussed Dixon, the price they were receiving for their milk, and their discontent. Milne summarized the remarks of the board members and then stated the issue as, "Are we going to go it on our own or are we going to knuckle under to the manager?"[61] At the end of the discussion, Milne said that Cheese & Dairy and Red Clover would abide by the wishes of the membership. He then led the farmers through a series of voice votes. The meeting's minutes recorded the votes:

Mr. Milne: (To stockholders) (1) are you in favor of the highest possible price?
Loud aye vote—No nayes.
(2) Are you in favor of getting as much information as possible?
Loud aye vote—No nayes.
(3) Are you in accord with the Board that has been taking all the guff and been pushed around and taken all they can take?
Loud aye vote—No nayes.[62]

The members gave a definitive answer when George Milne asked them about staying with County Creamery or breaking away. They preferred independence. In a September 19, 1963, letter to County Creamery, Cheese & Dairy's board announced its members' decision:

in view of the situation with regard to representation of T.C.D.A. on the T.C.C.A. board, the admission of the Tillamook Fluid Milk Shippers to the County Association, the misunderstanding concerning the payment for our bulk milk, and other good and sufficient reasons, and in light of the new County marketing agreement which provides for immediate cancellation, that T.C.D.A. should and does hereby inform you that its marketing agreements are hereby cancelled and terminated at this time.[63]

The farmers' danders were up. But could they succeed on their own?

CHAPTER 9

The Crusaders

After deciding to split from County Creamery, the farmers of Cheese & Dairy and Red Clover bought a full-page newspaper ad that announced,

> we shall now proceed with the marketing of our cheese independent of the Tillamook County Creamery Association . . . In a sense, we are crusaders, fighting to re-establish the fame and consumer demand for our cheese and other dairy products—the finest in America.[1]

What made these change agents think they could succeed on their own? It may have been hubris. It may have been that they figured they could do the marketing better than it had been done by County Creamery. It may have been that their enthusiasm made up for their lack of experience.

On a practical level, they knew they could hire attorneys and marketers. Also, they had total control of their cheese production. And making cheese in the Tillamook and Red Clover factories, not in the collection of six small outlying factories, would offer more consistent product quality. Red Clover had good cheesemakers, and given the close cooperation that existed between Red Clover and Cheese & Dairy, the organizations would get sellable cheese.

Cheese & Dairy was still plagued by the unauthorized loans that had used Cheese & Dairy's money and driven many of the discoveries that led to the split. In a September 11, 1963, letter to County Creamery, Cheese & Dairy said, "We tender you herewith assignment of all the notes and chattel mortgages securing the Alpenrose and Carnation loans in exchange for immediate payment by certified funds for full face value, which we understand to be $248,138.22 as of August

31, 1963, less unposted payments received in September, with proper credits for interest, and stand ready to give you the same non-recourse endorsement as was furnished by Alpenrose thereon."[2]

In other words, Cheese & Dairy offered County Creamery the same deal the member co-op had received years earlier: You are responsible for these loans, and you won't have any options if things don't work out. Not surprisingly, County Creamery did not accept the offer for the nonrecourse nor the demand for immediate repayment of loans totaling more than $2.2 million in today's dollars. It counteroffered "some form of credit for the loans."[3]

In October 1963, Cheese & Dairy and Red Clover terminated their marketing contracts with County Creamery. The split is mentioned in *The Tillamook Way*, but the book doesn't pinpoint the bad loans or Dixon's other actions as the causes. Instead, it says,

> Exactly what set it off is perhaps a case of no one being completely right and no one being completely wrong. Some Grade A producers were adamant in their demand that they remain in a closed pool. Dixon and some members of the board of directors were equally adamant that all members be permitted to join the pool. The dispute spilled over into the Willamette Valley after Dixon made the deal with Alpenrose Dairy, when valley producers were losing business to [County Creamery]. Those farmers complained to friends in the Tillamook Valley, many of whom were ready to accept any reason to attack Dixon and the [County Creamery] board because of the dispute.[4]

It is true that when Dixon made deals with Portland-area distributors, competing farmers in the Willamette Valley lost sources of sales, just as County Creamery bid at times for distribution deals that valley farmers won. If those valley farmers ever complained to Tillamook farmers, however, the incidences are lost to history. Dixon may have believed that outsiders had influence over Tillamook's farmers, given the milk law that resulted from statewide cooperation among farmers. He saw the strength in numbers that allowed the farmers to shape the language of the law. But Tillamook farmers were insular and not beholden to farmers in the Willamette Valley, nor would they have voted against their own interests solely to assist producers in another area of the state. The issue of a closed or open pool was a distraction from the real issues. Dixon, who had created a resistance he did not expect and could not manage, kept expressing concern about the pool possibly closing. Although Dixon invented the issue, it stuck in people's minds.

The two organizations settled into their new realities. Judge Combs had ruled that each side could continue to use areas of the large factory north of Tillamook. Even before the Cheese War, County Creamery and Cheese & Dairy shared equipment and production rooms—a system that had led to erroneous bookkeeping by County Creamery but was now necessary so that each group could produce its dairy products.

Cheese & Dairy made the cheese and ran the visitors' center; County Creamery kept the laboratory and its office in another area of the building. Cheese & Dairy bottled its milk at the facility; County Creamery's milk was bottled by Alpenrose in the Portland area. County Creamery made butter in the same room where Cheese & Dairy made ice cream.[5] The arrangement was awkward—like a divorced couple forced to continue living together, including taking turns using the kitchen—but it had been ordered by the court, and the two sides abided by it.

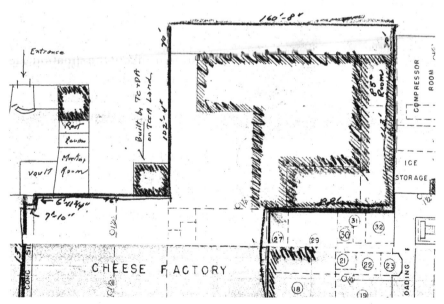

A segment of a factory floor plan, developed as an exhibit in the declaratory judgment lawsuit, notes that a small addition was "Built by TC&DA on TCCA land." The areas marked with jagged boundaries were owned by Cheese & Dairy but used by County Creamery. Courtesy of the author

Dividing the factory had some odd consequences. Ferd Becker's son, Jim, was a college student who worked at the factory for Cheese & Dairy in the summer. According to Jim, "Dixon would . . . walk through our factory quite often. His office was at the far end. He'd walk across to the end of the last vat through the curing room to the lab."[6] Because of the arrangement, it was easy for County Creamery to estimate Cheese & Dairy's volume of milk and production of cheese—and thus its financial health.

It was also easy for County Creamery's opponents to walk into its office and confront Dixon. Two Red Clover representatives, Bass Tone and Bert Quick, did just that in late August 1963. They wanted their factory's files, which County Creamery stored for it and for all of the factories.

But after the Granny Goose incident earlier in the year, Dixon had hired a former farmer, Merrill Maxwell, as a guard for the County Creamery office. George Milne recalled that "he stood in the County Creamery office with a revolver in a holster."[7] Tone and Quick pushed past the guard and went behind the counter. Dixon denied them access to their factory's files, despite the presence of a newspaper photographer.

Milne was fed up. He consulted Cheese & Dairy's lawyer, who confirmed the cooperatives' rights to their records. He talked to fellow

Beale Dixon, Bass Tone, Bert Quick, and guard Merrill Maxwell. *Headlight Herald,* September 1, 1963

Cheese & Dairy director Vern Lucas, a former marine who was also angry about the situation. He agreed to go down to the County Creamery office with Milne.

When they entered the office, "This guard wasn't going to let us in past the outer office," Milne said. "We just kinda moved him out of the way. I gave the guard a push, and he wouldn't stay out; he came back. So I gave him a *good* push. I got him clear out of the way. His gun fell out, and his glasses fell off. His hat came off. I remember Vern was so mad, he kicked the hat clear across the office.

"After that they settled down, and we went in and got our records. I had a whole list of what we had to have. It took us two or three hours. They didn't do anything. I'm sure they called McMinimee, who told them they had to let us have our records."[8]

NO MONEY, NO MILK

Multiple lawsuits began to unfold against Cheese & Dairy. Otto Schild sued; seventy-seven Shiveley Shippers sued; the Oregon Department of Agriculture sued. The lawsuits were related to County Creamery's deviation from its usual bookkeeping practices—changes that hurt Cheese & Dairy's cash flow. Dixon had shortened the time line for charging Cheese & Dairy's account for County Creamery–related expenses from thirty days to fifteen, but he had not tightened the calendar for revenue payments.[9] In a rare unanimous vote at an April 1963 Cheese & Dairy meeting, the directors passed Vern Lucas's motion: "This Board of Directors see the money for cheese be turned over in 60 days."[10] When that did not occur, Cheese & Dairy withheld its cheese from County Creamery.[11]

County Creamery needed Cheese & Dairy's cheese and milk for sales and as collateral when it sought bank loans for itself.[12] The established bookkeeping practice was for County Creamery to pay cash to Cheese & Dairy. To retaliate for Cheese & Dairy's action, however, County Creamery stopped paying the cash it owed Cheese & Dairy.[13] Instead, Dixon substituted credit on the books. His action choked Cheese & Dairy's cash flow. The situation worsened when Dixon told the County Creamery board "he did not know whether Creamery Association has received payment for Cheese and Dairy bulk milk delivered to Portland"[14] during the summer, and thus he did not give Cheese & Dairy credit for that milk. Cheese & Dairy's board believed County Creamery had been paid by the distributors and could indeed pay,[15] but with both cash and credit denied by County Creamery, Cheese & Dairy had no way to pay its farmer members.

The newly independent cooperative could have sought recourse from the Oregon Department of Agriculture or a judicial review; instead, on September 6, 1963, Cheese & Dairy sent a notice to County Creamery that all milk deliveries would cease until payment was made.[16]

"No money, no milk" was the rallying cry among the rebellious farmers. But many farmers were still recovering from not receiving advances in April, and the impact of the latest pay gap was severe. Farms were on the line.

The lack of milk checks rippled throughout the business community, too. When farm families had to economize, J. C. Penney didn't sell as many shirts and shoes, Safeway didn't sell as many groceries, and the Tillamook Coliseum didn't sell as many movie tickets. Some farmers couldn't pay their feed bills and were grateful that Buchanan Cellars, one of the feed suppliers, said, "We'll wait." Every Cheese & Dairy farm family was economizing, but for some, there wasn't much of a safety net.

Because Cheese & Dairy refused to ship its milk to County Creamery and did not yet have contracts with distributors, it had thousands of pounds of milk without a market. Cheese & Dairy converted all of its milk into cheese.

On September 12, 1963, Cheese & Dairy reported to its members, "Mr. Dixon admitted in a letter dated September 5, 1963, that a bookkeeping error had been made in the Creamery office and that $299,011.56 was not credited to Cheese and Dairy as it should have been."[17] Today, the error would amount to more than $2.7 million.

On the last day of September, Cheese & Dairy wrote to its members that August's milk checks were ready, despite no payment from County Creamery. But there was a catch: the checks were not mailed to the shippers with the letter. Cheese & Dairy had arranged for a line of credit with First National Bank, but the fledgling organization didn't want to use it unless absolutely necessary.[18] Cheese & Dairy membership began to drop, and membership in Shiveley Shippers and County Creamery began to grow.

By late September, Cheese & Dairy had signed a contract with Mayflower to deliver milk to the Portland market,[19] and in October, it told its farmers it was shipping sixty thousand pounds of milk daily.[20] Cheese & Dairy was still lacking County Creamery's payment, so it used its line of credit to pay its patrons. It did not pay members of the Tillamook Fluid Milk Shippers, however. The board excluded the nearly eighty Shiveley Shippers out of pique because they had switched to County Creamery and no longer had marketing agreements with Cheese & Dairy.

Seizing an opportunity to be viewed favorably, County Creamery sent checks to the Shiveley Shippers, saying, "We understand that Tillamook Cheese Dairy [sic] Association is holding up the check that they owe you for milk deliveries made by you to them during August. *We know that you have obligations to meet, and we are enclosing an advance check.*"[21] The letter noted that the funds were being loaned at .5 percent interest. Shippers could return the checks if they were not needed,[22] but nearly all of the Shiveley Shippers put their checks in the bank.

Next, seventy-seven members of the Shiveley Shippers banded together to pursue a court claim against Cheese & Dairy because of the lack of pay. In October 1963, Shiveley Shippers voted to assign its members' individual claims to County Creamery to be included in a lawsuit.

Otto Schild, one of the new Shiveley Shippers, did not cash his check from County Creamery.[23] Instead, he filed an individual suit against Cheese & Dairy for nonpayment for his milk. Cheese & Dairy explained to its patrons, "This court action will decide if T.C.&D.A. must pay Mr. Schild before T.C.C.A. pays us."[24] Schild won his lawsuit in February 1965.[25] In May 1965, McMinimee filed a lawsuit on the same issue on behalf of Gaylord Shiveley and the other Shiveley Shippers who had cashed County Creamery's checks. The lawsuit never saw the inside of a courtroom.[26]

Then, the Oregon Department of Agriculture stepped in to sue Cheese & Dairy over the issue. The department had other options under the Milk Marketing Act. It could have sued County Creamery alone because that co-op acted as an agent in selling milk for Cheese & Dairy but then failed to hand over the cash to pay Cheese & Dairy members.[27] The department could have sued both co-ops, each a milk handler, for jointly failing to pay producers. Instead, the department filed suit against Cheese & Dairy, by itself, focusing on the part of the Milk Marketing Act that governed buyers and sellers.[28] As the state's attorneys saw it, Cheese & Dairy sold the farmers' milk to County Creamery, and therefore Cheese & Dairy bore sole responsibility for paying producers.

The trial was held on December 8, 1964, at the Tillamook County Courthouse. The court ruled that a co-op must pay its members even if it wasn't paid itself.[29] Cheese & Dairy appealed the ruling in the State Department of Agriculture lawsuit but lost in 1966. Then it appealed that decision to the Oregon Supreme Court. Cheese & Dairy was ordered to set aside $125,000 as a contingency to cover a possible court judgment against it. At its December 2, 1966, board meeting, the directors explored ways to finance the required surety bond for the appeal.[30] The Department of Agriculture gave Cheese & Dairy an eight-day extension to post the bond, and at its December 7, 1966, meeting, the board approved mortgaging the cheese factory and reimbursing individuals who supported the appeal.[31]

The board raised $147,000—more than $1.4 million today. The list of thirty-four contributors to the bond fund included Joe Beeler, Harley Christensen, Hooker Jenck, Glenn Johnston, Hans Leuthold, Vern Lucas, Arnold Waldron, Doc Sayles, and Steve Steiner. It included Bob Blaser, Bert Quick, and Bass Tone. It included loyal farmers such as Joe Chatelain, Glen Koehler, Casper Naegeli, and Roy Redberg. The smallest contribution was $500; six farmers gave $10,000 each, or more than $86,000 each in today's dollars.[32] The list of donors did not include George Milne or Ferd Becker. By not contributing, both men signaled that they thought Cheese & Dairy should not spend more money and courtroom time on this issue.

In 1968, the Oregon Supreme Court ruled against Cheese & Dairy, saying it was obligated to pay its producers even though County Creamery was the marketing agent and received payment for the milk, but through an accounting procedure issued credit rather than paying cash to Cheese & Diary for its fluid milk. The chief justice, C. J. Perry, dissented from the majority opinion. He said County Creamery was acting as an agent, not a buyer, when selling the producers' milk to distributors.[33] He wrote, "it was the Creamery Association that wrongfully withheld the trust moneys and applied them to the purported debt of [Cheese & Dairy]."[34]

A petition for rehearing, based on Cheese & Dairy's argument that advances to producers by County Creamery "were loans, not payments" and thus "constituted deductible items under the terms of the contract," was denied.[35] When the Cheese War ended, the US Supreme Court was considering hearing the case. Meanwhile, County Creamery filed a trademark lawsuit against Cheese & Dairy that would be of major importance to both cooperatives. But always, farmwork demanded the rebels' attention, too.

MEANWHILE, BACK ON THE FARM . . .

"We kept the farm going by working a lot of hours and letting a lot of things go," Barbara Milne said.[36] George Milne milked, but sometimes it didn't happen until he got home late in the evening. Or he paid others to do his evening milking. Or, as Barbara Milne said, "There were times when Hans Leuthold or one of the Durrers would come over and milk when George had a late meeting. It just points out the personal sacrifices and the support we gave each other."[37]

Tom Tone, one of Bass Tone's sons, recalls many nights of milking for his dad because he was attending meetings.[38] Cows like regularity, though, and the disruption to their usual rhythm meant they didn't produce as much milk, which meant a drop in the next month's milk check. On Tillagem Farm, Milne was tired. Some meetings began at eight or nine o'clock at night—cow care was prioritized over the Cheese War—but the late starting times meant even later ending times, and the cows still expected to be milked before dawn the next day.

On days with no meetings, Milne raced to get some farmwork done. He cleared cow pies out of the loafing shed and laid new bedding. He cleaned the barnyard using a Ford 8N tractor with a scraper blade on the back. He filled feed troughs with silage and hay. He refilled mineral feeders. He spot-welded any broken field equipment. He ordered grain and selected bull semen for the artificial inseminator to use with cows ready to be bred. He doctored sick cows. He moved cows to different pastures. In the summer, he cut silage and made hay. Often, the list of chores wasn't completed at the optimal moment. Always, he seemed to be a day behind.

He said later, "I remember one spring, farmers came over and worked a lot of ground for me because I was planting field corn for the second year. That fall is when they harvested our corn by hand."[39]

Barbara Milne recalled, "The summer had been cool so the corn was slow to ripen, and then the rains came so early we couldn't get the field chopper out in the field. If George hadn't been so busy representing the Cheese & Dairy shippers, he would have gotten to the corn before the rain." Recognizing the crisis, Sharon Bennett, a farmer's wife, organized supporters into a harvesting crew.[40]

George Milne remembered, "There were more than twenty men at a time for about a week in November 1963. Some came and then went away again. It was miserable conditions and everyone came."[41]

Barbara Milne explained, "This was mud—cold and rainy, long hours. They had their own morning milkings and chores, and then they brought over their tractors and wagons. Steve Steiner said that we could use any piece of equipment he owned."[42]

STEVE STEINER

That generosity was notable because as Steiner's son, Nick, recalls, his dad got up every morning and wondered, "What can I do today to make a buck?"[43] One way was to serve as an unofficial bank for many borrowers. To finance a car, people went to the banks or to Steiner. He hauled hay into Tillamook, letting farmers feed it to their cows without paying for it until after winter ended. Along with the handshake deal came 10 percent interest. Steiner drove heavily loaded hay trucks, with about thirty tons on the truck and trailer, for most of his adult life, including thirty-one round trips of 420 miles each at age 70. He taught Hooker Jenck how to run a hay-hauling business, which was the start of the Jenck trucking company that continues today.[44]

As a child, Steve Steiner had lived in Tillamook before his family moved back to Switzerland. He returned on his own at 14, determined to be a farmer. With only a fifth grade education, he went on to be a success, owning Premium Farms and raising registered Guernseys that, like Hans Leuthold's cattle, won national awards. Because Steiner accepted cows in payment, his Guernsey herd expanded to include Holsteins.

Steiner was one of the farmers who always responded to Cheese & Dairy's appeals for money. He "didn't talk rah rah," according to his son, Nick. But during the Cheese War, Steiner loaned more than $45,000—more than $360,000 today—to the cause to pay for lawyers and expenses. As far as Nick knows, the money was never repaid. Nick says, "He stood by his friends, and that was good enough."[45]

Steve Steiner was captain of the Tillamook County Sheriff's Mounted Posse and posed on a parade day. Courtesy of Nick Steiner

Steiner was a cow man through and through. No surprise, then, that he used a phrase that came from observing the last few weeks before a cow calved, a time when her udder swelled as she got ready to deliver a calf and a steady supply of milk. When anything started to go right—whether or not it involved a cow—he liked to say, "Now we're making bag!" Steiner was helping Milne "make bag" by not charging for the use of his equipment. Nick remembers, "Steve loaned a Cat with a blade on the back and a bucket on the front . . . He off-loaded and gave a tutorial; next day, he got another call about the crew being short-handed. Steve came and ran the Cat."[46]

Nick Steiner explains the harvesting technique, "The crew cut through the middle of the field so they could cut both sides and work their way out."[47] Nick and his brother-in-law and the rest of the crew used machetes to cut the corn, stack it in their arms and carry it to the wagons. The Cat pulled the wagons out of the field. Then guys like Fib Johnston hooked tractors onto the wagons and drove them down the hill to the barn. Fib recalls, "The hill was so slick [with mud], it was like being on a ski slope."[48] Once the heavy wagons reached the barn, the corn was off-loaded and fed into field choppers. Then, converted manure spreaders carried the raw silage up a ramp and fed it into the silage pit.

One day of harvesting stood out. Barbara Milne said, "I was giving the guys lunch in the garage because they were covered with mud and didn't want to take off their outer clothing to come into the house. Some of the women sent over big kettles of spaghetti and meatballs and things. Marvin Pangborn was late coming. Everyone else was out in the field. He came about eleven o'clock with a big kettle of food that Esther, his wife, had sent, and he told me he was late because President Kennedy had been shot."[49]

George Milne said, "The rest of us learned about it in the garage at lunch."[50]

CHEESE SALES

While the "no money, no milk" lawsuits went through the court system, Cheese & Dairy was beginning to sell its own cheese. By late October 1963, Premium Brand Tillamook Cheese was available in the Portland market. It is unknown whether the name was selected because the farmers were familiar with Steve Steiner's Premium Farms, or because it was recommended by Cheese & Dairy's ad agency.

Vern Lucas led a sales committee that secured promotions in Fred Meyer's Oregon grocery chain. The farmers were pleased with the launch of Premium Brand Tillamook Cheese, but they knew they needed to focus on the populated Southern California market. Large wheels of cheese were popular, thanks to a 34,591-pound behemoth produced in Wisconsin for the 1964 World's Fair.[51] Fred Meyer contracted with a Wisconsin cheese producer to supply it with a huge wheel of cheese. Supporters of the rebels—including James Durrer, Robert Durrer, Bob Hurliman, Max Hurliman, John Nielsen, Yelta Vanderzee, Art VanLoo, and J. B. Williams—addressed the need for marketing like Wisconsin's in an October 6, 1963, letter to the *Headlight Herald*:

> It must have been painful to Tillamook dairymen to read the article on Fred Meyer's gigantic Wisconsin cheddar cheese. . . . This is just one more reason why the members of TC&DA feel they must produce and market their dairy products

Cheese & Dairy introduced Premium Brand Tillamook Cheese through ads like this one.
Headlight Herald, March 22, 1964

independently. For it is only through constantly working to manufacture a premium quality product and promoting it with an adequate advertising program that we can continue to have a successful dairy industry. . . . Tillamook can no longer afford to drift contentedly along on its past reputation.[52]

Tillamook's cheesemakers began to catch up. Bass Tone became Cheese & Dairy's milk grader and cheese inspector. The leaders of Cheese & Dairy learned quickly that store owners were more open to buying their cheese when a cheesemaker was in the room, and Tone was an excellent representative. The February 11, 1964, *Board Information* by the Cheese & Dairy Publicity Committee discussed a trip to Southern California, saying,

Four directors and Basil Tone, our cheese inspector, made a business trip to Los Angeles and met with about 100 brokers, buyers and food distributors who handle cheese sales in a market of more than 9 million people. At this cheese-cutting

Cheese & Dairy officials met with California grocery store owners to plan a huge cheese for their store. (left to right) Vern Lucas, George Milne, Bass Tone, and store owners Mr. and Mrs. Don Wetzel. *Headlight Herald*, March 22, 1964

demonstration . . . Bas [sic] Tone demonstrated cheese grading. During the four hour question and answer period, the directors emphasized the quality of our cheese and the buyers showed great interest.[53]

Tone was accompanied by Glenn Johnston, Hans Leuthold, Vern Lucas, and George Milne. The trip was Tone's first airplane ride. When the plane encountered turbulence, he was heard saying, "Hold her in the road, Joe, hold her in the road."[54] Tone enjoyed flirting with the flight attendant; according to his sons, he got her autograph on a napkin.[55]

The farmers returned with a contract to produce a ten-thousand-pound cheese, thought to be the largest cheese ever made in the west,[56] for a California supermarket. Cheese & Dairy and Red Clover were off to a good start in proving that proper marketing of cheese made in Tillamook would result in sales.

In response to the success of Premium Brand Tillamook Cheese in the marketplace, Dixon and County Creamery's representatives told cheese brokers that Cheese & Dairy did not have the right to use the word "Tillamook" on its cheese, and County Creamery would sue the brokers if they handled the competing cheese.[57] In light of the threat of lawsuits, sales of Premium Brand Tillamook Cheese plummeted. The executive committee of the board of directors of Cheese & Dairy told its members and patrons, "Because of threatening letters and other actions by the Tillamook County Creamery Association in the trade, T.C.&D.A. was forced to sell cheese at the [lower] unbranded price to meet payouts."[58]

Many years later, Dixon tried to explain County Creamery's action as an issue of quality. He told his biographer, "we were a little afraid that some of the cheese that they had made was insufficient quality."[59] Yet Premium Brand Tillamook Cheese won numerous industry awards during its existence.[60]

If the product had been left alone, its sales would have put money in Cheese & Dairy's coffers. The declaratory judgment, along with the "no money, no milk" lawsuits, had been expensive to litigate. Cheese & Dairy wasn't selling enough cheese and was feeling the financial pinch. The co-op became reliant on its bank for the bulk of its financing, but sometimes the decision-makers at First National needed persuading.

Barbara Milne recalled later, "We were at a Far West Classic basketball tournament in Portland with Dale Sayles. George had to call First National to see if it would keep financing us. No one knew which way it would go when George picked up the pay phone to call. We heard him talking like a good old guy. But when he hung up, we had financing."[61]

The next time funding was needed "because of an emergency that exists," the board formalized the "acceptance of private individual loans."[62] Several times during the Cheese War, when Cheese & Dairy was at its borrowing limit with its bank, farmers made personal guarantees backed by their farms. Even with the private loans, the cooperative was struggling to find money to keep going. Ferd Becker saw the bigger picture, according to the minutes of a February 12, 1964, Cheese & Dairy board meeting:

> As a . . . member of the Finance Committee to the Board of Directors, Mr. Becker feels that through the action taken by Mr. Dixon that our position in the future of holding our premium price of our cheese on the market may never again be regained even though additional expenses are incurred in sales advertising and promotion. The concern, worry . . . and physical effect on each member of our Association, our employees and others can never be repaid in full. Many of our patrons have their life savings invested in our Association and by this action may create a forced sale and a great loss to all members.[63]

Cheese & Dairy sought an injunction in early 1964 against County Creamery for relief from the marketing cooperative's letters to cheese brokers who handled Premium Brand Tillamook Cheese. The insurgent farmers received good news when Judge William East issued the injunction allowing Cheese & Dairy to label its cheese as Premium Brand Tillamook Cheese and to use "Tillamook" to refer to its corporate name and geographic location. Judge East said that County Creamery had to stop threatening Cheese & Dairy's brokers, dealers, distributors, customers, and potential customers. Then, in a new court action, County Creamery sued Cheese & Dairy for $250,000—more than $2.2 million today—over the Tillamook trademark. Cheese & Dairy promptly filed a counter lawsuit for $500,000, or nearly $5 million in 2022 dollars.[64]

THE TRADEMARK LAWSUIT

The trademark lawsuit was assigned to Chief Federal Judge Gus Solomon, who urged both sides to bring all trademark issues to arbitration rather than to trial. Industry groups also urged an out-of-court settlement. Cheese & Dairy's board agreed unanimously to arbitration, but County Creamery refused.

One of County Creamery's attorneys told the court, "the owners and board of directors of TCCA are unanimous in their stand and would insist on a court battle 'to the end.' "[65] Perhaps County Creamery knew that a trial would be more expensive for Cheese & Dairy than arbitration and yet another way to weaken the group's finances; word spread that Dixon said at a Central Cheese Association meeting that County Creamery "would soon have T. C. & D. A. broke."[66] Plus, Cheese & Dairy insisted that arbitration should include an accounting by Creamery "in full for all [Cheese & Dairy] funds they used over the year and 4,000,000 pounds of cheese they sold for us last year."[67]

County Creamery took out a full-page ad in *Shopping Smiles*, a Tillamook newspaper, to claim that Cheese & Dairy's "irresponsible course of conduct" had made arbitration impossible. County Creamery said it could not "submit to the suggested form of proceedings because in so doing control of the Tillamook trademark might fall into irresponsible hands."[68] The ad concluded, "We would only be postponing the day of reckoning and doing the community no service if we avoided this attack by resorting to arbitration."[69] The ad was co-signed with the names of the six small factories and the Shiveley Shippers group.

"Rejection of the proposal brought a flash of anger to Judge Solomon's face," reported the *Oregon Journal*: " 'If you have such a fine record and justice on your side, you shouldn't have any reluctance to submit to arbitration,' [Judge Solomon] snapped."[70] County Creamery's board of directors signed a letter that was published in Tillamook's paper, explaining its decision not to arbitrate by saying,

> We suggest that the best way to guarantee our future economic welfare is for the county's milk producers to resume the unified cooperative effort which experience has proved successful. With all of us working together again for the best interests of

all producers, with the cheese and fluid milk operations properly coordinated, all will be protected and all will profit.[71]

The Tillamook community was concerned about the animosity between the dairy groups, and several churches asked their congregations to work to end the legal battles.[72] They did not succeed. The trademark trial commenced in May, with Judge William East presiding because Judge Solomon said he "felt too keenly about the case."[73] Cheese & Dairy and Red Clover board members submitted statements about the impact of County Creamery's letters to buyers. Meanwhile, County Creamery accused Cheese & Dairy and Red Clover of not acting in good faith because while the trademark lawsuit was heading to court, the two cooperatives filed an antitrust lawsuit against County Creamery, and it began a long journey to an eventual trial in 1968.

Before the trademark trial, news leaked about County Creamery's purchase of 450,000 pounds of Minnesota cheese. Judge Solomon, who had not yet recused himself from the proceedings, said, "the people of Oregon will be unhappy to have 'Minnesota Cheese' marketed under the 'Tillamook' label if TCCA wins its right to sole ownership of the brand known throughout the country."[74] The cheese purchase weakened County Creamery's claim to sole use of the Tillamook trademark and harm to the brand from a competing cheese. At the trial, a former County Creamery employee testified, "the creamery association received green colored labels marked as 'Tillamook mild' and . . . he was told the labels were to be used in the packaging of Minnesota cheese."[75] The testimony forced Dixon to tell the court that he also had an order for another 175,000 pounds.

> Dixson [sic] told of buying the Minnesota cheese from Pure Milk
> Products Co., Winsted, Minn., recently in 40-pound squares. . . .
> "None of the cheese has been re-packaged or labeled nor moved
> out of the warehouse," he said. He said he hadn't decided about
> repackaging or labeling the cheese.[76]

If cheese from Minnesota could be sold with the Tillamook label, why couldn't a cheese made in Tillamook by a rival factory be labeled Tillamook? When the out-of-state purchase became public knowledge,

County Creamery was stuck with thirteen boxcars of cheese that undercut its legal claims.

Dixon's earlier sale to Granny Goose, which was allowed to add "Made with Tillamook Cheese" to the labels of its aerosol cheese spread, also became a problem for County Creamery. As Del Mayer, a young Cheese & Dairy board member who went on to be an attorney and judge, wrote to the editor of the Tillamook paper,

> If TCCA is now concerned that the name Tillamook might fall into irresponsible hands, perhaps they can appreciate the concern of TC&DA members when they learned that the Granny Goose Company had been given the exclusive right to use "Tillamook" on their product. This right was granted without the authorization or knowledge of either TC&DA or of the board of directors of TCCA. It is amazing that this group, which showed so little concern about the Granny Goose deal, now stands with righteous indignation and complains of infringement when TC&DA tries to market its products as "Premium Brand—made and aged by Tillamook Cheese and Dairy Association," which our trademark attorneys tell us we have the right to do.[77]

The trademark trial put a spotlight on the deep divide between the two groups. On one side of the divide, George Milne testified about Dixon, as reported by *The Oregonian* under a headline that read, "Tillamook Cheese Man Accused of Being 'Liar.'"[78] Milne said Dixon told farmers at a County Creamery membership meeting that he "had not cut the price of milk to the Carnation Co. A half an hour after the meeting, Milne told the court, Dixon admitted he had done so. Milne said, too, that he believed there was a lack of trust and confidence in Dixon." In contrast, Dixon testified in court that "he had offered to resign as manager of [County Creamery] but the association directors refused to accept his offer. He said, further, that he was 'besieged' by persons to continue as manager."[79]

Judge East ruled in favor of Cheese & Dairy, saying that the Premium Brand label did not infringe on the Tillamook trademark.[80] He went further, ruling that Cheese & Dairy owned the Tillamook trademark, with County Creamery having permission to use the word to label its cheese. As the *Oregon Journal* reported, "The side in the Tillamook Cheese dispute that had been willing to submit to arbitration emerged the winner over its rival."[81]

Judge East issued a warning along with his ruling in the trademark case, saying,

> Whatever may be the ultimate result of having two marketing agents for the Grade A fluid milk products of Tillamook County, I can make no prognosis, but I do know that the favorable and heretofore nationwide premium market for cheese marketing under the brand "Tillamook" cannot survive under two competing marketing agencies.[82]

He urged both parties to "settle upon a single marketing agent to market the cheese produced in Tillamook County under the famous brand of 'Tillamook.' "[83] In response, Cheese & Dairy offered to serve as the sole marketing agent and grading agent for all Tillamook cheese.[84] County Creamery rejected the offer, instead inviting Cheese & Dairy to return as a member cooperative, with County Creamery serving as the only marketing agent. County Creamery also offered to buy Cheese & Dairy's cheese inventory.[85] Cheese & Dairy then suggested using a third party to market and grade Tillamook's cheese.[86]

The judge's decision in the trademark case went into effect, but County Creamery appealed the ruling. In April 1965, a panel of three federal appeals court judges denied the appeal. County Creamery then asked for a hearing by the full US Court of Appeals Ninth Circuit. In May 1965, that request was denied, too. The decision said in part that Cheese & Dairy "never lost its common law rights to that trade-mark and that nothing which has occurred would operate to estop defendant from continuing to claim and use its trade-mark. Accordingly, we are of the opinion that the court correctly held that [Cheese & Dairy] owns the mark 'Tillamook' for cheese; that it has a further right to use the same, and that it has not infringed any trade-mark right which the plaintiff may have."[87]

County Creamery tried again, asking the US Supreme Court to hear its appeal. The Court declined.[88]

In October 1966, County Creamery redesigned its labels, adding an image of the *Morning Star*, a ship that had carried cheese to markets in the early days of Tillamook's cheese industry. Country Creamery also added the word "original." Cheese & Dairy immediately asked for a ruling on the use of the word. Judge Bruce Thompson, later to preside over the antitrust lawsuit, ruled that, based on Judge East's decision, County Creamery could not say "original." But it was allowed to continue using "genuine," as long as the label did not imply that it was the only producer of genuine Tillamook cheese.[89]

Cheese & Dairy's patrons were proud of their legal victory, believing that owning the trademark would establish their cooperative as a viable manufacturer of Tillamook cheese and lead to bigger sales. Their victory was not going to be as helpful as they forecast.

FIELD NOTE 6
Cheese War Truce

BY LINDA KIRK

For the afternoon of the DAR tea, the Cheese War entered a truce. With Louise McMinimee hosting, good manners prevailed, and no controversial topic intruded.

Members of the Tillamook chapter of the Daughters of the American Revolution held an annual tea to honor high school recipients of the DAR Good Citizen awards. Each of the three public high schools in the county sent the selected Good Citizen and her mother to the tea. I held the Good Citizen slot for Tillamook High School in central Tillamook County. At the tea, I would meet students representing Neah-Kah-Nie High School in north county and Nestucca High School in south county.

On a sunny day in the spring of 1968, I viewed dairy farms as I looked out the window of my mother's 1966 Ford LTD while she drove toward the home of Warren McMinimee, chief counsel for County Creamery. For five years, McMinimee had more than held his own in court against big-firm Portland attorneys hired by Cheese & Dairy.

I knew he would be at work, so I wasn't worried about making conversation with him. My worry was how best to conduct myself in an unfamiliar setting with unfamiliar people. I didn't want to spill food. I didn't want to go blank if a question came my way. I wanted to represent my high school well. More than that, I wanted to represent my family well.

Louise McMinimee had probably hosted her full share of events when her husband served as a state senator in the 1950s.[1] She may have been expecting to host more gatherings because Governor Tom McCall had recently appointed Warren McMinimee to the State Parks Advisory Committee.[2] Her house was ideal for entertaining. I had glimpsed the large red brick house many times, set back from the country road beyond a green lawn.

Elegant. Everything about Louise McMinimee and her house was elegant. The grounds were elegant. The furniture was elegant. Probably the tea itself was elegant, but I declined tea because I didn't want to risk dropping a china teacup. We DAR Good Citizens were not so elegant. We were dressed formally, but we looked like the rural high school seniors that we were. I wore a navy-blue dress with a green chiffon scarf at the neck and black pumps. I had learned to walk in heels without wobbling, so that gave me a small jolt of confidence.

I took cues from my mother, who showed no jitters. She had worked with our hostess on Methodist Church committees. She knew Louise McMinimee to be courteous, efficient, and generous. Mom said that the lawyer's wife had quietly taken care of replacing worn and faded curtains in the church's Sunday School classrooms.

After introductions, Louise McMinimee asked polite questions about my plans for the future. I had answers ready, and I delivered them in a steady voice. Education plans? "Oregon State University. Major in English education. I want to teach in a junior high." Why junior high? "Students in junior high can be challenging, but that age level is where I think I can make a difference." Displaying impeccable courtesy, McMinimee spoke with each honoree. Later, we three DAR Good Citizens posed for a photograph on an interior staircase. We thanked our hostess for a lovely afternoon and led our mothers to the parked cars.

Before a week passed, I mailed a thank-you note. It was a brief note in careful, correct English. I made no mention of the Cheese War. The truce held.

CHAPTER 10

The Lean Years

The ongoing court battles and setbacks in selling their cheese drained some of the energy from Cheese & Dairy's supporters. Even a victorious lawsuit hurt the organization's bottom line because the lawyers were expensive. The cooperative became dependent on its bank's financing. When Cheese & Dairy's general manager retired in 1964, the bank endorsed a candidate for the position, but he decided not to take the job. The bank did not approve of several other candidates for the leadership role. At one point in the 1964 search, Doc Sayles wrote to the board, offering to discuss having him manage the factory, but no action was taken. Then the bank's officers told Cheese & Dairy's board that they would accept George Milne.[1]

He was reluctant. His pregnant wife didn't want him to do it, and he didn't want to "work out" in town. But he remembered the support he had received from the farmers who helped him harvest his corn. He didn't want to abandon them, nor did he want Cheese & Dairy to fail, which it would unless the bank's loans and line of credit were available. In October 1964, he resigned as Cheese & Dairy's board president and began his new role.

Milne, wearing his one suit and necktie to his town job, relied on his new milkers to take over his farm's twice-daily milkings and the related chores. Milne tracked the daily pounds of milk recorded by the bulk milk hauler, and if the milkers hit several goals, such as Milne's usual volume of milk production as well as low leucocyte counts, they would receive bonuses.

Milne worked long hours as the factory's manager, leaving home early in the morning and returning after the evening milking. But every day, despite business, Milne checked the volume of milk produced by his cows. All was well, it seemed. In reality, though, the milkers weren't able to match Milne's volume and made up for it by running a garden hose through the open milk house door to the propped-up lid of the bulk tank. They poured in water until an acceptable volume was created.

"We found out about the water when the butterfat test dropped real low," Barbara Milne recalled later. The Babcock test had flagged a problem. "We asked for further testing by the factory's quality control inspector, and the test came back showing water in the milk."[2] Suddenly, the Milnes faced the demise of their Grade A farm. State laws, written to prevent adulterated milk from reaching the market as it had in the past, said that watered milk was classified as degraded milk. If the problem recurred, the milk could be sold as cheese milk, but it would be banned from the Grade A market. Tillagem Farm would be out of business.

After firing the hired hands, Milne did a daylight tour of the farm buildings. He looked for other damage and noticed that various maintenance chores had not been done. He hadn't inspected the calf barn yet, but an incoherent yell from one of his daughters alerted him to check it out.

Inside the barn, the young calves were standing on three-foot-deep compacted manure in their individual pens. All of the pens would need to be shoveled out. But that wouldn't have caused his daughter to sound distraught. Then he noticed that it was abnormally quiet back where the heifers were housed. These older, bigger calves had a large fenced area that spread from a wall on one side to a sliding door on the pasture side, allowing the animals to come and go when the door was open. The heifers weren't in the enclosure, which wasn't unusual, except that the door to their pasture was closed.

Milne noted that this pen, too, had not been cleared of manure. And then he saw cow noses poking out of the top of the deep manure in the pen. Because only the noses were visible, it meant the heifers were buried. It meant they had suffocated. All of those noses meant all of the heifers were dead.

When Milne saw the dead animals, his anguish and anger exploded. He was mad at the hired men, and he was mad at himself. Instantly, he knew he had tried to do too much. He had lost track of what he had told the farmer after the Oregon Dairymen's Association's quota meeting, choosing instead to fly without keeping his feet on the ground. He had forgotten that he was a farmer first. He vowed never to neglect his farm again.

So after about forty-five days on the job, Milne resigned. Cheese & Dairy's *Board Information* of December 7, 1964, said, "Due to an emergency situation on behalf of George Milne in his farm operation, he has reluctantly decided to resign as manager of TC & DA. Your Board regrets having to accept his decision and are now in search of a replacement."[3]

DROWNING IN DEBT

Dixon's unsecured, unauthorized loans continued to plague Cheese & Dairy. Carl Cadonau of Alpenrose Dairy had testified in Federal Court on November 30, 1964, that all of the loans to its store customers were good.[4] Cadonau testified at a hearing where the court decided to amend the antitrust case to include Alpenrose as well as him individually. His testimony on the health of the loans wasn't worth much, given that there was no paperwork to review and some loan recipients had already defaulted.

With more digging into the financials, the board was able to report to its patrons:

> The total loss to date on the Alpenrose store keeper notes is $22,000.00. The doubtful notes now a year past payment, total $18,486.00. If this total of $40,486.00 was available to TC & DA capital at the present time, it would make a big difference in the TC & DA financial picture.[5]

Indeed, it would make a big difference; in today's dollars, the $40,486 is equivalent to more than $367,000. Cheese & Dairy tracked County Creamery's finances because the rebel group wanted to be repaid for the unauthorized loans. In November 1964, Cheese & Dairy's board president, Harley Christensen, received a copy of County Creamery's audit results from an unknown person and said in a newspaper article, "This was an audit so qualified by the accountants as to express no opinion as to the validity of the financial statement."[6]

The bank declined to back Cheese & Dairy in paying its patrons for November 1964's milk. Cheese & Dairy sent a letter to all patrons on

December 31, 1964, notifying them of the postponement until February 1, 1965, but telling them that they could request a draw of up to 35 percent of their expected payment.[7] Cheese & Dairy began exploring a relationship with a different bank.[8]

Applications for the general manager job had tapered off from the two-hundred-plus that had flooded in when Ed Burke had retired in 1963, perhaps because potential applicants had heard about the organization's financial instability. However, Joe Larson was hired in early 1965 on a temporary basis and stayed for several months.

The challenge of building a solvent cooperative was nearly overwhelming, and the farmers on the board sometimes struggled to get Cheese & Dairy's business done in the regularly scheduled meetings. By 1965, the board had learned to recess each meeting to the call of the chairman—in other words, to leave the meeting open and eliminate time-consuming formal notices that might delay the date of the next meeting. Now each meeting began with adjournment of the previous meeting, giving the directors the flexibility to meet as often as needed.

Cheese & Dairy's finances were so shaky that its bank refused to provide further loans to help pay its farmers and staff.[9] The Cheese & Dairy board and membership began to talk about returning to County Creamery. But as Casper Naegeli asked at a special membership meeting, "What is to be accomplished if we go back to the same thing we left?"[10] Hooker Jenck led Cheese & Dairy's negotiations with County Creamery. At the February 17, 1965, board meeting, Jenck reported that County Creamery had rejected the Cheese & Dairy proposal to return and had instead counterproposed:

1. T.C. & D.A. & RED CLOVER dismiss all legal action.
2. T.C.&D.A. financial statements be made available to T.C.C.A.
3. T.C. & D.A. return to membership to T.C.C.A. with unification of assets of T.C.C.A. & T.C. & D.A.
4. Red Clover return to membership in T.C.C.A.[11]

The Cheese & Dairy board continued to ponder its options. The board needed to ease its patrons' concern about how they would be affected if Cheese & Dairy were insolvent. The patrons were nervous,

and some switched to Shiveley Shippers or returned to County Creamery in part because it looked as if their cooperative might not be around
to receive their milk or pay them for the milk it did process. The board
and manager were unsure how Cheese & Dairy would pay farmers for
their December 1964 milk. Larson said, "the Portland banks seemed
hopeless at this time," and Vern Lucas said later in the same meeting
that First National Bank "has not yet called their note."[12] The attorneys
wanted to be paid at least $14,000 of the total due to them; the coopera-
tive authorized payment, but only after Cheese & Dairy paid back its
bank loans.[13]

At a special Cheese & Dairy meeting, the board decided that farmers could be members of Cheese & Dairy without marketing agreements.[14] That is, the farmers could cancel their contracts with Cheese
& Dairy but still be Cheese & Dairy producers—ship milk to it—if they
chose. The offer was a way for the organization to retain its dwindling
membership while allaying the members' legitimate concerns about
staying with an organization that might not be able to pay them after
they shipped their milk to it. Should that occur, the farmer without
a marketing agreement could switch to another organization without
delay. The change also addressed the bank's concern about the dimin-
ishing number of shippers; perhaps farmers would stay if they knew
they could opt out at any time.

At the same meeting, Hans Leuthold said that First National Bank
"finally agreed to release all money as of March 1st which results from
Grade A sales of milk, bulk and local. Cheese & Dairy must sell half a
million lbs. of cheese immediately, the difference between 35 cents per
lb. and the sale price we can pay to our producers. The bank also wants
us to try and merge with Dairy Co-op."[15]

The farmers were more interested in rejoining County Creamery
than merging with Dairy Co-op, now known as Mayflower and at the
time Oregon's largest milk producer cooperative.[16] Every Cheese &
Dairy board meeting now included discussion of how to reach an agreement to return to County Creamery, although the board members had
also begun to talk to Mayflower about merging with that cooperative.[17]

Despite the dire straits, a core of farmers remained loyal to the cause.
At a membership meeting of the two cooperatives, "Bob Blaser told the
producers that the members of Red Clover said that Dixon could go

square to hell now—the same as he could have two years ago, and that Red Clover would accept any shippers that came."[18] At the same meeting, "Mrs. Ed Landis asked for a few moments of standing silence so that all might pray. This was granted and everyone complied."[19] Perhaps it helped; Cheese & Dairy's attorney sent a letter on March 1, 1965, reporting, "Carl Cadonau says that if we will send him a list of all the Portland store loans with their current balances, he thinks Alpenrose will get somebody like Beale [Dixon] to take them over."[20]

At the March 3, 1965, board meeting, Larson reported, "the bank encouraged liquidating the cheese inventory. We have persued [sic] every possible source of revenue and nothing definite could be presented at this time."[21] The board voted to pay for the December 1964 milk by mortgaging the cheese factory and equipment. George Milne wasn't on the board anymore, but he couldn't stay away. From the audience at the meeting, he began a question with an ominous phrase: "If, after 3/13/65 T.C. & D.A. still exists . . ."[22]

The March 13 annual meeting loomed large for the cooperative because negotiations to join Mayflower Farms were to be settled by then; patrons who had canceled their marketing agreements would not have their memberships terminated until after the meeting so they could vote, and the members would weigh in on returning to County Creamery.

But President Leuthold reported at the meeting that Mayflower wasn't interested in a merger "at this time."[23] And when the motion to return to County Creamery was made, it was defeated by twelve votes, 51 to 63. At the same meeting, George Milne was voted back onto the board.

Cheese & Dairy no longer had enough milk to justify the cost of making cheese at the big factory. Mida Wyss, the mother-in-law of Vern Lucas, wrote in her diary on Saturday, March 13, 1965, "The big factory will close tomorrow and all of Cheese & Dairy cheese milk will go to Red Clover Monday."[24] Red Clover's board pledged to "market Premium Brand Tillamook Cheese."[25]

It was a gloomy period for Cheese & Dairy. After its factory was shuttered, President Hans Leuthold was quoted on March 31 in *The Oregonian* discussing the co-op's decreasing number of producers: "the association currently has 90 to 100 members; and . . . it formerly had about 300 members. He said some of the Cheese & Dairy members had returned to the Tillamook County Creamery Association."[26] That same day, the general manager, Joe Larson, resigned, writing, "Due to recent cost analysis of a reduced operation where your business is reduced to one-half the volume of last year, I feel you cannot afford the office force and a general manager."[27] Cheese & Dairy would go four months without a general manager until hiring A. J. Swett, who owned a farm and had been Tillamook's mayor.[28]

While the rebellious farmers were limping along, Beale Dixon wasn't having a carefree spring, either. Mida Wyss wrote in her diary at the end of March, "It's rumored that Beale Dixon secured a permit to 'carry a gun.' He surely must be pretty much scared, if he would only leave it would solve a lot of County problems."[29]

On April 30, 1965, some of Cheese & Dairy's patrons, including George Milne and Glenn Johnston, followed through on the offer to have their marketing contracts canceled. It was a bittersweet moment for them. Previously, they had given their all to the cause. Now, their loyalty bumped into the reality of needing to protect themselves if their co-op folded. For Milne and Johnston, it was never a question of not supporting Cheese & Dairy. They remained active, involved milk shippers. To the end of the Cheese War, they and others were hoping that Cheese & Dairy would prevail. For George Milne, however, the risk to his farm couldn't be tolerated.

The board continued its search for operating capital and ways to pay existing debts. It had the right to mortgage the plant to producers, and some of the farmers signed onto a mortgage that raised funds for Cheese & Dairy.

Good news began to filter into the board meetings. Foremost Milk Company expressed interest in Cheese & Dairy's milk,[30] and negotiations began. Mayflower told the board it would accept "any, all surplus at the classII [sic] price,"[31] helping Cheese & Dairy move its extra Grade A milk. Trumpy Cheese, a Wisconsin company, bid on buying 355,000 pounds of cheese,[32] and Arden Farms began exploratory talks with Cheese & Dairy. Beale Dixon wrote to Cheese & Dairy, and according to the April 20, 1965, board minutes expressed "concern and interest in purchasing $74,497.90 of these [store] notes of which are [sic] all current." The Cheese & Dairy minutes reported that Dixon made no comment regarding the bad notes,[33] but repayment of the equivalent of more than $659,000 in today's dollars would have definitely improved Cheese & Dairy's bottom line.

Although the financial picture was getting better, the continuing level of stress was affecting relationships. One board member, Floyd Woodward, resigned, saying, "Do [sic] to the fact that I can no longer bow down to Mr. Lucas and Mr. Leuthold, I hereby submit my resignation as Ex[ecutive] Sec[retary] and board member."[34] County Creamery paid Cheese & Dairy more than $70,000 as reimbursement on most of the Portland store loans, but ironically "There remains, [sic] several Portland store notes in which T.C.C.A. is not interested due to the insecure status of the notes."[35]

Because the cash flow improved, the Tillamook cheese factory reopened on May 24, 1965, and the Cheese & Dairy producers voted to "lease all or substantially all of Tillamook Cheese & Dairy Association assets" to Foremost, should that company want to come to Tillamook. The motion passed, 33 to 30.[36] Cheese & Dairy continued to negotiate with Foremost and to respond to actions that would interfere with sales of Premium Brand Tillamook Cheese. In mid-1965, Cheese & Dairy sent a letter to a broker in Los Angeles:

> you informed Certified Grocers that the offices of TC&DA and TCCA are now "the same" and for that reason you are in a position to know that until 1966 neither TC&DA nor TCCA will have available any 40 pound sharp cheese blocks nor 25 pound sharp cheese wheels or daisies. Such information is not true insofar as TC&DA is concerned . . . Under the circumstances, if the information we have received is correct, and you have deliberately given false information to Certified Grocers so as to interfere with the sale of TC&DA's cheese in the Los Angeles area, you are certainly in violation of TC&DA's rights. We intend to take action against you.[37]

Cheese & Dairy was still searching for financial stability. In June, the board offered "8% for a maximum of 1/4 million dollars" for producer loans to the co-op.[38] In September, however, Foremost signed an agreement to buy, age, and market all cheese produced by both Cheese

& Dairy and Red Clover.[39] Then the board authorized Foremost to use an assumed business name, "Tillamook Cheese Co." when selling Tillamook cheese.[40] At last, the struggling cooperative had a stable, large-scale conduit for Premium Brand Tillamook Cheese. Cheese & Dairy's finances would be healthier. The organization could continue to exist. Everyone breathed easier.

Cheese & Dairy's finances had improved enough that Great Western National Bank, in Portland, wanted its business. First National Bank declined to compete to retain the account, and Cheese & Dairy moved its accounts to its new bank.[41] Then, on January 1, 1966, Red Clover merged with Cheese & Dairy, closing its factory and shipping to the factory north of town. The inefficiency of the small cheese factory, plus the available space in the large factory, made the merger a necessary but painful decision.

While the Foremost relationship worked well enough for eighteen months, Cheese & Dairy didn't want to continue splitting profits with Foremost. With its improved finances and a new banking relationship, the board had the money in 1967 to buy back its inventory and do its own marketing, and it announced the amicable end of its Foremost contract.[42]

To gain more milk and grow production, Cheese & Dairy found a Washington cooperative, Cow Milkers Incorporated, willing to truck milk to Tillamook. Cheese & Dairy Board President Hans Leuthold said, "We are hopeful that through greatly increased sales we will now be able to better our producer payout and bring more money in Tillamook county [sic] generally."[43]

Despite occasional good news, it seemed as if Cheese & Dairy were suffocating, dying slowly like those heifers. The cooperative pinned its hopes for survival on its antitrust lawsuit.

THE ANTITRUST LAWSUIT

Cheese & Dairy and Red Clover had brought federal antitrust lawsuits against County Creamery in May 1964. Both cooperatives claimed that County Creamery "contracted, combined and conspired"[44] to restrain interstate commerce and marketing as well as conspiring "to monopolize the dairy products market."[45] Cheese & Dairy asked for triple damages of nearly $8 million, or nearly $72 million today; Red Clover sought $668,000, or nearly $6 million today.[46]

On February 16, 1965, a *Headlight Herald* news article announced that County Creamery had filed separate countering suits for $10 million—more than $88.5 million each today—against Cheese & Dairy and Red Clover. The article noted, "The net current assets of the Red Clover organization total approximately $13,000, according to Red Clover's President Basil Tone."[47] According to the article, Cheese & Dairy and Red Clover's suits totaled $8.4 million. "This amount plus Tillamook County Creamery Association's $20 million suits filed this week are almost $1 million more than total assessed valuation of the entire county of Tillamook."[48]

The Cheese & Dairy and Red Clover antitrust lawsuits began winding their way through courtroom maneuvers and delays. Some of the rebels agreed with Hans Leuthold, who stated that, "the law suits . . . are the greatest lever that Cheese & Dairy has . . . T.C.C.A. fears the anti-trust suits."[49] County Creamery tried to prevent the antitrust lawsuits from going to trial, but the US Court of Appeals Ninth Circuit ruled in March 1966 that they could proceed. Later, County Creamery tried to have its attorney, Warren McMinimee, removed from the list of defendants. As noted in the *Headlight-Herald*, the court found that "genuine factual issues exist concerning the role played by McMinimee which, if resolved one way, would exculpate him from liability and, if decided the other way, might subject him to liability."[50] The court ruled that McMinimee would continue to be a defendant in the case.[51]

County Creamery appealed the lower court's decision to make a summary judgment—a judgment without a full trial—of Alpenrose Dairy's possible role "to restrain interstate trade or commerce" and "to monopolize a certain part of such trade or commerce."[52] The appeal court panel said, "It appears to us that [affidavits about Alpenrose's role] are sufficient to present a genuine issue of fact as to whether Alpenrose Dairy, Inc. was a co-conspirator."[53] Alpenrose and its manager, Carl Cadonau, continued to be included in the lawsuits.

The pretrial date was set for November 13, 1967, after the judge denied a motion for delay by County Creamery. In 1968, four years after being filed, the case was finally heard in Portland. Judge Bruce

Thompson of Reno, Nevada, an antitrust expert who had ruled in 1966
on County Creamery's redesign of its label, presided over the trial.

In the antitrust case, the plaintiffs outlined a series of actions by
County Creamery that had damaged their organizations, restrained
interstate commerce, and conspired to monopolize a segment of the
dairy industry. Cheese & Dairy's list included:

- Restrained interstate commerce in the marketing of cheese, milk,
  and milk products.
- Conspired as individuals and with Carl Cadenau [sic] of Alpen-
  rose Dairy to monopolize part of the dairy industry.
- Prevented TCDA from marketing its products.
- Denied TCDA its full representation on the County Creamery
  board.
- Refused to pay over to TCDA the credit balance of TCDA's
  Grade A milk account held by County Creamery, a sum of about
  $771,527.
- Refused to pay over to TCDA the credit balance of TCDA's
  cheese account, a sum of about $711,128.
- Refused to pay over to TCDA the credit balance of TCDA's feed
  department account, a sum of about $300,000.
- Credit balances arbitrarily withheld by County Creamery totaled
  more than $2.5 million. Triple damages equal more than $7.7
  million.
- Attempted to intimidate a major creditor to destroy TCDA's line
  of credit.
- Attempted to intimidate TCDA's suppliers or patrons.
- Threatened legal action against TCDA's agents, brokers, and
  customers.
- Possessed about four million pounds of TCDA's cheese, sold it,
  and refused to give an accounting to TCDA.[54]

In March 1968, Cheese & Dairy's office manager, Philip Kelly, wrote
to patrons about the trial, saying, "Our attorneys and members who
have attended the trial in Portland are generally pleased with the course
of the proceedings and are optimistic toward the outcome."[55]

Farmers drove from Tillamook to downtown Portland for the trial. It required a lot of effort and time. Attendees lost the workday and had to travel about two hours each way, plus navigate downtown Portland's traffic and parking fees, but the trial represented a do-or-die moment and was reported as such by the *Headlight Herald*:

> During the last recess, one dairyman said . . . to a reporter, "Whoever loses in this case is going to get hurt. If it's me I don't know what I'll do. I've worked hard to build up my ranch. If I lost it, I might lose my head and do something violent."[56]

At the conclusion of the testimony, Judge Thompson read a lengthy statement, saying in part, "There isn't any law, there isn't any Court, that could even come close to a solution of the problems you have down in Tillamook County."[57] The judge described the situation as "an unholy mess." He warned the sides that they were "playing with fire." He told them that whichever side was ruled against would go out of business. He added that he was not afraid to make a ruling, but he would not make a ruling for at least two months, and he urged the two sides to reach a settlement in that period or risk bankruptcy.[58]

In an April 11, 1968, article in the *Headlight Herald* on the judge's posttrial statement, he was quoted suggesting two options:

1. Form two cooperatives, one for cheese producers and one for grade-A milk producers.
2. Do away with the cheese cooperative all together and have all dairy farmers become grade-A milk producers.[59]

Then, in recognition of Dixon being the focal point for all of the issues, as well as an impediment to cooperation and healing, Judge Thompson also suggested that Beale Dixon retire.[60] The judge's final suggestion was to remove Warren McMinimee from the settlement negotiations: "He has been too close to the controversy to be objective. He has been named as a defendant in this very lawsuit. And there are a good many others who are better qualified by disinterest and impartiality effectively to assist you in working out your problems."[61]

Judge Thompson concluded, "we are dealing with an economic civil war in Tillamook County . . . I truly entreat you people, you good people, to think about this; get together and solve your problems by mutual accommodation, which is the only way they will ever be solved."[62]

When the Cheese War ended five months later, the antitrust lawsuit decision was still pending, and that was the fate of an accounting lawsuit, too.

THE ACCOUNTING LAWSUIT

In May 1965, a year after filing the antitrust suit, Cheese & Dairy launched a lawsuit against County Creamery to force it to give an accounting of the funds that it had not paid to Cheese & Dairy, citing the "manipulation of accounting books by TCCA."[63]

Cheese & Dairy asserted that Creamery had yet to pay $2,306,036, or more than $20 million today, from various assets, sales, and debt. Payment of that missing money would ease Cheese & Dairy's financial bind and reassure its patrons that it was viable. Cheese & Dairy filed the suit in Multnomah County, home to Portland, to find a neutral courtroom—or perhaps to do some judge shopping. In July 1965, County Creamery filed a motion to change the venue from Multnomah County to Tillamook County. Both sides exaggerated the ease or difficulty of a trial in Portland. County Creamery claimed it would be a hardship on its farmers to go to Portland to testify; the plaintiffs assured the court that travel would not be a problem. The court settled on Tillamook but assigned the case to Judge Albert R. Musick, a circuit court judge from Washington County, west of Portland.

The lawsuit experienced many delays between 1965 and the trial in early 1968. County Creamery filed motions for postponement, numerous counterclaims, and objections to the form, time, or place of the lawsuit's claims.[64] Otto Schild filed an affidavit for the defense, stating that the plaintiff held documents needed by the defense; in a similar affidavit, this time for the plaintiff, Vern Lucas said the defendant had possession of documents needed by the plaintiff. One court filing was titled "Amended Reply to Defendant's Eighth Affirmative Answer, Partial Defense and Counterclaim and Defendant's Ninth Affirmative Answer, Partial Defense and Counterclaim."

Cheese & Dairy's general manager at the time, Donald E. McMullen, wrote to members and patrons on March 23, 1967,

We have also been informed that Judge Musick has signed an Order in our favor to the effect that T.C.C.A.'s Plea in Abatement to our Accounting Suit was not legally sufficient. We are now very hopeful of an earlier trial date because of this. I will keep you informed on our progress.[65]

Yet another delay was requested in a September 8, 1967, affidavit by Warren McMinimee's law partner, Douglas E. Kaufman, who wrote of County Creamery's attorney, "Warren A. McMinimee has taken ill and has been advised by his doctor that his health would be imperiled if he were to proceed to engage in the trial of any cases at this time."[66]

At last, the trial began on January 16, 1968. Cheese & Dairy was represented by Edwin Peterson, who later became chief justice of the Oregon Supreme Court.

"I was testifying one time in the accounting lawsuit," Milne remembered years later, "and McMinimee dragged out the Cheese & Dairy minutes. He had me read them out loud. They had to do with setting the price for some milk. He said we were taking over and setting milk prices, which was TCCA's business, because we were under contract to them.

"He asked if we had set the price. And I said, 'Yes, that's correct.' He was gloating and said, 'You don't have the authority to do that.' I looked at him and said, 'We've always done it. It's always been our authority because we aren't setting the price to the farmer, we're setting the price to the stores.'

"Peterson, our lawyer, had told us at lunch that day that cross examination is tricky. A good witness can foul up a lawyer. So what the heck, I tried to be a good witness."[67]

Dixon was grilled by Cheese & Dairy's attorney, with Judge Musick, who had an extensive background as a business attorney, leaning over from his high bench to question Dixon closely, too. Dixon recalled to his biographer, "And it was very, very difficult to explain those things to the court. I would say now that most people, most judges are not bookkeepers. Never were, or never will be."[68]

Barbara Milne remembered a different version of the courtroom testimony. "Dixon was testifying; McMinimee was leading him through his questions. Dixon would say, 'This is what happened . . .' and the judge would say, 'But Mr. Dixon, didn't you hear the minutes read into the record?' Dixon would say, 'Yes,' and Judge Musick would point out, 'They say differently.' Dixon would say, 'Well, this is right.' Then the judge would ask, 'Weren't you at the next meeting when the minutes were approved?' and Dixon would say, 'Yes, I was. But what I remember now is right.'"[69]

Dixon also recalled testifying at trials, including the accounting lawsuit:

> I don't mind telling you that I came home from coarse situations in Portland during some of those periods when I thought it would be much easier to just run off the road and end things. Or, I was on the stand here in Tillamook for seven straight days. And there were times when I thought I ought to get up out of my chair and walk straight out the front door of the courthouse and keep right on walking straight for the ocean and right out into the ocean. No one, unless they've been through a situation like that, can realize.
>
> And yet, I would have farmers come to me and say, "Beale, I don't see how you can stand it. I don't see how you can be on the witness stand and answer all the questions and know what the answers are and be consistent in the answers." And I would just simply say, "There's only one thing you can do, and that is to just simply tell them exactly what the facts are."[70]

In February 1968, Judge Musick advised County Creamery to withdraw its counterclaims against Cheese & Dairy,[71] boosting rebel hopes that the judge understood that County Creamery's claims in the larger lawsuit were also invalid.

Barbara Milne herself came to Judge Musick's attention, thanks to an attempt by McMinimee to block her from attending the trial. After the court had adjourned for the day, Barbara Milne was getting ready to leave the courtroom when one of the other women still in the room alerted her that McMinimee was talking to the judge about her.

Barbara Milne remembered, "McMinimee told the judge that I should not be allowed in the courtroom because I was taking notes and would tell my husband what was going on in the trial, and he was scheduled to testify later."[72] She always took notes, whether at church or a trial, as a way to pay attention, list information she wanted to learn more about, and record everything that had occurred. In the early days of the Cheese War, farmers sat in her living room planning their strategy while she stood in the dining room, her ear almost touching the closed folding door separating the men from her as she wrote notes of things to discuss later with her husband.

As McMinimee suspected, she planned to tell her husband exactly what had been said that day. After McMinimee's protest, she recalled, "The judge looked at him and said, 'Don't even talk to me about that. She is a citizen, and she has every right to be in the courtroom.' I told the woman that I would be there the next day if I had to crawl up the aisle with my pencil between my teeth!"[73]

After the accounting trial concluded, the farmers waited for the judge's decision. George Milne was optimistic, but the judge got sick and took a leave of absence from the bench.[74] Eight months later the Cheese War was over, and the pending decisions in the antitrust and accounting lawsuits no longer mattered.

Tourists Swarm the Factory

BY LINDA KIRK

Two miles north of downtown Tillamook, the sprawling Tillamook cheese factory could be seen by everyone driving on Highway 101. Built parallel to the highway in 1949, the cheese plant stretches longer than a football field. In the 1960s, a welcoming wall of windows invited drivers to leave the highway, walk into the factory, and look around. The invitation was accepted by fifty thousand travelers every year.[1]

Soon after the factory opened, male guides offered tours. In 1957, women took over guiding.[2] They led tours until the cheese factory was remodeled and expanded in the 1990s.[3] Then, in place of tours, the factory offered viewing windows, video footage, a café, and hand-dipped ice cream cones. More than a million tourists stopped by the cheese factory in 2016.[4] In 2018, County Creamery held a grand opening for a new, larger tourist facility. Installed above the entrance is a giant photo of a cow—a cow the cooperative named Flower.[5]

Back when groups of visitors followed guides through the cheese factory, my older sister, Cathy, led tours in 1965 and 1966 during her summer breaks from college. My stint as a cheese guide came in 1968, just before Cheese & Dairy went out of business.

Arriving at the cheese factory on my first day of work, I could see that the staff was swamped. Anita Beeler, my supervisor, quickly introduced me to the other guides and then put me to work filling trays with cheese samples. For the rest of that day, and all of the next, I sat on a stool in a back corner of the sales area, cutting cheese cubes and stabbing them with toothpicks.

From the corner, I watched as waves of tourists crowded into the visitor area. As each wave grew, voices filled the room. It was a room that easily held twenty-five milling visitors, but it grew uncomfortably crowded when fifty or sixty people pressed in. Every thirty minutes, a cheese guide opened the door to the vat room, where milk became cheese. The guide raised her white bullhorn and announced, "The next tour will leave in five minutes." The crowd shifted to face the guide. Then the guide opened the door, letting in a whiff of freshly cooked cheese curds, and started the tour.

At home, I studied a brochure that described Tillamook's cheese-making process. I wrote facts on a note card that fit in the pocket of my white uniform. I felt nervous about leading tours, but ready, too. Before the end of the week, Anita let me take a group of tourists through the plant. I waited by a vat where paddles stirred heated milk. I took a deep breath and spoke loudly into the bullhorn, "Bacteria culture, coloring, and rennet are added to the milk. Color is extracted from annatto seeds. Rennet causes the milk to coagulate."[6] If anyone asked about rennet, I was ready to say that the factory used rennet made from the stomachs of veal calves. If no one asked, I would not elaborate on rennet.

I led my group to the last vat. I said, "Here the cheesemakers are flipping the curds." Two cheesemakers, working on opposite sides of the vat, leaned far over the vat's walls. They wore white shirts and pants, white hats like soda jerks', and brown rubber boots. They reached both hands to the bottom of the vat and, muscles straining, lifted warm, heavy, slippery, unwieldy slabs of solidified curds, and flipped them over.

Later in the tour, we looked through windows into the packaging room, where women cut and wrapped cheese after stripping wax from forty-pound cheese blocks. "Packages of Premium Brand cheese are distributed to grocery stores throughout the West," I said. In the cold-storage room, I pointed to shelves of cheese wheels and two-pound rectangular baby loaves. "Here we age the cheese from sixty days for mild cheddar to nine months for sharp. Cheese inspectors regularly take random core samples and taste the samples to monitor the cheese."

Seven days a week, customers crowded the sales counter. The quietest day that summer was Labor Day—maybe because tourists thought the factory was closed. It was the first day that the soft-serve ice cream machine did not overheat. Not once. That was one Labor Day bonus. Another was that we were all paid double time. My hourly wage jumped to $2.50.

On Labor Day, I had time to think about the tourists who left Highway 101 every day and came into the cheese factory. I had an impres-
sion of people who were road-weary and looking for a diversion. The
visitors who stopped in the morning saw a factory humming with activ-
ity. By late afternoon, the day's milk was transformed into cheese. The
vats were empty; the cheesemakers were gone. Despite the inactivity,
the afternoon visitors seemed satisfied with their tours. Most people
listened attentively. The most frequent question was, "Do you have a
lot of mice here?"

During my weeks at the cheese factory, I talked with hundreds of
people, but no one person stood out. Unlike my sister, I did not meet
a famous person. Cathy led a tour that included Mark Hatfield, who
was then Oregon's governor. She said Hatfield was so handsome and
such an attentive listener that she almost forgot her spiel. Little did she
know that Hatfield had firsthand knowledge of tour-guiding: while a
high school senior in Salem, Hatfield had led tours of Oregon's capitol.[7]

Near the end of September, I worked my last day as a cheese guide.
Fall term registration at Oregon State University was coming up in a few
days. I said goodbye to Anita and then drove west through the parking
lot. I turned left onto Highway 101. On the seat beside me, wrapped in
white paper, was a two-pound wedge of sharp cheddar cheese.

CHAPTER 11

The End

On September 26, 1968, the *Headlight Herald* printed a large headline above its nameplate that read, "Creameries Reach Agreement."

In smaller print were the words "TCCA Surviving Association."[1]

For the rebellious farmers, 1968 saw the death of their dream. The loss seemed to be reflected in the country's national tragedies, with Americans buffeted by riots in cities and the assassinations of Martin Luther King Jr. and Robert F. Kennedy. In Tillamook, the end of the Cheese War was not violent or deadly, but it was personal. It deeply affected the farmers, their families, and their community.

By early 1968, the loyal members of Cheese & Dairy had read the writing on the wall, and their energy was at an all-time low. On February 6, 1968, L. M. Thorpe, Cheese & Dairy's final general manager, had written to members and patrons asking them to continue shipping milk to "enable us to generate cash . . . to make this, your co-operative, a going concern." He concluded by writing,

> I wish to express my personal appreciation and admiration for this co-operatives', [sic] owners, shippers, YOU. The way this group has remained steadfast and determined in the face of adversity and harassment is unique, outstanding and wonderful. And I am certain you are correct in your principles and right in your views, and will win this conflict in the end. Believe me you deserve to![2]

It wasn't going to happen. The defiant farmers ran out of money. The manager's letter also alerted shippers that milk checks that had been due February 1 would be paid February 15, but they would be written for 40 percent of the outstanding payables. The remaining 60

percent "will be paid on March 1, 1968. If we should succeed in arrang-
ing a more favorable financing program, these dates on milk payables
will, of course, be brought back to a current status."[3]

Cheese & Dairy did not lose the Cheese War because it was wrong;
it lost because it lacked the cash flow to keep operating while waiting
for the antitrust and accounting lawsuit decisions. All of the lawsuits
and appeals had taken time and money, and Cheese & Dairy's coffers
were finally empty. Perhaps if Cheese & Dairy had stayed with Foremost, the co-op would have had time to gain more financial stability
before the last legal pushes, but that was water under the bridge now.

In December 1967, according to *The Tillamook Way*, County
Creamery had decided on nine necessary steps for reunification:

Dissolution of member organizations
Merger into a county organization
Elect directors by districts within the county
TCCA to take over assets of merging organizations
Inventories of cheese to be paid for with cash according to grade
Present member groups to settle own accounts
Feed department allocations to be released by member associations
New board to be responsible for operations
All pending lawsuits to be canceled.[4]

Cheese & Dairy's board wrote to its patrons and shippers on June
14, 1968, about a special meeting of the membership, to be held June
25, 1968, with the agenda "1. To vote upon the question of dissolving
Tillamook Cheese & Dairy Association. 2. To vote upon selling all or
substantially all the Tillamook Cheese & Dairy Association assets, real
and personal property."[5]

The end of Cheese & Dairy was clearly imminent and finally
occurred in September. From April to September 1968, Cheese &
Dairy's board had waited for Judge Bruce Thompson's decision in the
antitrust lawsuit. During that period, the board offered several settlement ideas to County Creamery, just as it had in 1965, but the offers
were rejected.

Five months had passed since the judge took the antitrust case
under advisement. No decision had been forthcoming. Meanwhile,

no decision had been rendered in the accounting lawsuit. Philip Kelly, Cheese & Dairy's office manager, said on March 30, 1968, "We are impatiently waiting the day when the fruits of labor can be returned to the producer instead of attorneys and lenders."[6]

That day didn't come.

THE SETTLEMENT

The settlement between the two creameries totaled more than $1.2 million, or more than $9.6 million today. It was one of the largest cash deals in the history of Tillamook County to that date.[7] County Creamery's settlement had three components, all designated as payments to creditors:

Cheese & Dairy's cheese inventory: $500,000
Cheese & Dairy's facilities: $466,000
Cheese & Dairy's remaining debts: $235,000

Creditors filed more than two hundred claims. One of the smallest amounts was $1.90, owed to 4-H Club Local Leaders. Walter E. Heller & Company expected the largest payout, $540,000.[8] Heller advertised in 1969 that it loaned money to businesses when "you've reached your borrowing limit with ordinary money sources."[9] Cow Milkers Association was owed more than $27,000. To pay off the debt, County Creamery agreed it would make daily payments:

to W. E. Heller Co. and to Cow Milkers Association, in the order of their respective security, the purchase price under this agreement for all such pledged cheese which is graded and delivered to TCCA on that day.[10]

Cheese & Dairy patrons expected reimbursement of their $25 membership fees and any loans they had given to Cheese & Dairy. Joe Beeler's $27,034 claim topped the list of eighty-six farmer creditors. Next came G&R Dairy and Hooker Jenck, who were each owed more than $10,000. Seven shippers expected to receive more than $5,000: Wilsona Farms (Leuthold family), Joe Chatelain, Steve Steiner, Carl

Tohl, Vern Lucas, Zinzer Brothers, and Harley Christensen.[11] Ironically, the victors in the Cheese War would also pay $27,644 to Cheese
& Dairy's Portland legal firm.[12]

In another irony, County Creamery took out a loan to acquire
Cheese & Dairy.

> Beale Dixon . . . reports that the purchase was accomplished
> by means of a term loan on inventories, but that the Creamery
> Association expects to arrange additional financing through
> a mortgage loan to complete sewage disposal facilities and
> building and machinery improvements which will make the plant
> completely modern with the latest cheesemaking techniques.[13]

The *Headlight Herald* editorialized, "Wounds won't be healed overnight, just because an agreement has been signed, but time will help."[14]
A County Creamery ad in the same issue featured the Tillamook brand
name and proclaimed it to be "The People's Choice in Tillamook."[15]

Dixon recalled to his biographer:

> And then we took over what remained of the interest of the
> producers in the Tillamook Cheese and Dairy Association. I
> believe that at that point, they had lost enough money that those
> producers only received about 50 percent of their face value of
> their investment in that association. But at least they got it back
> on a solid footing, and the certificates were revolved on that
> basis as other certificates were revolved. And that brought them
> back into the association.[16]

Certificates were also called capital allocations or debentures. Barbara Milne explained,

> Every year, shippers to Creamery got *x* number of dollars a month.
> At the end of the year, there was a profit to be divided up. The
> IRS said we got it and we had to pay tax on it, but we didn't get it
> during the first ten years of shipping. For that decade, the profit
> was kept; then it was returned. The co-op used it for buildings
> and equipment. So the co-op was always ten years behind on

payments. When something happened like the Shiveley Shippers splitting off, that affected the debentures for the entire group."[17]

Farmers were keenly aware of their debentures. They were like a forced savings account that would help them in the future. Based on the coming debenture payment, a farmer might plan to reroof the barn or buy a few more cows. The purchase and sale agreement between County Creamery and Cheese & Dairy included language that addressed debentures:

> TC&DA, as a former member patron of TCCA, is the owner of and is entitled to certain patronage allocations and capital equities in TCCA. In order to distribute such TC&DA interests among the former TC&DA patrons entitled to share therein, TCCA shall issue and distribute to such former patrons TCCA creamery division capital reserve certificates in the total amount of such TC&DA interests ... All such certificates shall be revolved by TCCA with, in the same manner and in the same proportion as all other presently issued.[18]

Despite the language in the agreement, however, "At the time Cheese & Dairy went bankrupt, Creamery kept those ten years of profit," Barbara Milne later recalled. "Dixon said, 'We'll pay off all your debts, but we'll keep those 10 years of profit.'"[19] Joe Jenck, Hooker's son, recalls, "Other dairymen knew Dixon stole the debentures."[20] Cheese & Dairy farmers didn't protest losing their debentures, however. They didn't have any votes on the County Creamery board; they were the losers; they didn't have any political clout; they had no stomach for another battle or lawsuit; they didn't have money to hire an attorney; and they were grateful that the

Beale Dixon in 1975 as he neared retirement. *Headlight Herald*, April 9, 1975

winners were letting them return. But more than fifty years later, they remember their unpaid debentures.

CHANGES IN THE DAIRY INDUSTRY

Almost immediately after the agreement, County Creamery adopted policies imposed by state dairy industry regulators that required all milk to meet Grade A standards, whatever its final use. A few months before County Creamery bought out Cheese & Dairy, the Oregon Department of Agriculture had started discussing upgrades to the standards of "manufacturing grade," or cheese, milk. An August 1, 1968, article in the *Headlight Herald* noted that "temperature standards for manufacturing grade milk, a leukocyte count standard along the same line as that for grade A milk and an increase in the bacteriological standard for this milk will be discussed."[21]

As Ed Yates, County Creamery's head cheesemaker in the 1960s, said in *The Tillamook Way*, "Who would have envisioned that all the milk in Tillamook County would one day be Grade A?"[22] It was a sea change in the industry. The new standard achieved Judge Thompson's suggestion after the antitrust suit to end the system of two types of shippers. Indeed, all cow milk today meets the same high standard, no matter what its end use will be.

Dixon claimed to have foreseen the flaws in the two-milk system, telling his biographer,

> But I could see these youngsters and farmers producing some mighty fine milk manufacturing for cheese, that were not permitted to market their milk as grade A. But on the other hand, the grade A producers could produce all they wanted and have their milk go into cheese or butter and powder. And I began to see the unfairness of it. And I began to think that all milk should be grade A and all farmers should share in all markets for milk. Because after all, milk was milk, and there really was no reason to have a different quality of milk for cheese, or butter and powder.[23]

The state's new refrigeration requirement could only be achieved by using bulk tanks. Installing a tank, however, also meant paying for

Barbara and George Milne in the early 1970s. Courtesy of the Milne family

a new building, complete with electricity. The expense of the tank and the building gave some cheese milk producers an incentive to retire. Others, such as Red Clover's Bob Blaser and his wife, Helen, chose to sell their dairy cows and run beef on their farms until they retired. The Blasers had never gone Grade A, and they weren't going to start now.[24]

The Milnes did not want to support County Creamery. So George Milne took another precaution: he transferred ownership of his cows to his wife so she would be free to sell the milk to any processor. The Milnes met with Bob Ely, who had gone to work for the Oregon Department of Agriculture, to transfer ownership and assign the quota to her.[25] Then the Milnes chose to ship to Farmers Cooperative Creamery of McMinnville, also known as Darigold. That co-op was glad to send bulk tank trucks from the Willamette Valley to Tillamook every day to pick up the milk that was suddenly available from the Milnes and other farmers.

Eventually, most of the Cheese & Dairy farmers who remained in dairying shipped their milk to County Creamery. Hooker Jenck was one of the first to return. Dave Leuthold, Hans's son, held out for some years, shipping to a Guernsey cow cooperative before returning to County Creamery. George Milne always shipped his milk to Darigold until, opting for semi-retirement, he switched to raising beef cattle for the last fifteen years of his farming career.

AFTERMATH

If Grade A certification had been required in 1960, the Cheese War might never have happened. Or perhaps it would have happened anyway; Dixon might still have pushed for using Cheese & Dairy's money to make unsecured loans to stores to gain sales. Cheese & Dairy still would have protested his moves.

Dixon said in his oral history interview in 1987, "Times change, and jobs change. The thing that is necessary to make an organization go changes from generation to generation. And so I was only hopeful that I would do my part in improving and helping make Tillamook Cheese a little more secure. And I feel gratified in the progress we made." He added, "I didn't realize [the marketing of Grade A milk] was going to be such a factor in my life when I came to Tillamook. And it did become probably the biggest problem, or perhaps I can say, the biggest accomplishment that I ever made for the producers."[26]

George Milne reflected, "At least the Grade A farmers had the milk stabilization law. The quota created value and potential wealth for farmers."[27] Indeed, it helped the Milnes when they were ready to retire. "When we sold the herd years later," Barbara Milne said, "we got more than $10 per pound of quota."[28]

When the dust settled, McMinimee remained as County Creamery's attorney, despite the advice of Judge Thompson in the antitrust lawsuit. In 1989, Dixon talked about his legal advisor in an interview with his biographer, Gerry Hysmith.

Dixon: With all of the accusations and lawsuits that were brought, I should mention Warren McMinimee in connection with that. Our board turned to Warren to help us through various lawsuits that were made. And there had been statements made that, well, he was well paid for what he did. And yet knowing what other attorneys were charging and knowing what he charged us, I really think that he had a lot of just personal desire to help save the Tillamook County Creamery Association. And when you get involved in something like that, it was wonderful to have Warren on our side.
Hysmith: He did a fine job.
Dixon: He did. He really did. He doesn't overlook anything.[29]

McMinimee admitted, according to *The Tillamook Way*, "that there were many times when he wasn't at all certain TCCA was going to win."[30] Barbara Milne said, "After Cheese & Dairy ended, McMinimee said that if he had worked with the rebels, we would have had this wrapped up long ago. I'm completely convinced that if they hadn't had McMinimee, we would have won. And if we had not had George, they would have won very easily."[31]

After Cheese & Dairy folded, the losing farmers had to cope with their new reality. They had given nearly everything to achieve autonomy—and they had failed. Hans Leuthold was "very discouraged," according to Dave Leuthold.[32] Glenn Johnston "felt foolish, like he wasted his time," said Fib Johnston.[33] Steve Steiner told his son, Nick, that only the lawyers made money on the Cheese War.[34] Hooker Jenck focused his pride on leaving the farm for his family, according to his son.[35]

Some of the men continued to get together, like veterans meeting to talk—or not—about their war experiences, knowing that only someone who has been there could understand. Others of the group continued their established traditions of playing cards together regularly or going on yearly hunting trips.

George Milne did not hang out with the guys. The Cheese & Dairy experience had either hurt him too much, or taught him to keep his head down, or left him feeling that he should stick to family and farming. Perhaps he was as focused in defeat as he had been in battle. For Milne, it was easiest to revert to the self-contained farmer he had been before circumstances had demanded more of him. Certainly, neither George nor Barbara Milne wanted to think about the loss, and Barbara Milne didn't want to risk having her husband taken away from her again.

"Later," Barbara Milne said, "I was working on the county's land use plan with Vic Affolter, the county planner. He had grown up on a small farm in south Tillamook County, and his parents shipped to Creamery. He told me that everybody felt George was a good guy; he was sincere, he was honest—but he was mistaken."[36]

She said, "We were so naive."[37] And her husband responded, "Oh, gosh, yes."[38]

Barbara Milne said, "We were right; we did the best we could; it was over. It was like having a tiger by the tail. You're afraid you'll get bitten. But when we let go, it didn't bite us at all."[39]

"Only once do I remember feeling there were people who didn't want to speak to me or who wanted to leave me out. The one time was when I was a room mother at South Prairie Elementary School with Mrs. Arnold Walker after the fight. I started to talk to her at a meeting and she said, 'I can't talk to you. My husband doesn't want me to talk to you.'"[40]

Old-timers remember who chose which side. A few agree with the County Creamery farmer who was overheard by Joe Jenck, Hooker's son, telling a newcomer years later, "We never should have let those sons of bitches back in."[41] Not surprisingly, others agree with Tom Tone, one of Bass Tone's sons, who says, "We got out-snookered by crooked men."[42]

The dream of autonomy led to a bruising disillusionment at the end of the Cheese War, with rebel families and friends in need of healing. The process went well for some but never occurred for others. Meanwhile, Tillamook Cheese has thrived, and both George Milne, the proud farmer and reformer, and Beale Dixon, who really, really wanted to succeed, would be glad.

I Was a Teenage Creditor

BY LINDA KIRK

When I was 18, Cheese & Dairy owed me $89.03, but I never received a paycheck. Instead of issuing payments, Cheese & Dairy sold its assets to County Creamery for more than a million dollars, closed its books, and quit operating. My unpaid claim was included in a master list of creditors prepared by Cheese & Dairy in 1968 and attached to the back pages of the final book of minutes maintained by the cooperative.

It is thanks to Anita Neilson and the Johnstons that the minutes exist today. Anita and her husband, Bob Neilson, shipped milk to Cheese & Dairy at the same time that she held a job working for Beale Dixon in the County Creamery office. Neilson said later that someone in the County Creamery office asked her to haul the minutes ledgers to the dumpster. Instead, Neilson took the ledgers home. After storing the ledgers at her house for many years, she took them to her neighbors, Fib and Rita Johnston. Neilson knew that Fib Johnston and his father, Glenn Johnston, supported Cheese & Dairy throughout the Cheese War. The Johnstons were surprised to receive the minutes but agreed to keep them. Over the following three decades, they thought about tossing out the minutes books, but it didn't seem right. Then, in 2015, I asked the Johnstons if my sister and I could meet them at their house for an interview about the Cheese War. On the day of the interview, I phoned Rita Johnston to confirm our meeting. She asked if we wanted Cheese & Dairy minutes books. Yes, we wanted them!

The stack of ledgers the Johnstons gave us included minutes of meetings held from 1951 to 1968. The day we received the books, Marilyn and I stayed up late reading minutes and talking. Our father attended most of the meetings. It was not surprising to see his name, but it was a more powerful experience than I expected. This was our father's history. We could read in the minutes what he said and did.

That night, I didn't stay awake long enough to read all the entries. It was the next day that I felt a jolt of surprise. On a thirteen-page list of final creditors, there was my name: Linda Milne.[1] How could I be a creditor? My only direct association with Cheese & Dairy was when I worked for the co-op as summer help. The explanation was that Cheese & Dairy was collapsing while I was giving tours at the factory. Later in September, when I was registering for fall term classes at Oregon State University, County Creamery was negotiating to buy Cheese & Dairy. The two sides announced an agreement that included County Creamery assuming the failing co-op's assets and debts.[2] One of those debts was my final paycheck. The creditor list included nineteen former employees. At $89.03, my payroll claim was small, but not the smallest. That creditor was Valerie Moody, whose claim was $81.37. The largest payroll checks, a bit more than $330, went to O. N. Sheldon and cheese-maker Fritz Baumgartner.

My life as a creditor was brief and uneventful. I was oblivious to the events unfolding at the Tillamook branch of First National Bank on October 6, 1968,[3] when officials from Cheese & Dairy met with Beale Dixon, County Creamery's manager, to make it official that Cheese & Dairy was out of business. They signed documents, they probably shook hands, and then they all went back to work—at the cheese factory and on their farms.

Later that fall, my mother forwarded my final paycheck. When the envelope arrived, I may have noticed that it was from County Creamery, not Cheese & Dairy. I know I didn't call home to ask questions. My building had one phone for forty-two students, and long-distance calls were expensive. Maybe I wrote a letter asking my parents to explain. Even so, a check is a check. I probably walked down Monroe Street to the bank and cashed the County Creamery paycheck. Then I went back to my desk and opened my biology textbook, untroubled by my stint as a teenage creditor.

Epilogue

> I think it's clear that the cooperative model has allowed relatively smaller farms, from specific regional areas, to survive in a way they probably would not have if they were not organized as cooperatives.
>
> —Gordon Edgar

> After the fight ended, Warren McMinimee insisted that County Creamery become a producer co-op, like Cheese & Dairy had been. That straightened out the bylaws and the accounting and depreciation. County Creamery became a better outfit.
>
> —George Milne

With reunification, County Creamery's farmers and staff needed to respond to changes in environmental, organizational, and marketing requirements. One major change occurred when a Federal Milk Marketing Order came to Oregon. FMMOs seek to provide orderly marketing of milk, from the farm to processors to consumers by dictating the price of milk.[1] Oregon's quota system continued to operate alongside the FMMO from 1970 to 1987. In 1987, when fewer than one-third of farmers participated in the state quota system, it ended. Like other states, Oregon now operates with "minimum milk price regulations enforced by Federal Milk Marketing Orders based on a system of mandatory dairy price reporting, milk pricing formulas, price discrimination based on the end-use of raw milk and equity payments from a revenue sharing pool."[2]

Cooperative-owned processing plants are allowed to pay less than the minimum price; non-cooperative facilities must pay at least the minimum unless they have agreed in advance with their suppliers to pay a different price. The price paid by consumers for the products does not correlate with what was paid to the producers by the handlers. Indeed, farmers' payments have dropped while retail prices have risen.[3] It is a complicated system, to put it mildly. But when cooperatives such as County Creamery or Vermont's Cabot Creamery create value-added products like cheese, ice cream, and yogurt, they are less vulnerable to the fluid milk price set by a milk marketing order.[4]

Still, all dairy farmers live with great uncertainty about whether their hard work will pay off. Farmers have tried to make up for low prices with greater volumes of milk, but in recent years Americans have been drinking less milk.[5]

At least one cooperative, Darigold—also known as Northwest Dairy Association—is trying something different. In 2020, it told its members that the pricing of its internal quota system would change. It is "reinvesting a portion of farmer profits in new equipment and products, raising the penalty on overproduction and opening the option for farms to sell their 'base' to other farms."[6] The base arrangement looks a lot like Oregon's 1960s quota system. Darigold is hoping its strategy will create value, inspire other organizations to enact similar steps, reduce the glut of milk on the market, and raise the milk price in the long run.

Modern dairy farmers have been dealing with changes like this for as long as they have been milking cows. For example, in the late 1960s, the state of Oregon required them to install bulk tanks. The tanks, which replaced the once-ubiquitous ten-gallon milk cans, hastened the closure of Tillamook's small cheese factories because tanker trucks could haul milk efficiently from farmers' bulk tanks to Tillamook's big factory. The small output of the factories was another factor. In 1963, Beaver had thirty-five patrons providing cheese milk; Hebo had eighteen, Central thirty, and Red Clover forty.[7] By the late 1960s, membership declined as cheese-milk farmers went Grade A or quit dairying. The lower volume of production resulted in higher manufacturing costs that reduced the factories' profit margins. The outlying factories didn't have modern cold storage facilities, and it remained difficult for all cheesemakers to maintain the highest-quality standards.

In early 1969, the six remaining small factories closed. Hebo Cheese Factory became a home; Beaver became a home and business, Mohler became a winery, and Oretown became a manufacturing plant for salad dressing. Some former cheese factories are empty and crumbling.

The closure of the factories meant Tillamook County Creamery Association no longer needed to be a marketing cooperative, splitting income and expenses among its eight cooperatives. As a marketing cooperative, County Creamery had a multilayered structure. It worked with the boards of Mohler or Cloverdale, not directly with the farmers, and it was always interested in retaining the loyalty of each factory's board members. When County Creamery became a producer cooperative, it established primary relationships with its members, even if they were not on the board. Additionally, expenses and income are not parceled out proportionally to member cooperatives, which means that the bookkeeping is simplified and more understandable.

ENVIRONMENTAL ISSUES

The state's requirement for wastewater systems was another factor in the closure of the small factories. County Creamery had to invest in a wastewater system at the Tillamook factory.[8] It had a reliable volume of year-round water, thanks to construction of a dam in the hills east of the factory on a tributary of the Kilchis River. The wastewater system and water supply, plus the central location, made Tillamook's cheese factory the logical place to make, store, and ship cheese and other dairy products.

The new wastewater system was emblematic of the industry's growing awareness of environmental issues centered around water. Tillamook County is fittingly known as the land of many waters:[9] five rivers flowing into Tillamook Bay with about 665 stream miles;[10] other rivers emptying into Nehalem, Netarts, and Nestucca Bays; streams and sloughs abounding; and the infamous annual rain that soaks the ground and swells the waterways to flood level nearly every winter. As awareness of groundwater pollution has grown, Tillamook has been in the crosshairs, both because it contains a lot of cows and because it contains a lot of water.

All along, people had noticed the pollution but accepted it as part of their way of life. For example, most factories were sited next to waterways for a water supply and easy discharge of excess whey. When

Tom Tone, one of Bass Tone's sons, was a child, he liked to fish on the Trask River at Red Clover because he caught fish fattened on whey.[11] By the late 1960s, Oregon's state government, as well as the federal government, began to issue regulations to keep the flow of whey and farm pollutants, from chemicals to manure to sediment, from reaching the waterways.

On the farms, cow herds were smaller in the old days, which meant that a pile-and-wait-for-dry-weather manure system worked. Manure continues to be a handy boost for pastures and field corn, which many Tillamook farmers grow today, thanks to hybrid seeds that mature more quickly than in George Milne's time—although as farmer Joe Jenck says, "Our 72-day corn takes 150 days in Tillamook."[12]

A 2011 bioenergy study estimated that Tillamook's cows "generate approximately 233 million gallons of manure per year."[13] The state required Tillamook farmers to build containment systems—tanks— that stopped biosolids from draining into rivers, irrigation systems, or ponds. And the state told farmers like Joe Jenck that, to remedy sediment problems, they had to plant trees and fence off riverbanks to reinforce the riparian zones of their properties so nothing would escape into the waterways and harm aquatic life. Dikes and flood gates had to be improved so fish could move upstream to spawn.[14]

Despite these steps, Tillamook farmers and the state cope with the real possibility that unintentional pollution will reach the waterways. In 2017, a dairy accidentally poured 190,000 gallons of sludge into the Tillamook River.[15] One of the fishermen who discovered it told the *Headlight Herald*, "It looked like hundreds of gallons a minute." Another said, "It was significant . . . It wasn't just some little thing—it was really heavy." The farm was fined $17,000. A news release issued jointly by the farmer and County Creamery said that it wouldn't occur again because a second valve had been added. Within one month, three other local farms had spills.[16] And the same farm that produced the large 2017 spill had a smaller spill in 2019.[17]

County Creamery itself has not been exempt. A local oyster farmer and the Northwest Environmental Defense Center joined a suit filed by the US Environmental Protection Agency asserting cow manure was contaminating the oyster beds in Tillamook Bay. In a 1992 consent decree, EPA fined County Creamery $240,000 for violating its wastewater discharge permit, and the cooperative volunteered to spend $25,000 annually for four consecutive years to install fences that would keep animals out of the rivers bordering members' properties.[18] In 2015, the Oregon Department of Environmental Quality fined County Creamery $56,532 for exceeding its wastewater discharge permit limitations at the factory. A County Creamery spokesperson noted that the cooperative upgraded its equipment.[19]

The herds of cows are getting larger. Many farmers want to establish CAFOs—confined or concentrated animal feeding operations—to provide maximized feed and nutrients to the herds, keep the cows sheltered in the winter and sometimes year-round, and produce the most milk possible. But CAFOs mean concentrated waste material. CAFOs are jointly regulated in Oregon by the Department of Agriculture and the Department of Environmental Quality. They are also regulated by federal agencies. Each dairy farm must develop an Animal Waste Management Plan, approved by the Oregon Department of Agriculture, before receiving a CAFO permit. The state inspects each farm regularly.[20] Tillamook has also joined an industry environmental group, Farmers Assuring Responsible Management, to preemptively address issues such as animal welfare.[21]

Seeing a business opportunity, a company built a manure digester near Tillamook to convert sludge into biogas. The leftover waste has fewer pathogens, which provided faint comfort when a 2019 spill poured three hundred thousand gallons of treated manure into Anderson Creek, which empties into the Tillamook River, which then drains into Tillamook Bay.[22] Although two companies tried to run the digester, it wasn't economically sustainable, and it shut down.[23] Today, Tillamook hosts two private digesters, one for a CAFO of three to four thousand cows next to town, the other for a group of farmers who financed the digester themselves.[24]

Manure disposal wasn't a consideration when George Milne started farming in 1948. He had 15 registered Jerseys on thirty-eight acres and grew his herd to include 150 Holstein cows, 50 heifers ready to breed and add to the herd, and 30 to 40 calves, all on 182 acres. When he retired, it was a large farm. Now, most Tillamook herds have at least twice as many cows.[25] Yet the eighty or so remaining County Creamery members are an 87 percent drop from the six hundred Tillamook farmers in 1963.[26]

Statewide, the number of dairy farms has declined nearly 94 percent between 1965 and 2017.

1965: 12,500
2017: 645[27]

Between 2002 and 2007, an average of three dairy farms went out of business each month.[28]

Meanwhile, Oregon farmers' milk production has grown. The remaining Oregon farmers care for about 124,000 cows that produce 2.6 billion pounds of milk and make dairy the state's fourth-largest commodity.[29] To accomplish more with less, dairy farmers offer their cows carefully calibrated nutrition, breed them with gender-specific semen to increase the number of female calves that can be added to the herd, and use technology to handle parts of the daily milkings.

In 2018, Oregon's farms added more than $473 million to the state's economy.[30] The typical Oregon farmer was nearly 60 years old, owned about three hundred acres, and milked 350-400 cows in an average small- to medium-sized herd.[31] The Tillamook farmers of 1900 would be stunned that their annual production of a hundred thousand pounds of butter and/or cheese each year has morphed into more than 34 million pounds of cheese annually. Likewise, Tillamook farmers of the 1960s would be shocked that most of Tillamook County Creamery Association's milk and products aren't generated in Tillamook.[32]

MARKETING TILLAMOOK CHEESE

As Tillamook's market share grew, County Creamery faced a big decision: become ubiquitous in supermarkets or remain a high-end treat in the gourmet section. Its board chose to make its products available everywhere. In the early 2000s, Board President Joe Rocha explained the decision in a remarkably candid statement for the very private organization.

The board of directors . . . figured out that we could not sell the milk that we produced here turned into cheese and keep everybody happy and keep it a little artisan place. We were too big for that . . . So we already knew that the Safeways of the world would have to sell our cheese. Well, the problem is the Safeways of the world want you in all of their stores, or they don't want to deal with that kind of thing. So we have to supply those people.[33]

Today, Tillamook Cheese is available in Safeway stores everywhere. It is provided as a snack on airplanes and sold on US military bases in the Middle East. Mission accomplished—except, success led to another problem: not enough product to meet the demand, despite hard-working cows and smart farmers.

Another issue was getting the cheese to the markets. As then-CEO Strunk said in a 2012 article about shipping dairy products from Tillamook, "Mile-marker 'zero' on the West Coast is probably the most difficult place to distribute [from] to the entire US."[34]

To cope with supply and transportation issues, County Creamery built the Columbia River Processing Plant near Boardman, a small northeastern Oregon town in Morrow County. In 2001, County Creamery began buying milk from Threemile Canyon Farms, a Boardman-area CAFO megadairy that milks about thirty-three thousand cows that generate 2 million pounds of milk daily. Threemile Canyon is licensed to house seventy thousand cows[35] and operates a manure digester.[36] In fact, Morrow County now boasts the greatest number of cows of any Oregon county.[37] For several years, Tillamook also bought milk from Lost Valley Dairy, another Boardman-area CAFO megadairy. It was licensed for thirty thousand cows.

By 2013, the two eastern Oregon dairies supplied more than half of Tillamook's milk, according to the Oregon Food Bank's "Tillamook County Community Food Assessment."[38] Lost Valley Dairy was shuttered by the state in 2018 after numerous environmental violations.[39] Tillamook continues to buy milk from Threemile Canyon and several other area dairies.

Tillamook's Morrow County facility turns the Boardman milk into 55 million pounds of cheese each year.[40] A separate company's Idaho plant creates Tillamook's shredded and sliced cheeses from the eastern Oregon cheese. The same company packages the cheese for Idaho distribution and commodity sales, and a company in Utah packages it for the southwest markets. In 2014, the Tillamook plant was producing cheese, ice cream, and sweet whey. Today, according to Tillamook's website, its butter, yogurt, sour cream, cream cheese spreads—as well as some of its cheeses, ice cream, and new products—are made by contracted manufacturers outside of Tillamook.

Tillamook Cheese owns the Bandon Cheese brand, having purchased its factory on the southwest Oregon coast in 2000. When the purchase of the factory and the brand was complete, County Creamery sent letters to Bandon-area businesses, warning them that they might not be allowed to continue using Bandon in their business names. The businesses protested. A Bandon, Oregon, city councilor said, "If we have to trademark our city, we'll trademark our city."[41] Even the town of Bandon, Ireland, opposed County Creamery's assertion of its exclusive right to the use of place names. The issue faded away, though, in part because County Creamery closed the Bandon factory. In 2004, *Willamette Week* newspaper noted that Tillamook was labeling so-called Bandon organic cheeses as "Oregon Coast Cheese," but the products were made in Wisconsin with Wisconsin milk. A spokesperson explained that the slogan was being used "for brand recognition." The newspaper also said that the Bandon name had been changed in 2003 to "Oregon Coast Foods."[42] Today, County Creamery makes Bandon cheese in Boardman, offering it in two-pound, nonorganic blocks at a lower price point than the similar-looking blocks of Tillamook Cheese.

Again in 2004, Tillamook Cheese was overly protective of its name, protesting the twenty-eight-year use of the Tillamook place name as part of the business name of Tillamook Country Smoker, a local meat product maker. For a time, County Creamery sold Tillamook Country Smoker products in its catalog and factory store. When the meat business's market share grew, however, County Creamery objected to Tillamook Country Smoker's use of the geographic name and sent a cease-and-desist notice. Tillamook Country Smoker asked for a declaratory judgment, which was granted, and it continues to use its brand name today.[43]

In 2012, former CEO Strunk said, "We're now well over a $500 million company, and there are different expectations when you're this size company."[44] One change is that Tillamook's corporate headquarters moved to Portland.[45] Another difference is the size of the marketing budget. In 2011, Tillamook Cheese introduced a multimillion-dollar marketing campaign. It was quite a change from the ad budget in 1919, when Tillamook promoted its cheese by spending $16,000 on "newspapers and de luxe billboards . . . along the Pacific Coast."[46] Advertising had begun the previous year and resulted in a "price 4 cents per pound higher than any other cheese sold in the Los Angeles market."[47]

Today's advertising, combined with tasty products, has been effective. *Dairy Foods* magazine reported that in 2021, Tillamook was 37 on the "Dairy 100," the magazine's list of North America's top processors of dairy foods and beverages.[48] A 2020 survey found that 4.68 million Americans used one pound or more of Tillamook's natural or imported cheese that year,[49] and Tillamook's medium cheddar is America's top-selling natural cheese among those aged at least 60 days.[50] Tillamook's ice cream continues to grow in popularity nationwide.[51]

Tillamook Cheese's marketing continues to highlight the farmers of Tillamook who still own the cooperative but do not provide even half of the raw material. The discrepancy between marketing and reality led to a 2019 lawsuit charging that Tillamook's ads spurred consumers to pay more for its products without letting the buyers know that some items weren't produced with milk from the cows and settings featured in the marketing.[52] The lawsuit has not progressed through the court system.

Today, Tillamook has reached $1 billion in sales[53] and has received a third-party designation as a Certified B Corporation by meeting standards in governance, workers, customers, community, and the environment.[54] In mid-2021, Tillamook County Creamery Association paid more than $4 million for a closed Wisconsin cheese factory.[55] Although no plans have been announced for the site, the 117-acre plot in Chilton, north of Milwaukee, has room to expand and easy access to midwestern transportation hubs.

Because of Tillamook's market growth, though, it has had to make some compromises. Taste is one of them. For most of its history, Tillamook's cheese was manufactured with milk from cows that ate lush grass near the ocean, ignoring the ninety-plus inches of rain that fell on them every year. With most of the milk for Tillamook's products now originating more than two hundred miles east of Tillamook in a region that receives an average of fewer than fourteen inches of rain a year, the resulting cheese has a very different terroir. Although terroir is most frequently associated with wine, it is important for dairy products, too. The "breed of the animals, what they eat, and their environment—a 'microbial ecosystem'—combine to produce a distinctive flavor."[56] Longtime fans of the cheese can detect the difference between products made with Tillamook's milk and those made with Boardman's milk—or perhaps, in the future, with Wisconsin's milk. Ironically, the industrialization of milk production has altered the unique flavor that made people love Tillamook Cheese in the first place.

To reemphasize the flavor of cheese made from coastal milk, Tillamook is leaning into a new market, as explained in 2012:

> "It's going to be expansion into new markets with high-end products, not two-pound baby loaves," Rocha said. "It's going to be chunks of three-year-old cheese that we do great. The kind that you would be used to going to the cheese counter or deli and paying $10-$12 a pound for."[57]

Currently, Tillamook offers "Maker's Reserve," a brand category that includes white, aged, extra sharp cheddar. These are artisanal cheeses and probably use milk from Tillamook's own cows. Tillamook also offers Farmers' Collection, which it describes as "special occasion cheese for every occasion."[58] Under the current marketing strategy, gourmet cheese will be a small part of the cooperative's overall production.

Small-scale cheese production has not disappeared from Tillamook County. Nestucca Bay Creamery in south Tillamook County is a farm-based operation that sells artisanal cheeses with Tillamook's terroir from its storefront in Cloverdale as well as online and at area farmers' markets. The creamery doesn't rival Tillamook Cheese, but it is reminiscent of the small factories that launched Tillamook's dairy industry.

In 2004, Tillamook Cheese's board of directors voted to require its members to stop using recombinant bovine growth hormone (rBGH); the decision was challenged by some of the farmers, with support from Monsanto, the manufacturer of rBGH. In 2005, the majority of the members voted to retain the ban.[59] Tillamook does not offer any organic products, even though a handful of Tillamook farmers produce organic milk that they sell outside the county,[60] but the absence of artificial growth hormones has given Tillamook's products credibility with a growing segment of consumers.[61]

A Tillamook farmer of the 1960s would have needed an extraordinary crystal ball to predict sales success with cheese spreads; several styles of yogurt; sliced, shredded, and snack cheeses; cream cheese; and sour cream. Yes, ice cream and butter were sold back then, but only locally. No one predicted that Tillamook would offer shredded mozzarella, but its role as a pizza topping has made that flavor the nation's most-eaten cheese.[62] Cheesemakers didn't make Colby-Jack cheese, much less blends of various flavors, but they are available in dairy cases everywhere now. Today, as consumer tastes latch onto new trends, flavors, sizes, convenience, and packaging, Tillamook Cheese is a multifaceted maker of dairy products.

Having its focus on grocery supply chains may have helped Tillamook survive the market upheavals that accompanied the coronavirus pandemic. Some commodity milk producers had to dump their product because the commercial demand—restaurants, group living, institutional facilities—shrank and the supply chain was disrupted.[63] As the pandemic continued, milk consumption grew as families remained at home, drinking milk by the glass and using dairy products in their cooking.[64] Meanwhile, Tillamook Cheese continued to turn its milk into products for grocery stores.

Tillamook Cheese has grown into a large business, made better because the Cheese War laid important groundwork for its organizational structure and the marketing on which Tillamook has built its modern reality.

Notes

PREFACE

1 Cheese & Dairy board meeting minutes, May 1966, author's private collection.
2 Cheese & Dairy board meeting minutes, June 15, 1966, author's private collection.
3 Nick Steiner, interview with author, May 7, 2015.

FIELD NOTE 1

1 Trust for Public Land, "137 Acres on Kilchis Point Protected."
2 H. S. "Beale" Dixon, oral history interview with Gerry Hysmith, March 13, 1987, OH 87.4, Tillamook County Pioneer Museum, Tillamook, Oregon.
3 Harry C. Elliot, Tillamook County Pioneer Museum, Tillamook, Oregon.

CHAPTER 1

1 Dupuis, *Nature's Perfect Food.*
2 Mendelson, *Milk.*
3 Valenze, *Milk.*
4 Manchester and Blayney, "Milk Pricing in the United States."
5 Sanderson, "Drop in Milk Prices Rekindles Old Battle Flames," 1.
6 Tib Johnston, telephone interview with Linda Kirk, June 22, 2017.

CHAPTER 2

1 Parr, *Pacific Northwest Cheese,* 43.
2 Heintzelman, "Evolution of an Industry."
3 Allen, "Tillamook Cheddar Cheese."
4 Heintzelman, "Evolution of an Industry," 77-81.
5 Collins, *Cheese Cheddar.*
6 Collins, *Cheese Cheddar.*
7 Satterfield, *The Tillamook Way,* 33.
8 Collins, *Cheese Cheddar.*
9 Satterfield, *The Tillamook Way,* 32.
10 Collins, *Cheese Cheddar.*
11 "1918 Creameries."
12 Collins, *Cheese Cheddar,* 183.
13 Skinner, *Circular 94,* 10.
14 Taylor, *Persistent Callings,* 155.

15 Bushman, "Cheesemaker's Daughters," 26-28.
16 Cornell University Extension Service, "Milk Facts."
17 Parr, *Pacific Northwest Cheese*, 56.
18 George Milne, interview with author, 1993.
19 Dave Leuthold, interview with author, May 1, 2015.
20 Leuthold, interview with author, May 1, 2015.
21 George Milne, interview with author, 1993.
22 Owens, "Evaluation of Some Structure, Conduct and Performance Characteristics," 82.
23 Owens, "Evaluation of Some Structure, Conduct and Performance Characteristics," 228.
24 Owens, "Evaluation of Some Structure, Conduct and Performance Characteristics," 243.
25 H. S. "Beale" Dixon, Grade A Shippers Association special meeting minutes, Robert H. Ely secretary, April 3, 1956, 25, author's private collection.
26 Joe Jenck, interview with author, June 6, 2015.
27 "Klamath Rancher Selected as 'Grassman of the Year,'" 3.
28 Dixon, Grade A Shippers Association annual meeting minutes, 1959.
29 Dixon, Grade A Shippers Association annual meeting minutes, 1959.
30 Barbara Milne, interview with author, 1993.

CHAPTER 3

1 Satterfield, *The Tillamook Way*, 88.
2 "Northwest's Largest Cheese Plant."
3 H. S. "Beale" Dixon, oral history interview with Gerry Hysmith, March 13, 1987, OH 87.4, Tillamook County Pioneer Museum, Tillamook, Oregon.
4 Documents gathered by author. "Ex-Bank Cashier Indicted," 20; "Surety Company Pays $6000"; "Scotts Mills Bank In Hands of State."
5 Satterfield, *The Tillamook Way*, 88.
6 Nick Steiner, interview with author, May 7, 2015.
7 Satterfield, *The Tillamook Way*, 89.
8 Satterfield, *The Tillamook Way*, 89.
9 Fib Johnston, interview with author, May 2, 2015.
10 George Milne, interview with author, May 15, 1993.
11 Dave Leuthold, interview with author, May 1, 2015.
12 Jim Becker, interview with author, June 8, 2015.
13 Barbara Milne, handwritten note, author's private collection.
14 Satterfield, *The Tillamook Way*, 89.
15 "Tillamook County Producers Split Over Question Of Fluid Milk Sales."
16 Anita Neilson scrapbook entry, author's private collection.
17 TCA annual meeting minutes, R. E. Deaver secretary *pro tem*, February 16, 1952, 27, author's private collection.
18 Dixon, oral history interview, March 13, 1987.
19 GASA board meeting minutes, May 9, 1955, 6, author's private collection.
20 GASA annual meeting minutes, February 21, 1957, 40, author's private collection.
21 Becker, interview with author, May 29, 2020.
22 Becker, interview with author, May 29, 2020.

23 Becker, interview with author, May 29, 2020.
24 Tillamook County Jersey Breeders and Tillamook Guernsey Cattle Club, ad in *Headlight Herald* (Tillamook, OR), May 20, 1962, 11.
25 Becker, interview with author, May 29, 2020.
26 Becker, interview with author, June 8, 2015.
27 Becker, interview with author, June 8, 2015.
28 Becker, interview with author, June 8, 2015.
29 Becker, interview with author, June 8, 2015.
30 Becker, interview with author, May 6, 2015.
31 Becker, interview with author, June 8, 2015.
32 Becker, interview with author, June 8, 2015.
33 Ferd J. Becker, letters to editor, *Headlight Herald* (Tillamook, OR), 1963.
34 Cheese & Dairy meeting minutes ledgers, author's private collection.
35 GASA annual meeting minutes, February 19, 1959, 79, author's private collection.
36 GASA annual meeting minutes, February 19, 1959, 79, author's private collection.
37 Johnston, interview with author, May 2, 2015.
38 Leuthold, interview with author, May 1, 2015.
39 Barbara Milne, interview with author, May 15, 1993.
40 Johnston, interview with author, April 25, 2015.
41 GASA annual meeting minutes, February 19, 1959, 80, author's private collection.
42 Barbara Milne, interview with author, May 15, 1993.
43 Sanderson, "Drop in Milk Prices Rekindles Old Battle Flames," 1.
44 Kinnaman v. Bailey, 241 Or. 634, 406 P.2d 145 (1965), https://law.justia.com/cases/oregon/supreme-court/1965/241-or-634-0.html.
45 GASA annual meeting minutes, February 20, 1958, author's private collection.
46 Manchester and Blayney, "Milk Pricing in the United States."
47 GASA board meeting minutes, November 18, 1957, author's private collection.
48 GASA board meeting minutes, November 10, 1958, author's private collection.
49 GASA board meeting minutes, November 10, 1958, author's private collection.
50 County Creamery and Member Associations, Secretary's Report in *Annual Report, 1959-1960*, author's private collection.
51 Bianco, "Hoffa Says Support Given Cheese Strikers," 10.
52 George Milne, interview with author, May 15, 1993, author's private collection.
53 Bianco, "Hoffa Says Support Given Cheese Strikers."
54 Bianco, "Hoffa Says Support Given Cheese Strikers."
55 GASA special membership meeting minutes, June 23, 1959, 88, author's private collection.
56 "Farmers Help Tillamook Plant," photo in *The Oregonian*, July 2, 1959.
57 Hiestand, "Problems of Small Business."
58 "Wage Boost Ends Tillamook Strike," 1.
59 George Milne, interview with author, May 15, 1993.
60 County Creamery and Member Associations, Secretary's Report in *Annual Report, 1959-1960*, author's private collection.
61 "Wage Boost Ends Tillamook Strike," 1.
62 County Creamery and Member Associations, Secretary's Report in *Annual Report, 1959-1960*, author's private collection.
63 "Bomb Blasts," 1.

64 H. S. "Beale" Dixon, secretary's report in *Tillamook County Creamery Association and Member Associations Annual Report, 1961-62*, author's private collection.
65 TCA board meeting and special patron meeting minutes, May 15, 1961, 116, author's private collection.
66 H. S. "Beale" Dixon, undated letter to Kenneth E. Carl of the Oregon Department of Agriculture, author's private collection.
67 TCA annual meeting minutes, February 18, 1961, author's private collection.
68 George Milne, interview with author, December 26, 1989.
69 GASA board meeting minutes, October 2, 1961, author's private collection.
70 GASA board meeting minutes, October 2, 1961, author's private collection.
71 George Milne, interview with author, December 26, 1989.
72 George Milne, interview with author, December 26, 1989.
73 "Trouble in Tillamook," *Northwest Dairy News*, June 28, 1963, 4.
74 Cheese & Dairy organizational board meeting minutes, January 4, 1962, 2, author's private collection.
75 Barbara Milne, interview with author, May 15, 1993.
76 Judge Bruce Thompson, posttrial comments, April 4, 1968, Oregon State Archives, Salem; Tillamook Cheese & Dairy Association v. Tillamook County Creamery Association et al., 358 F.2d 115 (9th Cir. 1966).

FIELD NOTE 3

A portion of this essay was first printed in *Oregon Humanities* and is reused with permission.

1 DiTomaso and Healy, *Weeds of California and Other Western States*, 383.

CHAPTER 4

1 "Disagreement at Hearing on Milk," 5.
2 George Milne, interview with author, May 15, 1993.
3 Milne, interview with author, May 15, 1993.
4 GASA board meeting minutes, March 21, 1961, author's private collection.
5 GASA board meeting minutes, April 17, 1961, author's private collection.
6 Steusloff, "Dairymen See Price for Class I Milk," 1.
7 GASA board meeting minutes, April 17, 1961, author's private collection.
8 Sanderson, "Legislation to Prevent Milk-Price War," 13.
9 Oregon State Archives, Salem, *Oregon Laws 1961*, chap. 529, 966-74.
10 Testimony, Oregon State Legislature hearing, April 10, 1961, Oregon State Archives, Salem.
11 Testimony, Oregon State Legislature hearing, April 10, 1961, Oregon State Archives, Salem.
12 The preceding two paragraphs draw on information from Oregon State Archives, Salem, *Oregon Laws 1961*, chap. 529, 966-74, sections 16, 17, 21, 22, 24.
13 Steusloff, "Dairymen See Price for Class I Milk," 1.
14 "Legislation to Prevent Milk-Price War," 13.
15 "Market Pool Turned Down in Milk Vote," 1.
16 US Tariff Commission, *Cheddar Cheese*.
17 Ad, *Headlight Herald* (Tillamook, Oregon), May 5, 1963, 12.
18 GASA board meeting minutes, June 6, 1960, author's private collection.

19 GASA board meeting minutes, March 6, 1961, author's private collection.
20 "Dairy Suit Trial Surprise."
21 Steusloff, "Dairymen Seek Law Changes Aiding Producer," 1.
22 Oregon State Archives, Salem, *Oregon Laws 1961*, chap. 529.
23 Curley's Dairy, Inc. v. Dairy Cooperative Association, 202 F. Supp. 481 (D. Or. 1962), https://law.justia.com/cases/federal/district-courts/FSupp/202/481/1733968/.
24 Morgan, "Milk Producers, Processors Vie," 1.
25 GASA board meeting minutes, December 10, 1956; February 9, 1959; February 8, 1960; April 11, 1960; April 25, 1960, author's private collection.
26 GASA board meeting minutes, February 9, 1959, 77, author's private collection.
27 GASA board meeting minutes, March 9, 1959, 85, author's private collection.
28 GASA board meeting minutes, March 9, 1959, 85, author's private collection.
29 "Trouble in Tillamook," 4.
30 "Trouble in Tillamook," 4.
31 "Trouble in Tillamook," 4.
32 "Trouble in Tillamook," 4.
33 "Trouble in Tillamook," 4.
34 GASA board meeting minutes, October 9, 1961, author's private collection.
35 GASA board meeting minutes, November 6, 1961, author's private collection.
36 TCDA board meeting minutes, January 4, 1962, author's private collection.
37 TCDA board meeting minutes, February 6, 1962, author's private collection.
38 Cheese & Dairy board meeting minutes, March 12, 1962, 8, author's private collection.
39 H. S. "Beale" Dixon, oral history interview with Gerry Hysmith, March 13, 1987, OH 87.4, Tillamook County Pioneer Museum, Tillamook, Oregon.
40 Fib Johnston, interview with author, April 25, 2015.
41 Glenn Johnston, letter to the editor, *Headlight Herald* (Tillamook, OR), February 10, 1963, 4.
42 Cheese & Dairy board meeting minutes, May 27, 1964, author's private collection.
43 Jim Becker, interview with author, June 8, 2015.
44 Nick Steiner, interview with author, May 27, 2020.
45 Steiner, interview with author, May 27, 2020.
46 Johnston, interview with author, May 2, 2015.
47 Steiner, interview with author, May 7, 2015.
48 Steiner, interview with author, May 27, 2020.

CHAPTER 5

1 Jim Becker, interview with author, June 18, 2015.
2 Nick Steiner, interview with author, May 7, 2015.
3 Barbara Milne, interview with author, May 15, 1993.
4 Fib Johnston, interview with author, May 2, 2015.
5 Rita Johnston, interview with author, May 2, 2015.
6 Rita Johnston, interview with author, May 2, 2015.
7 Joe Jenck, interview with author, June 6, 2015.
8 Fib Johnston, interview with author, April 25, 2015.
9 Rita Johnston, interview with author, April 25, 2015.

10 Jenck, interview with author, June 6, 2015.

11 Jenck, interview with author, June 6, 2015.

12 Fib Johnston, interview with author, April 25, 2018.

13 Fib Johnston, interview with author, April 25, 2018.

14 Cheese & Dairy board meeting minutes, May 15, 1962, 11, author's private collection.

15 Cheese & Dairy, approved handwritten addition to special board meeting minutes, June 5, 1962, 14.

16 Cheese & Dairy board meeting minutes, May 15, 1962, 11, author's private collection.

17 Cheese & Dairy special board meeting minutes, June 5, 1962, 13, author's private collection.

18 Cheese & Dairy special board meeting minutes, June 5, 1962, 13, author's private collection.

19 Cheese & Dairy board meeting minutes, June 5, 1962, 13, author's private collection.

20 Cheese & Dairy board meeting minutes, June 19, 1962, 15, author's private collection.

21 Cheese & Dairy board meeting minutes, June 5, 1962, 14, author's private collection.

22 Cheese & Dairy special board meeting minutes, June 5, 1962, 14, author's private collection.

23 Cheese & Dairy special board meeting minutes, June 5, 1962, 14, author's private collection.

24 Cheese & Dairy special board meeting minutes, June 5, 1962, 14, author's private collection.

25 H. S. "Beale" Dixon, oral history interview with Gerry Hysmith, March 13, 1987, OH 87.4, Tillamook County Pioneer Museum, Tillamook, Oregon.

26 Fib Johnston, telephone interview with Linda Kirk, June 22, 2017.

27 Satterfield, *The Tillamook Way*, 89.

28 Cheese & Dairy meeting minutes, June 19, 1962, 15.

29 County Creamery bylaws, Article V, Section 1 (amended 1955), author's private collection.

30 Satterfield, *The Tillamook Way*, 92.

31 George Milne, interview with author, May 15, 1993.

32 Satterfield, *The Tillamook Way*, 92.

33 Cheese & Dairy special board meeting minutes, July 26, 1962, 21, author's private collection.

34 Cheese & Dairy special board meeting minutes on July 26, 1962, 21, 22, author's private collection.

35 Cheese & Dairy board letter to members on August 2, 1962, author's private collection.

36 Cheese & Dairy board meeting minutes, August 13, 1962, 23, author's private collection.

37 "Local Rite to Be Held July 1 for McMinimee."

38 "Plaque to Honor McMinimee," A-5.

39 Becker, interview with author, June 8, 2015.

40 Fib Johnston, interview with author, May 2, 2015.

41 Steiner, interview with author, May 7, 2015.

42 Dave Leuthold, interview with author, May 1, 2015.

43 "Folks You Should Know."

44 Jenck, telephone interview with Linda Kirk, March 23, 2015.

45 Dodge, *Deadly Wind*, 61–62.

46 Jenck, telephone interview with Linda Kirk, May 1, 2015.

47 Walt Beeler, interview with author, May 6, 2015.

48 Cheese & Dairy, *Board Information*, October 11, 1962, author's private collection.

49 "Declaratory Judgment."

50 "Controversy of Dairy Groups Hits Courts Here," 1.

51 "Controversy of Dairy Groups Hits Courts Here," 1.

52 Cheese & Dairy special membership meeting minutes, September 5, 1962, 32, author's private collection.

53 Cheese & Dairy, *Board Information*, September 18, 1962, author's private collection.

54 Cheese & Dairy board meeting minutes, September 5, 1962, 27, author's private collection.

55 County Creamery, *Tillamook Cheese News*, October 1962, author's private collection.

56 Cheese & Dairy marketing contract, author's private collection.

FIELD NOTE 4

1 Gipson, *Old Yeller*, 110, 121.

CHAPTER 6

1 George Milne, interview with author, May 15, 1993.

2 Barbara Milne, interview with author, May 15, 1993.

3 Cheese & Dairy membership meeting minutes, August 27, 1962, author's private collection.

4 Cheese & Dairy membership meeting minutes, August 27, 1962, author's private collection.

5 Cheese & Dairy membership meeting minutes, August 27, 1962, author's private collection.

6 Millard Bailey, Otto Schild, and Karl Zweifel, letter to TCDA patrons, August 31, 1962, author's private collection.

7 Letter, September 16, 1962, author's private collection.

8 Cheese & Dairy special board meeting minutes, September 5, 1962, author's private collection.

9 Cheese & Dairy special board meeting minutes, September 5, 1962, author's private collection.

10 Unknown, note at top of recall letter, author's private collection.

11 Barbara Milne, interview with author, May 15, 1993.

12 George Milne, interview with author, May 15, 1993.

13 George Milne, interview with author, May 15, 1993.

14 Cheese & Dairy special evening membership meeting minutes, September 5, 1962, author's private collection.

15 Cheese & Dairy special evening membership meeting minutes, September 5, 1962, author's private collection.

16 TCDA board meeting minutes, September 5, 1962, author's private collection.

17 Cheese & Dairy board meeting minutes, January 11, 1963, author's private collection.

18 Oregon State Archives, Salem, *Oregon Laws 1963*, chap. 442, Section 21 (1), 698.

19 Oregon State Archives, Salem, *Oregon Laws 1963*, chap. 442, Section 21 (3), 698.

20 Oregon State Archives, Salem, *Oregon Laws 1963*, chap. 442, Section 21 (5), (b), 699.

21 Cheese & Dairy, *Board Information*, August 1, 1962, author's private collection.

22 George Milne, interview with author, May 15, 1993.

23 Claude Steusloff, "Milk Stabilization Bill," 1.

24 George Milne, interview with author, May 15, 1993.

25 George Milne, interview with author, May 15, 1993.

26 George Milne, interview with author, May 15, 1993.

27 George Milne, interview with author, May 15, 1993.

28 *Tillamook Cheese News* (October 1962), 2, author's private collection.

29 Holley, "Tillamook County Producers Split."

30 *Northwest Dairy News* (Bellingham, WA), September 14, 1962.

31 "Threat of Milk Price War."

32 George Milne, letter to the editor, *Headlight Herald* (Tillamook, OR), February 3, 1963.

33 H. S. "Beale" Dixon, oral history interview with Gerry Hysmith, March 13, 1987, OH 87.4, Tillamook County Pioneer Museum, Tillamook, Oregon.

34 County Creamery newsletter, February 1963 issue, author's private collection.

35 Board of Directors, Tillamook County Creamery Association, letter to the editor, *Headlight Herald* (Tillamook, OR), January 27, 1963.

36 George Milne, letter to the editor, *Headlight Herald* (Tillamook, OR), February 3, 1963.

37 Milne, letter to the editor.

38 George Milne, interview with author, May 15, 1993.

39 Linda Kirk, interview with author, November 16, 2015.

40 "Agriculture Laws for 1963-65 Reviewed."

CHAPTER 7

1 Cheese & Dairy board meeting minutes, January 11, 1963, 49, author's private collection.

2 Cheese & Dairy, *Board Information*, April 3, 1963, author's private collection.

3 "New Secretary Manager on Job," *Shopping Smiles*, April 4, 1962, author's private collection.

4 "Ely Resigns as TCDA Official."

5 County Creamery newsletter, March 29, 1963, author's private collection.

6 Letter from County Creamery to patrons, January 16, 1963, author's private collection.

7 Cheese & Dairy, *Board Information*, February 14, 1963, author's private collection.

8 Cheese & Dairy, *Board Information*, February 14, 1963, author's private collection.

9 Cheese & Dairy, *Board Information*, February 14, 1963, author's private collection.

10 Barbara Milne, interview with author, May 15, 1993.
11 Barbara Milne, interview with author, May 15, 1993.
12 George Milne, interview with author, May 15, 1993.
13 Barbara Milne, interview with author, May 15, 1993.
14 George Milne, interview with author, May 15, 1993.
15 Cheese & Dairy, *Board Information*, February 14, 1963, author's private collection.
16 Minutes, special joint meeting of the Cheese & Dairy and Red Clover boards, August 19, 1963, 3, author's private collection.
17 George Milne, interview with author, May 15, 1993.
18 Barbara Milne, interview with author, May 15, 1993.
19 George Milne, interview with author, May 15, 1993.
20 George Milne, interview with author, May 15, 1993.
21 Fib Johnston, interview with author, May 2, 2015.
22 Nick Steiner, interview with author, May 7, 2015.
23 Minutes, special joint meeting of the Cheese & Dairy and Red Clover boards, August 19, 1963, 2, author's private collection.
24 H. S. "Beale" Dixon, oral history interview with Gerry Hysmith, March 13, 1987, OH 87.4, Tillamook County Pioneer Museum, Tillamook, Oregon.
25 TCA board meeting minutes, January 20, 1958, 80, author's private collection.
26 County Creamery and Member Associations, *Annual Report*, H. S. Dixon, secretary, Calendar Year 1962, author's private collection.
27 Minutes, special joint meeting of the Cheese & Dairy and Red Clover boards, August 19, 1963, 2, author's private collection.
28 Pat and Mike Tone, interview with author, June 3, 2016.
29 Barbara Milne, interview with author, May 15, 1993.
30 Minutes, special joint meeting of the Cheese & Dairy and Red Clover boards, August 19, 1963, 2, author's private collection.
31 TCA board meeting minutes, January 16, 1951, 1, author's private collection.
32 Tippens, "TCCA Manager Discloses Move."
33 "Trouble in Tillamook," *Northwest Dairy News* (Bellingham, WA), June 28, 1963.
34 Ferd Becker, letter to editor, *Headlight Herald* (Tillamook, OR), February 10, 1963, 4.
35 Cheese & Dairy, *Board Information*, January 21, 1963, author's private collection.
36 Barbara Milne, interview with author, May 15, 1993.
37 "New Motion Filed for Re-Hearing in Dairy Action."
38 Cheese & Dairy, *Board Information*, August 13, 1963, author's private collection.
39 Satterfield, *The Tillamook Way*, 89.
40 County Creamery annual meeting minutes, February 16, 1963, author's private collection.
41 Cheese & Dairy, ad in *Shopping Smiles*, September 26, 1963, author's private collection.

FIELD NOTE 5

1 "Tillamook County."

CHAPTER 8

Epigraph from Joe Bianco, "Family Feud," 36.

1 Joe Beeler, letter to the editor, *Headlight Herald* (Tillamook, OR), January 27, 1963.

2 Dale M. Sayles, letter to the editor, *Headlight Herald* (Tillamook, OR), February 10, 1963, 4.

3 Bert Quick, letter to the editor, *Headlight Herald* (Tillamook, OR), February 3, 1963.

4 *Board Information*, January 3, 1963, author's private collection.

5 George Milne, interview with author, May 15, 1993.

6 Hiestand, "Problems of Small Business," 1758-59; US Department of Labor, *Legislative History*, 2:1758-59.

7 George Milne, interview with author, May 15, 1993.

8 Barbara Milne, interview with author, May 15, 1993.

9 Cheese & Dairy annual meeting minutes, February 16, 1963, 57, author's private collection.

10 Cheese & Dairy annual meeting minutes, February 16, 1963, 57, author's private collection.

11 Cheese & Dairy annual meeting minutes, February 16, 1963, 59, author's private collection.

12 George Milne, interview with author, May 15, 1993.

13 George Milne, interview with author, May 15, 1993.

14 Cheese & Dairy special board meeting minutes, April 25, 1963, 2–4, author's private collection.

15 "Tankers Roll," 1.

16 Cheese & Dairy, *Board Information*, May 3, 1963, author's private collection.

17 "Reward Is Offered in Threat Case," 1.

18 Jim Becker, interview with author, May 8, 2015.

19 George Milne, interview with author, May 15, 1993.

20 "Trouble in Tillamook," 4.

21 Bianco, "Family Feud Splits Member from Tillamook Creamery Group," 36.

22 Bianco, "Family Feud Splits Member from Tillamook Creamery Group," 36.

23 County Creamery and Member Associations, Annual Report, 1962; Secretary's Report, H. S. "Beale" Dixon, author's private collection.

24 Cheese & Dairy special board meeting minutes, April 25, 1963, 3, author's private collection.

25 Cheese & Dairy, *Board Information*, May 6, 1963, author's private collection.

26 "Milk Tankers Idled," photo caption, *Headlight Herald* (Tillamook, OR), May 12, 1963, 1.

27 "Tillamook Creameries Import Eastern Cheese."

28 George Milne, interview with author, May 15, 1993.

29 Cheese & Dairy board meeting minutes, May 1 and 6, 1963, author's private collection.

30 "Tankers Roll."

31 Letter to Cheese & Dairy patrons, May 15, 1963, author's private collection.

32 Letter to Cheese & Dairy patrons, May 15, 1963, author's private collection.

33 George Milne, interview with author, May 15, 1993.

34 "Dairy Suit Trial Surprise."

35 Tippens, "TCCA Manager Discloses Move."
36 Barbara Milne, interview with author, May 15, 1993.
37 Unidentified courtroom witness, author's private collection.
38 Unidentified courtroom witness, author's private collection.
39 "Dairy Suit Trial Surprise," 1.
40 Barbara Milne, interview with author, May 15, 1993.
41 Liz Hurliman, interview with author, May 2, 2015.
42 Barbara Milne, interview with author, May 15, 1993.
43 "Dairy Suit Trial Surprise," 1.
44 "Tillamook Dairy Case Rule Made."
45 "Tillamook Dairy Case Rule Made."
46 Cheese & Dairy, *Board Information*, July 29, 1963, author's private collection.
47 Cheese & Dairy, *Board Information*, August 13, 1963, author's private collection.
48 Joe Jenck, telephone interview with author, July 16, 2017.
49 Dave Leuthold, interview with author, May 1, 2015.
50 County Creamery Board Minutes as recalled by TCDA, August 14, 1963, 1, author's private collection.
51 County Creamery Board Minutes as recalled by TCDA, August 14, 1963, 2, author's private collection.
52 County Creamery Board Minutes as recalled by TCDA, August 14, 1963, 2, author's private collection.
53 County Creamery Board Minutes as recalled by TCDA, August 14, 1963, 3, author's private collection.
54 Cheese & Dairy and Red Clover joint meeting minutes, August 19, 1963, 6, author's private collection.
55 "Tillamook Creameries Import Eastern Cheese."
56 "Cheese Trademark Fuss Continues," 4.
57 "Judge Changes Opinion on Dairy Lawsuit Points," 1.
58 Cheese & Dairy board meeting minutes, August 19, 1963, 1, author's private collection.
59 Cheese & Dairy board meeting minutes, August 19, 1963, 5, author's private collection.
60 Cheese & Dairy board meeting minutes, August 19, 1963, 6, author's private collection.
61 Cheese & Dairy board meeting minutes, August 19, 1963, 3, author's private collection.
62 Cheese & Dairy board meeting minutes, August 19, 1963, 6, author's private collection.
63 Cheese & Dairy, *Board Information*, September 26, 1963, author's private collection.

CHAPTER 9

1 Ad, *Shopping Smiles* flyer, *Headlight Herald* (Tillamook, OR), September 26, 1963, 15.
2 Cheese & Dairy, *Board Information*, including September 11, 1963, letter to County Creamery, September 12, 1963, author's private collection.
3 Cheese & Dairy, *Board Information*, September 12, 1963, author's private collection.

 4   Satterfield, *The Tillamook Way*, 90–91.
 5   *The Tillamook Way*, 92.
 6   Jim Becker, interview with author, June 8, 2015.
 7   George Milne, interview with author, May 15, 1993.
 8   George Milne, interview with author, May 15, 1993.
 9   TCDA board meeting minutes, April 8, 1963, 3, author's private collection.
10   TCDA board meeting minutes, April 8, 1963, 3, author's private collection.
11   Otto Schild v. Tillamook Cheese & Dairy Association, Findings of Fact and
     Conclusions of Law, Tillamook County Circuit Court, February 5, 1965, 2.
12   Otto Schild v. Tillamook Cheese & Dairy Association, 2.
13   Otto Schild v. Tillamook Cheese & Dairy Association, 3.
14   Cheese & Dairy, *Board Information*, September 12, 1963, author's private
     collection.
15   "TCDA Board Says," 1.
16   Cheese & Dairy, letter to County Creamery, September 5, 1963, *Board
     Information*, September 6, 1963, author's private collection.
17   Cheese & Dairy, report to members regarding Dixon letter admitting
     bookkeeping error, *Board Information*, September 12, 1963, author's private
     collection.
18   Cheese & Dairy, *Board Information*, September 30, 1963, author's private
     collection.
19   Cheese & Dairy, *Board Information*, September 26, 1963, author's private
     collection.
20   Cheese & Dairy, *Board Information*, October 16, 1963, author's private collection.
21   County Creamery letter, September 30, 1963, author's private collection.
22   County Creamery letter, September 30, 1963, author's private collection.
23   Otto Schild v. Tillamook Cheese & Dairy Association.
24   Cheese & Dairy, *Board Information*, February 11, 1964, author's private
     collection.
25   Otto Schild v. Tillamook Cheese & Dairy Association.
26   Gaylord Shiveley v. Tillamook Cheese & Dairy Association, Complaint
     (Tillamook County Circuit Court, February 19, 1965).
27   "Tillamook Cheese & Dairy Ass'n v. State Dept. of Agriculture U.S. Supreme
     Court."
28   "Tillamook Cheese & Dairy Ass'n v. State Dept. of Agriculture U.S. Supreme
     Court."
29   Otto Schild v. Tillamook Cheese & Dairy Association.
30   Cheese & Dairy board meeting minutes, December 2, 1966, author's private
     collection.
31   Cheese & Dairy board meeting minutes, December 7, 1966, author's private
     collection.
32   State Department of Agriculture v. Tillamook Cheese and Dairy Association,
     appeal, April 10, 1968.
33   Perry, "Dissent by Chief Justice," 37.
34   Perry, "Dissent by Chief Justice," 39.
35   State Department of Agriculture v. Tillamook Cheese and Dairy Association,
     argued October 4, 1967, filed April 10, 1968, 4442 P.2d 608, Oregon State
     Archives, Salem.

36 Barbara Milne, interview with author, May 15, 1993.
37 Barbara Milne, interview with author, May 15, 1993.
38 Tom Tone, interview with author, June 3, 2016.
39 George Milne, interview with author, May 15, 1993.
40 Barbara Milne, interview with author, May 15, 1993.
41 George Milne, interview with author, May 15, 1993.
42 Barbara Milne, interview with author, May 15, 1993.
43 Nick Steiner, interview with author, May 7, 2015.
44 Steiner, interview with author, May 7, 2015.
45 Steiner, interview with author, May 7, 2015.
46 Steiner, interview with author, May 7, 2015.
47 Steiner, interview with author, May 7, 2015.
48 Fib Johnston, interview with author, April 25, 2015.
49 Barbara Milne, interview with author, May 15, 1993.
50 George Milne, interview with author, May 15, 1993.
51 Edgar, *Cheddar*.
52 Art Van Loo, the Durrer brothers, Bob Hurliman, Max Hurliman, Yelta Vanderzee, John Nielsen, and J. B. Williams, letter to the editor, *Headlight Herald* (Tillamook, OR), October 6, 1963.
53 Cheese & Dairy, *Board Information*, February 11, 1964, author's private collection.
54 George Milne, interview with author, May 15, 1993.
55 Pat, Mike, and Tom Tone, interview with author, June 3, 2016.
56 Photo caption, *The Oregonian* (Portland, OR), May 24, 1964.
57 "Tillamook Cheese Label Spurs $100,000 Lawsuit," 9.
58 Cheese & Dairy, *Board Information*, July 1, 1964, author's private collection.
59 H. S. "Beale" Dixon, oral history interview with Gerry Hysmith, March 13, 1987, OH 87.4, Tillamook County Pioneer Museum, Tillamook, Oregon.
60 Photo caption, *Headlight Herald* (Tillamook, OR), March 1, 1964; ad, *Headlight Herald*, August 7, 1966.
61 Barbara Milne, interview with author, May 15, 1993.
62 Cheese & Dairy board meeting minutes, January 22, 1964, author's private collection.
63 Cheese & Dairy board meeting minutes, February 12, 1964, author's private collection.
64 "Use of TC&DA Label Allowed in Dairy Suit."
65 "Cheese 'War' Heads for Court Showdown."
66 Cheese & Dairy board meeting minutes, February 12, 1964, author's private collection.
67 "Tillamook Unit Rejects Offer of 'Arbitration.'"
68 Ad, *Shopping Smiles* flyer.
69 Ad, *Shopping Smiles* flyer.
70 *Oregon Journal* (Portland, OR), May 13, 1964.
71 County Creamery Board, letter to the editor, *Headlight Herald* (Tillamook, OR), May 17, 1964, author's private collection.
72 "Arbitration Unacceptable in County Dairy Dispute," 1.
73 "Arbitration Unacceptable in County Dairy Dispute," 1.
74 "Arbitration Unacceptable in County Dairy Dispute," 1.

75 "Court Hears Cheese Case."
76 "Cheese Fuss Continues," 4.
77 Del Mayer, letter to the editor, *Headlight Herald* (Tillamook, OR), May 24, 1964.
78 "Tillamook Cheese Man Accused of Being 'Liar.'"
79 "Tillamook Cheese Man Accused of Being 'Liar.'"
80 "Use of TC&DA Label Allowed in Dairy Suit."
81 "TC&DA Wins Ruling in Trademark Case," 2.
82 "Cheese and Dairy Assn. Win," 8.
83 "Cheese and Dairy Assn. Win," 8.
84 "Cheese Unit Offers Aid."
85 "Creamery Rejects Peace Proposal," J3.
86 "Dairy Group Asks Ruling."
87 Tillamook County Creamery Association v. Tillamook Cheese and Dairy Association, 345 F.2d 158 (9th Cir., May 20, 1965).
88 "Lower Courts Upheld in Cheese Suit."
89 "Court Ruling Clarifies Point in Cheese Battle."

FIELD NOTE 6

1 "Local Rite to Be Held July 1 for McMinimee, Dead at 78."
2 "McMinimee Is Named to Park Commission."

CHAPTER 10

1 George Milne, interview with author, May 15, 1993.
2 Barbara Milne, interview with author, May 15, 1993.
3 Cheese & Dairy, *Board Information*, December 7, 1964, author's private collection.
4 Cheese & Dairy, *Board Information*, December 7, 1964, author's private collection.
5 Cheese & Dairy, *Board Information*, December 7, 1964, author's private collection.
6 "Cheesemaker Earnings Statement Challenged."
7 Cheese & Dairy, *Board Information*, December 31, 1964, author's private collection.
8 Cheese & Dairy board meeting minutes, January 12, 1965, author's private collection.
9 Cheese & Dairy board meeting minutes, January 12, 1965, author's private collection.
10 Cheese & Dairy board meeting minutes, January 12, 1965, author's private collection.
11 Cheese & Dairy board meeting minutes, February 17, 1965, author's private collection.
12 Cheese & Dairy board meeting minutes, March 10, 1965, author's private collection.
13 Cheese & Dairy board meeting minutes, March 3, 1965, author's private collection.
14 Cheese & Dairy special meeting minutes, February 27, 1965, author's private collection.

15 Cheese & Dairy special meeting minutes, February 27, 1965, author's private collection.

16 Owens, "An Evaluation of Some Structure, Conduct and Performance Characteristics," 165.

17 Cheese & Dairy board meeting minutes, March 3, 1965, author's private collection.

18 Cheese & Dairy and Red Clover joint meeting minutes, February 27, 1965, author's private collection.

19 Cheese & Dairy and Red Clover joint meeting minutes, February 27, 1965, author's private collection.

20 James O. Goodwin, letter to Cheese & Dairy, March 1, 1965, author's private collection.

21 Cheese & Dairy special board meeting minutes, March 3, 1965, author's private collection.

22 Cheese & Dairy special board meeting minutes, March 3, 1965, author's private collection.

23 Cheese & Dairy membership meeting, March 13, 1965, author's private collection.

24 Mida Wyss, diary entry, Saturday, March 13, 1965, collection of Janet Lucas Walker.

25 Cheese & Dairy membership meeting, March 13, 1965, author's private collection.

26 "Tillamook Plant Shuts."

27 Joe Larson, letter to patrons, March 31, 1965, author's private collection.

28 "Swett Appointed Manager of TCDA."

29 Mida Wyss, diary entry, Wednesday, March 31, 1965, collection of Janet Lucas Walker.

30 Cheese & Dairy board meeting minutes, March 24, 1965, author's private collection.

31 Cheese & Dairy board meeting minutes, March 24, 1965, author's private collection.

32 Cheese & Dairy board meeting minutes, March 30, 1965, author's private collection.

33 Cheese & Dairy board meeting minutes, April 20, 1965, author's private collection.

34 Floyd Woodward, resignation note, May 5, 1965, author's private collection.

35 Cheese & Dairy board meeting minutes, May 19, 1965, author's private collection.

36 Cheese & Dairy board meeting minutes, May 21, 1965, author's private collection.

37 Buckhorn, Blore, Klarquist, and Sparkman, letter to brokers, July 20, 1965, author's private collection.

38 Cheese & Dairy board meeting minutes, June 29, 1965, author's private collection.

39 "Foremost Dairy Inks Contract to Age, Market TCDA Cheese," 1.

40 Cheese & Dairy board meeting minutes, September 23, 1965, author's private collection.

41 Cheese & Dairy board meeting minutes, November 17, 1965, author's private collection.

42 "TC&DA to Do Own Cheese Marketing," 1.

43 "TC & DA to Triple Its Cheese Plant Output," 1.

44 "Tillamook Cheese Group Amends Antitrust Suit," 4M.

45 "Tillamook Cheese Group Amends Antitrust Suit," 4M.
46 "'Tillamook' Name Challenged."
47 "TCCA Claims $20 Million Damages in Dairy Dispute."
48 "TCCA Claims $20 Million Damages in Dairy Dispute."
49 Cheese & Dairy board meeting minutes, January 12, 1965, author's private collection.
50 "Lawyer Remains as Defendant in Cheese Trial."
51 Tillamook Cheese Dairy Association v. Tillamook County Creamery Association, 358 F.2d 115 (9th Cir., March 17, 1966).
52 Tillamook Cheese Dairy Association v. Tillamook County Creamery Association.
53 Tillamook Cheese Dairy Association v. Tillamook County Creamery Association.
54 "More Defendants Named in New TC&DA Complaint," 1.
55 Cheese & Dairy letter to patrons, March 1968, author's private collection.
56 Magmer, "Dairymen Told, 'Go Home, Settle Feud,'" 1.
57 Bruce Thompson, post-trial statement, Tillamook Cheese & Dairy Association v. Tillamook County Creamery Association, Civil No. 64-222, April 4, 1968, author's private collection.
58 Thompson, post-trial statement, 1, 5, 6.
59 Magmer, "Dairymen Told, 'Go Home, Settle Feud,'" 1.
60 Magmer, "Dairymen Told, 'Go Home, Settle Feud,'" 1.
61 Thompson, post-trial statement, 5.
62 Thompson, post-trial statement, 7.
63 "Tillamook Cheese Group Demands Accounting, Judgment from Rival Creamery Unit," 8.
64 Cheese & Dairy board meeting minutes, January 19, 1966, November 7, 1966; letters to patrons Fall 1966, author's personal collection.
65 Donald E. McMullen, letter to Cheese & Dairy patrons, *Board Information*, March 23, 1967, author's private collection.
66 Douglas E. Kaufman (McMinimee law partner), affidavit, September 8, 1967, Oregon State Archives, Portland.
67 George Milne, interview with author, May 15, 1993.
68 H. S. "Beale" Dixon, oral history interview with Gerry Hysmith, March 13, 1987, OH 87.4, Tillamook County Pioneer Museum, Tillamook, Oregon.
69 Barbara Milne, interview with author, May 15, 1993.
70 H. S. "Beale" Dixon, oral history interview with Gerry Hysmith, March 13, 1987.
71 L. M. Thorpe, letter to Cheese & Dairy members and patrons, February 14, 1968, author's private collection.
72 Barbara Milne, interview with author, May 15, 1993.
73 Barbara Milne, interview with author, May 15, 1993.
74 George Milne, interview with author, May 15, 1993.

FIELD NOTE 7

1 Cheese & Dairy ad in *Headlight Herald* (Tillamook, OR), December 1, 1963.
2 Tillamook Cheese Association board meeting minutes, January 15, 1957, 73, author's private collection.
3 Satterfield, *The Tillamook Way*, 11.
4 Oberst, "Tillamook Creamery Opens New Visitor Center."
5 Powers, "An Udderly Delicious Experience Awaits in Tillamook."

6 Tillamook Cheese Factory, "Instructions for Guides," 1953, author's private collection.
7 Walth, "Mark of Distinction," C-1.

CHAPTER 11

1 "Creameries Reach Agreement," 1.
2 L. M. Thorpe (general manager), letter to Cheese & Dairy patrons, February 6, 1968, author's private collection.
3 L. M. Thorpe (general manager), letter to Cheese & Dairy patrons, February 6, 1968, author's private collection.
4 Satterfield, *The Tillamook Way*, 94.
5 Cheese & Dairy, letter to patrons, June 14, 1968, author's private collection.
6 Cheese & Dairy, *Board Information*, March 30, 1968, author's private collection.
7 "Creamery Sale Completed Tues.," 4.
8 Tillamook Cheese & Dairy Association, List of Creditors, author unknown, 1968, 1, author's private collection.
9 Advertisement, Walter F. Heller & Company, 105 West Adams Street, Chicago, 1969.
10 Purchase and Sale Agreement, Cheese & Dairy and County Creamery, September 23, 1968, 2.
11 Tillamook Cheese & Dairy Association, List of Creditors, 3, 4.
12 Tillamook Cheese & Dairy Association, List of Creditors, 2.
13 "Creamery Sale Completed Tues.," 1.
14 Editorial, "Double Good News."
15 Advertisement, Tillamook County Creamery Association, Tillamook, OR, 1968, 24.
16 H. S. "Beale" Dixon, oral history interview with Gerry Hysmith, March 13, 1987, OH 87.4, Tillamook County Pioneer Museum, Tillamook, Oregon.
17 Barbara Milne, interview with author, May 15, 1993.
18 Purchase and Sale Agreement, Cheese & Dairy and County Creamery, Item #15, September 23, 1968, 3.
19 Barbara Milne, interview with author, May 15, 1993.
20 Joe Jenck, interview with author, June 6, 2015.
21 "Upgrading of Milk Standards Is Proposed."
22 Satterfield, *The Tillamook Way*, 89.
23 Dixon, oral history interview.
24 Helen Blaser, interview with author, June 13, 2016.
25 Barbara Milne, interview with author, May 15, 1993.
26 Dixon, oral history interview.
27 George Milne, interview with author, May 15, 1993.
28 Barbara Milne, interview with author, May 15, 1993.
29 Dixon, oral history interview.
30 Satterfield, *The Tillamook Way*, 93.
31 Barbara Milne, interview with author, May 15, 1993.
32 Dave Leuthold, interview with author, May 1, 2015.
33 Fib Johnston, interview with author, May 2, 2015.
34 Nick Steiner, interview with author, May 7, 2015.

35 Jenck, interview with author, June 6, 2015.
36 Barbara Milne, interview with author, May 15, 1993.
37 Barbara Milne, interview with author, May 15, 1993.
38 George Milne, interview with author, May 15, 1993.
39 Barbara Milne, interview with Linda Kirk, May 4, 2013.
40 Barbara Milne, interview with author, May 15, 1993.
41 Jenck, interview with author, June 6, 2015.
42 Tom Tone, interview with author, June 3, 2016.

FIELD NOTE 8

1 Tillamook Cheese & Dairy Association, List of Creditors, author unknown, 1968, author's private collection.
2 "Creamery Sale Completed Tues.," 1.
3 Purchase and Sale Agreement, Cheese & Dairy and County Creamery, September 23, 1968, 5.

EPILOGUE

Epigraphs: Gordon Edgar, interview with editor at Chelsea Green Publishing, retrieved from www.chelseagreen.com/2015/cheddar-history-gordon-edgar/; George Milne, interview with author, May 15, 1993.
1 Manchester and Blayney, "Milk Pricing in the United States," 7.
2 Newton, "How Milk Is Really Priced in the U.S."
3 Kardashian, *Milk Money*.
4 Rural Business–Cooperative Service, *Cooperative Benefits and Limitations*.
5 Bentley, "Trends in U.S. Per Capita Consumption of Dairy Products, 1980-2012."
6 McClain, "Darigold's New Strategy."
7 Ad in *Headlight Herald* (Tillamook, OR), April 28, 1963.
8 "Creamery Sale Completed Tues."
9 "Tillamook History."
10 Tillamook Estuaries Partnership, *Tillamook Bay Water Trail Online Guidebook*.
11 Tom Tone, interview with author, June 3, 2016.
12 Joe Jenck, interview with author, June 13, 2020.
13 Tetra Tech, *Tillamook County Bioenergy Feasibility Study Report*, 1.
14 Jenck, interview with author, June 13, 2020.
15 Wolfe, "Major Dairy Waste Spill Slams Tillamook River."
16 Wolfe, "Major Dairy Waste Spill Slams Tillamook River."
17 Dorsey, "Massive Manure Spill in Tillamook Bay."
18 "Creamery Will Pay Wastewater Penalty," 7.
19 "DEQ Fines Tillamook Creamery."
20 Jenck, interview with author, June 13, 2020.
21 https://assets.ctfassets.net/j8tkpy1gjhi5/5A2C18Xbmr5kJq2IAqcATw/a76793d635373ca6eafe4aae5e6cb8df/TCCA_2020_stewardship_report_032921.pdf.
22 Hale, "Manure Spill Splashes 300,000 Gallons near Tillamook Bay."
23 Jenck, interview with author, June 13, 2020.
24 Jenck, interview with author, June 13, 2020.
25 Jenck, interview with author, June 13, 2020.

26 Cheese & Dairy ad in *Headlight Herald* (Tillamook, OR), April 28, 1963.

27 Figures from the US Department of Agriculture's National Agricultural Statistics Service.

28 Figures from the US Department of Agriculture's National Agricultural Statistics Service.

29 "Map of Oregon Dairy Farmers."

30 "Map of Oregon Dairy Farmers."

31 Oregon Dairy and Nutrition Council, *2020 State of the Oregon Dairy Industry*.

32 Tillamook Corporation, *Tillamook County Creamery Association 2018 Comprehensive GRI Data*.

33 Swindler, "50 Jobs Lost."

34 Swindler, "50 Jobs Lost."

35 Three Mile Canyon Farms, "Quality Dairy Produced Responsibly."

36 Jenck, interview with author, June 13, 2020.

37 Oregon Dairy and Nutrition Council, *2020 State of the Oregon Dairy Industry*.

38 Oregon Food Bank, "Tillamook County Community Food Assessment," 2014, 5.

39 Douglas, "After Mega-Dairy Was Shut Down, Oregon Lawmakers Consider a Moratorium on New Operations"; Plaven, "Cleanup Permit Transferred to New Owners of Controversial Dairy."

40 "Travel Oregon: Places to Go, Boardman."

41 Happ, "TCCA Stirs Up a Kettle Full of Trouble."

42 Albright, "Something's Rotten in Tillamook."

43 Happ, "Tillamook Country Smoker Gets Trademark Win in Court."

44 Swindler, "50 Jobs Lost."

45 Bell, "How Tillamook's Cheese, Ice Cream and a New Portland Office Will Propel It Past $1b in Sales."

46 "Tillamook Proceeds with Plans to Add to Fame of Cheese," 22.

47 "Tillamook Proceeds with Plans to Add to Fame of Cheese," 22.

48 "Dairy 100."

49 "US Population: How Many Pounds of Tillamook Natural/Imported Cheese."

50 "Tillamook Sharpness Secret."

51 "10 Largest Ice Cream Companies in the United States."

52 "Tillamook Creamery Sued for Misleading Marketing."

53 "Top Private Companies: Tillamook County Creamery Association."

54 "Tillamook Earns Distinction."

55 Tillamook Wisconsin LLC, Calumet County, Wisconsin, Land Records, Deed #562100, 7.6.21.

56 Percival and Percival, *Reinventing the Wheel*.

57 Swindler, "50 Jobs Lost."

58 https://www.tillamook.com/products/cheese/farmers-collection

59 Gray, "Dairy Dilemma," 4.

60 Jenck, interview with author, June 13, 2020.

61 Jenck, interview with author, June 13, 2020.

62 Geiger, "Mozzarella and Cheddar Are the Tops."

63 Dumas, "Milk Production Grew Just as Demand Tanked."

64 McClain, "Iconic 'Got Milk?' Campaign Returns."

Bibliography

"10 Largest Ice Cream Companies in the United States." Zippia website. Accessed January 29, 2022. https://www.zippia.com/advice/largest-ice-cream-companies/.

"Agriculture Laws for 1963-65 Reviewed." *Capital Press* (Salem, OR). July 12, 1963.

Albright, Mary Ann. "Something's Rotten in Tillamook." *Willamette Week* (Portland, OR). August 3, 2004. https://www.wweek.com/portland/article-3470-somethings-rotten-in-tillamook.html.

Allen, Cain. "Tillamook Cheddar Cheese." In *The Oregon History Project*. Portland: Oregon Historical Society, 2006.

"Arbitration Bid Vetoed In Cheese Dispute." *Oregon Journal* (Portland, OR). May 13, 1964.

"Arbitration Unacceptable in County Dairy Dispute" *Headlight Herald* (Tillamook, OR). May 17, 1964.

Bell, Jon. "How Tillamook's Cheese, Ice Cream and a New Portland Office Will Propel It Past $1B in Sales." *Portland Business Journal* (Portland, OR). December 13, 2017.

Bentley, Jeanine. "Trends in U.S. Per Capita Consumption of Dairy Products, 1980-2012." *Amber Waves*. June 2014. https://www.ers.usda.gov/amber-waves/2014/june/trends-in-us-per-capita-consumption-of-dairy-products-1970-2012/.

Bianco, Joe. "Family Feud Splits Member from Tillamook Creamery Group." *The Oregonian* (Portland, OR). April 21, 1963.

———. "Hoffa Says Support Given Cheese Strikers; Early Settlement of Tillamook Tiff Rumored." *The Oregonian* (Portland, OR). July 2, 1959.

"Bomb Blasts Home, Auto of Tillamook Dairy Chief." *The Oregonian* (Portland, OR). May 20, 1960.

Bushman, Eva M. "The Cheesemaker's Daughters: Life in a 1920s Tillamook Cheese Factory." *Oregon Coast Magazine*. September–October 2007.

"Cheese and Dairy Assn. Win Right to Use 'Tillamook' Label in Federal Court Decision." *Headlight Herald* (Tillamook, OR). June 28, 1964.

"Cheese Fuss Continues." *Oregon Journal* (Portland, OR). May 22, 1964.

"Cheesemaker Earnings Statement Challenged." *Oregon Journal* (Portland, OR). November 20, 1964.

"Cheese Trademark Fuss Continues." *Oregon Journal* (Portland, OR). May 22, 1964.

"Cheese Unit Offers Aid." *The Oregonian* (Portland, OR). July 5, 1964.

"Cheese 'War' Heads for Court Showdown." *Portland Reporter* (Portland, OR). May 13, 1964.

Collins, Dean. *Cheese Cheddar*. Vol. 1 of *The Cheddar Box in Two Volumes*. Portland, OR: *Oregon Journal*, 1933.

"Controversy of Dairy Groups Hits Courts Here." *Headlight Herald* (Tillamook, OR). October 14, 1962.

"Court Hears Cheese Case." *The Oregonian* (Portland, OR). May 27, 1964.

"Court Ruling Clarifies Point in Cheese Battle." *Headlight Herald* (Tillamook, OR). October 30, 1966.

"Creameries Reach Agreement." *Headlight Herald* (Tillamook, OR). September 26, 1968.

"Creamery Rejects Peace Proposal." *Oregon Journal* (Portland, OR). July 9, 1964.

"Creamery Sale Completed Tues." *Headlight Herald* (Tillamook, OR). October 10, 1968.

"Creamery Will Pay Wastewater Penalty." *Albany Democrat-Herald* (Albany, OR). May 20, 1992.

"Dairy Group Asks Ruling." *The Oregonian* (Portland, OR). July 17, 1964.

"Dairy 100." *Dairy Foods Magazine.* August 9, 2021.

"Dairy Suit Trial Surprise as Case Rested by TCDA." *Headlight Herald* (Tillamook, OR). May 26, 1963.

"Declaratory Judgment." Legal Information Institute. Accessed October 25, 2021. https://bit.ly/3fWikWw.

"DEQ Fines Tillamook Creamery $56,532 for Wastewater Violations." *Headlight-Herald* (Tillamook, OR). May 28, 2015.

"Disagreement at Hearing on Milk." *Headlight Herald* (Tillamook, OR). June 24, 1962.

DiTomaso, Joseph M., and Evelyn A. Healy. *Weeds of California and Other Western States.* Vol. 1. Berkeley: University of California Press, 2007.

Dodge, John. *A Deadly Wind: The 1962 Columbus Day Storm.* Corvallis: Oregon State University Press, 2018.

Dorsey, Hilary. "Massive Manure Spill in Tillamook Bay." *Headlight Herald* (Tillamook, OR). July 24, 2019.

Douglas, Leah. "After Mega-Dairy Was Shut Down, Oregon Lawmakers Consider a Moratorium on New Operations." Food and Environmental Reporting Network. April 5, 2019. https://thefern.org/2019/04/after-mega-dairy-was-shut-down-oregon-lawmakers-consider-a-moratorium-on-new-operations/.

Dumas, Carol Ryan. "Milk Production Grew Just as Demand Tanked." *Capital Press* (Salem, OR). April 24, 2020.

Dupuis, Melanie. *Nature's Perfect Food: How Milk Became America's Drink.* New York: New York University Press, 2002.

Edgar, Gordon. *Cheddar: A Journey to the Heart of America's Most Iconic Cheese.* Chelsea, VT: Chelsea Green, 2015.

Editorial, "Double Good News." *Headlight Herald* (Tillamook, OR). October 10, 1968.

"Ely Resigns as TCDA Official; Burke Appointed." *Headlight Herald* (Tillamook, OR). March 24, 1963.

"Ex-Bank Cashier Indicted." *Morning Oregonian* (Portland, OR). July 7, 1932.

"Folks You Should Know." Newsletter, 1941.

"Farmers' Collection." Tillamook website. Accessed January 28, 2022. https://www.tillamook.com/products/cheese/farmers-collection.

"Foremost Dairy Inks Contract to Age, Market TCDA Cheese." *Headlight Herald* (Tillamook, OR). September 5, 1965.

Geiger, Corey. "Mozzarella and Cheddar Are the Tops." *Hoard's Dairyman Intel.* October 19, 2018. https://hoards.com/article-24266-mozzarella-and-cheddar-are-the-tops.html.

Gipson, Fred. *Old Yeller.* New York: Harper & Brothers, 1956.

Gray, Thomas W. "Dairy Dilemma: Ban on rBGH Use by Tillamook Sparks Conflict." *Rural Cooperatives* 73, no. 6 (November–December 2006).

Hale, Jamie. "Manure Spill Splashes 300,000 Gallons Near Tillamook Bay." *The Oregonian* (Portland, OR). July 23, 2019.

Happ, Joe. "TCCA Stirs Up a Kettle Full of Trouble." *Headlight Herald* (Tillamook, OR). December 23, 2003. https://www.tillamookheadlightherald.com/tcca-stirs-up-a-kettle-full-of-trouble/article_fc18bf44-53ac-5dfe-a850-f63e3f35ba5e.html.

———. "Tillamook Country Smoker Gets Trademark Win in Court." *Headlight Herald* (Tillamook, OR). August 3, 2004.

Heintzelman, Oliver H. "The Evolution of an Industry: The Dairy Economy of Tillamook County, Oregon." *Pacific Northwest Quarterly* 49, no. 2 (1958): 77-81. www.jstor.org/stable/40487297.

Hiestand, Edgar W. "The Problems of Small Business in the Field of Organized Labor." In *Legislative History of the Labor-Management Reporting and Disclosure Act of 1959*, vol. 2, 1758-59. Washington, DC: US Department of Labor, 1959.

Holley, Robert A. "Tillamook County Producers Split over Question of Fluid Milk Sales." *Northwest Dairy News* (Bellingham, WA). September 14, 1962.

"Judge Changes Opinion on Dairy Lawsuit Points." *Headlight Herald* (Tillamook, OR). August 18, 1963.

Kardashian, Kirk. *Milk Money: Cash, Cows, and the Death of the American Dairy Farm*. Lebanon, NH: University Press of New England, 2012.

Kerr, Robert M. *Tillamook Cheese & Dairy Ass'n v. State Dept. of Agriculture U.S. Supreme Court, Transcript of Record with Supporting Pleadings*. The Making of Modern Law. Gale: 2011.

"Klamath Rancher Selected as 'Grassman of the Year.'" *Albany Democrat-Herald* (Albany, OR). October 25, 1955.

"Lawyer Remains as Defendant in Cheese Trial." *Headlight Herald* (Tillamook, OR). March 27, 1966.

"Local Rite to Be Held July 1 for McMinimee, Dead at 78." *Headlight Herald* (Tillamook, OR). June 24, 1987.

"Lower Courts Upheld in Cheese Suit." *Headlight Herald* (Tillamook, OR). November 14, 1965.

Magmer, James. "Dairymen Told, 'Go Home, Settle Feud.'" *Headlight Herald* (Tillamook, OR). April 11, 1968.

Manchester, Alden, and Donald Blayney. "Milk Pricing in the United States." *Agricultural Information Bulletin* 761 (February 2001).

"Map of Oregon Dairy Farmers." Oregon Dairy Farmers Association. Accessed October 30, 2021. https://oregondairyfarmers.org/about/dairy-farmers-map/.

"Market Pool Turned Down in Milk Vote." *Capital Press* (Salem, OR). October 27, 1961.

McClain, Sierra Dawn. "Darigold's New Strategy Means Big Changes for Some Members." *Capital Press* (Salem, OR). March 16, 2020.

———. "Iconic 'Got Milk?' Campaign Returns." *Capital Press* (Salem, OR). August 6, 2020.

"McMinimee Is Named to Parks Commission." *Headlight Herald* (Tillamook, OR). April 16, 1967.

Mendelson, Anne. *Milk: The Surprising Story of Milk Through the Ages*. New York: Knopf, 2008.

"Milk Facts." Cornell University Extension Service. Accessed October 24, 2021. http://www.milkfacts.info/Milk%20Processing/Heat%20Treatments%20and%20Pasteurization.htm.

"Milk War Bill Earns Support." *The Oregonian* (Portland, OR). April 26, 1961.

"More Defendants Named in New TC&DA Complaint." *Headlight-Herald* (Tillamook, OR). August 16, 1964.

Morgan, Genevieve. "Milk Producers, Processors Vie over Reducing Minimum Wage." *Capital Press* (Salem, OR). May 18, 1962.

"New Motion Filed for Re-Hearing in Dairy Action." *Headlight Herald* (Tillamook, OR). August 25, 1963.

Newton, John. "How Milk Is Really Priced in the U.S." American Farm Bureau Federation. July 15, 2019. https://www.fb.org/market-intel/how-milk-is-really-priced-in-the-u.s.

"1918 Creameries." *Headlight Herald* (Tillamook, OR). June 23, 1976.

"Northwest's Largest Cheese Plant Opened at Tillamook." *The Oregonian* (Portland, OR). October 30, 1949.

Oberst, Gail. "Tillamook Creamery Opens New Visitor Center." *Oregon Coast Magazine*. June 2018. https://oregoncoastmagazine.com/2018/06/20/tillamook-creamery-opens-new-visitor-center/.

"Oregon Department of Agriculture Considers Permitting New Mega-Dairy, Easterday Farms, While Small Dairy Farmers Dump Milk." Common Dreams. May 13, 2020. https://www.commondreams.org/newswire/2020/05/13/oregon-department-agriculture-considers-permitting-new-mega-dairy-easterday.

Oregon Food Bank. "Tillamook County Community Food Assessment." Portland: Oregon Food Bank, 2013.

Oregon Rural Areas Development Committee. *Oregon Community of Tomorrow: Agriculture*. Corvallis: Cooperative Extension Service, Oregon State University, 1970.

Oregon State Archives. *Oregon Laws 1961*. Salem: Oregon State Archives, 1961.

Oregon State Archives. *Oregon Laws 1963*. Salem: Oregon State Archives, 1963.

Owens, Thomas Richard. "An Evaluation of Some Structure, Conduct and Performance Characteristics of the Portland-Vancouver Fluid Milk Market." PhD thesis, Oregon State University, 1962.

Parr, Tami. *Pacific Northwest Cheese*. Corvallis: Oregon State University Press, 2013.

"Patrick Criteser Is Named the 8th CEO of Tillamook Co-op." *Dairy Foods Magazine*. August 13, 2012.

Percival, Bronwen, and Francis Percival. *Reinventing the Wheel: Milk, Microbes, and the Fight for Real Cheese*. Berkeley: University of California Press, 2017.

Perry, C. J. "Dissent by Chief Justice in Tillamook Cheese and Dairy Association v. State Department of Agriculture, recorded in US Supreme Court Transcript of Record with Supporting Pleadings, April 10, 1968." In *The Makings of Modern Law*. Portland, OR: Stevens-Ness, 2008.

"Plaque to Honor McMinimee." *Headlight Herald* (Tillamook, OR). February 17, 1988.

Plaven, George. "Cleanup Permit Transferred to New Owners of Controversial Dairy." *Capital Press* (Salem, OR). April 10, 2020.

Powers, Ann. "An Udderly Delicious Experience Awaits in Tillamook." *Oregon This Week*. June 3, 2019.

"Reward Is Offered in Threat Case." *Headlight Herald* (Tillamook, OR). May 12, 1963.

Rural Business–Cooperative Service. *Cooperative Benefits and Limitations: Farmer Cooperatives in the United States*. Cooperative Information Report 1, Section 3. Washington, DC: US Department of Agriculture, 1990. https://www.rd.usda.gov/files/cir1sec3.pdf.

Sanderson, William. "Drop in Milk Prices Rekindles Old Battle Flames." *The Oregonian* (Portland, OR). April 25, 1961.

———. "Legislation to Prevent Milk-Price War Gets General Approval of Dairy Industry Men." *The Oregonian* (Portland, OR). April 26, 1961.

Satterfield, Archie. *The Tillamook Way: A History of the Tillamook County Creamery Association*. Tillamook, OR: County Creamery Association, 2000.

"Scotts Mills Bank in Hands of State." *Capital Press* (Salem, OR). April 29, 1932.

Skinner, Joshua John. *Circular 94* 76-100. Washington, DC: US Department of Agriculture.

"Special Cheese For Every Occasion." Tillamook website. Accessed January 29, 2022. https://www.tillamook.com/products/cheese/farmers-collection.

Steusloff, Claude. "Dairymen See Price for Class I Milk at Minimum of $6.21." *Capital Press* (Salem, OR). June 2, 1961.

———. "Dairymen Seek Law Changes Aiding Producer." *Capital Press* (Salem, OR). January 20, 1961.

———. "Milk Stabilization Bill to Be Proposed to State Legislature by Dairy Industry." *Capital Press* (Salem, OR). January 11, 1963.

"Surety Company Pays $6000." *Morning Oregonian* (Portland, OR). December 1, 1932.

"Swett Appointed Manager of TCDA." *Headlight Herald* (Tillamook, OR). July 25, 1965.

Swindler, Samantha. "50 Jobs Lost." *Headlight Herald* (Tillamook, OR). January 12, 2012. https://www.tillamookheadlightherald.com/news/jobs-lost/article_5d3b6832-3bd1-11e1-8a4f-0019bb2963f4.html.

"Tankers Roll; Trial Opening Is Due Monday." *Headlight Herald* (Tillamook, OR). May 19, 1963.

Taylor, Joseph E., III. *Persistent Callings: Seasons of Work and Identity on the Oregon Coast.* Corvallis: Oregon State University Press, 2019.

"TC&DA to Do Own Cheese Marketing." *Headlight Herald* (Tillamook, OR). April 2, 1967.

"TC&DA to Triple Its Cheese Plant Output." *Headlight Herald* (Tillamook, OR). April 27, 1967.

"TC&DA Wins Ruling in Trademark Case." *Oregon Journal* (Portland, OR). June 26, 1964.

"TCCA Claims $20 Million Damages in Dairy Dispute." *Headlight Herald* (Tillamook, OR). February 16, 1965.

"TCDA Board Says: 'No Money, No Milk' as Supply Is Halted." *Headlight Herald* (Tillamook, OR). September 8, 1963.

Tetra Tech. *Tillamook County Bioenergy Feasibility Study Report.* Pittsburgh: Tetra Tech, August 2011.

"Threat of Milk Price War Hangs over Dairymen." *Headlight Herald* (Tillamook, OR). December 30, 1962.

"Tillamook Cheese Group Amends Antitrust Suit." *The Oregonian* (Portland, OR). August 15, 1964.

"Tillamook Cheese Group Demands Accounting, Judgment from Rival Creamery Unit." *The Oregonian* (Portland, OR). May 18, 1965.

"Tillamook Cheese Label Spurs $100,000 Lawsuit." *The Oregonian* (Portland, OR). January 28, 1964.

"Tillamook Cheese Man Accused of Being 'Liar.'" *The Oregonian* (Portland, OR). May 23, 1964.

Tillamook Corporation. *Tillamook County Creamery Association 2018 Comprehensive GRI Data.* Tillamook, OR: Tillamook Corporation, 2018. https://www.tillamook.com/assets/3831/src/TCCA_2018_Comprehensive_GRI_Data.pdf.

"Tillamook County." American Courthouses. Accessed October 26, 2021. http://www.courthouses.co/us-states/o-u/oregon/tillamook-county/.

"Tillamook County Producers Split Over Question Of Fluid Milk." *Northwest Dairy News* (Bellingham, WA). September 14, 1962.

"Tillamook Creameries Import Eastern Cheese." *The Oregonian* (Portland, OR). May 22, 1964.

"Tillamook Creamery Sued for Misleading Marketing." *Headlight Herald* (Tillamook, OR). August 20, 2019.

"Tillamook Dairy Case Rule Made." *Oregon Journal* (Portland, OR). July 29, 1963.

"Tillamook Earns Distinction as a Certified B Corporation." *PR Newswire.* November 17, 2020.

Tillamook Estuaries Partnership. *Tillamook Bay Water Trail Online Guidebook.* Garibaldi, OR: Tillamook Estuaries Partnership, 2010. https://www.tbnep.org/water_trail_guidebooks/tillamook-bay-63.pdf.

"Tillamook History." City of Tillamook. Accessed October 30, 2021. https://tillamookor.gov/tillamook-history/.

"'Tillamook' Name Challenged; Court Fight Looms." *The Oregonian* (Portland, OR). May 13, 1964.

"Tillamook Plant Shuts." *The Oregonian* (Portland, OR). March 31, 1965.

"Tillamook Proceeds with Plans to Add to Fame of Cheese." *Oregon Daily Journal* (Portland, Oregon). April 19, 1919.

"Tillamook Sharpness Secret." Tillamook website. Accessed December 2, 2021. https://www.tillamook.com/products/cheese/sharpness-story.

"Tillamook Unit Rejects Offer of 'Arbitration.'" *The Oregonian* (Portland, OR). May 16, 1964.

Tippens, Jerry. "TCCA Manager Discloses Move to Curb Loss of Market Rights." *Oregon Journal* (Portland, OR). May 23, 1963.

"Top Private Companies: Tillamook County Creamery Association." Business Journals. Accessed November 4, 2021. https://www.bizjournals.com/profile/company/org_ch_38b08e0497a883d74679fc67c40cfe7d.

"Tracing the History of Cheddar with Cheesemonger Gordon Edgar." Chelsea Green Publishing. Accessed October 31, 2021. www.chelseagreen.com/2015/cheddar-history-gordon-edgar/.

"Travel Oregon: Places to Go, Boardman." Oregon Tourism Commission. Accessed October 30, 2021. https://traveloregon.com/places-to-go/cities/boardman/.

"Trouble in Tillamook: Dispute over Market Rights Divides a Dairymen's Co-op." *Northwest Dairy News* (Bellingham, WA). June 28, 1963.

Trust for Public Land. "137 Acres on Kilchis Point Protected (OR)." March 11, 2002. https://www.tpl.org/media-room/137-acres-kilchis-point-protected-or.

"Upgrading of Milk Standards Is Proposed." *Headlight Herald* (Tillamook, OR). August 1, 1968.

"US Population: How Many Pounds of Tillamook Natural/Imported Cheese Have You Used in the Last 7 Days?" Statistica Research Department. July 2, 2021. https://www.statista.com/statistics/286252/amount-of-tillamook-natural-cheese-eaten-in-the-last-7-days-in-the-us/.

US Tariff Commission. *Cheddar Cheese.* TC Publication 175. Washington, DC: US Tariff Commission, 1966. https://www.usitc.gov/publications/22/pub175.pdf.

"Use of TC&DA Label Allowed in Dairy Suit." *Headlight Herald* (Tillamook, OR). May 24, 1964.

Valenze, Deborah. *Milk: A Local and Global History.* New Haven, CT: Yale University Press, 2011.

"Wage Boost Ends Tillamook Strike." *Albany Democrat-Herald* (Albany, OR). July 8, 1959.

Walth, Brent. "Mark of Distinction." *The Oregonian* (Portland, OR). December 29, 1996.

Wolfe, Jordan. "Major Dairy Waste Spill Slams Tillamook River." *Headlight Herald* (Tillamook, OR). April 20, 2017.

Wunsch, Nils-Gerrit. "The Leading Ice Cream Brands of the United States in 2021, Based on Sales." Statistica. November 18, 2021. https://www.statista.com/statistics/190426/top-ice-cream-brands-in-the-united-states/.

Index

Organization meetings are sorted by year, month, and day at beginning of index. Organization main headings use the most common abbreviations or shortened names found in the text. *See* cross-references lead to these from long-form names. See page xiii for a key to the dairy organizations. Figures are indicated by bolded page numbers.

NUMBERS

May 9, 1955 GASA board meeting, 29
February 21, 1957 GASA board meeting, 30
1959 GASA annual meeting, 21–22
February 1959 GASA board meeting, 53
March 9, 1959 GASA board meeting, 53
June 23, 1959 GASA board meeting, 35
June 6, 1960 GASA board meeting, 49
March 21, 1961 GASA board meeting, 45
April 10, 1961 GASA board meeting, 21–22
April 17, 1961 GASA board meeting, 46
1962 County Creamery annual meeting, 8–10
May 15, 1962 Cheese & Dairy board meeting, 61
June 5, 1962 Cheese & Dairy board meeting, 61–63
June 13, 1962 County Creamery general meeting, 63–64
July 26, 1962 Cheese & Dairy special meeting, 65
August 13, 1962 Cheese & Dairy board meeting, 65
August 27, 1962 Cheese & Dairy member meeting, 73
September 5, 1962 Cheese & Dairy board member recall meeting, 74, 76–77
January 1963 ODA annual meeting, 80–82
February 16, 1963 Cheese & Dairy annual meeting, 100
April 1963 Cheese & Dairy board meeting, 121
April 25, 1963 Cheese & Dairy board meeting, 101
August 14, 1963 County Creamery board meeting, 110–15
August 19, 1963 Cheese & Dairy board meeting, 89–90, 115–16
February 17, 1965 Cheese & Dairy board meeting, 143
March 3, 1965 Cheese & Dairy board meeting, 145
March 13, 1965 Cheese & Dairy annual meeting, 145

A

accounting, County Creamery, 65, 87–91, 122
accounting lawsuit, 152–55, 160–61
aerosol cheese spread, 99–100
Agriculture, Oregon Department of, 46, 48, 61, 78, 86, 101, 123–24, 165, 175
Albany Democrat-Herald, 20
Alder Vale Creamery, **13**
Alpenrose Dairy
    and County Creamery, 49, 52, 53–54, 70, 104, 108, 117–19, 142, 149–50
    and GASA fluid milk, 54
    and Grade A milk, 7
    and loan programs, 49, 52, 55, 65, 66, 74, 108, 117–18, 142, 145
Anderson Creek, 175
Animal Waste Management Plan, 175
antitrust lawsuit, 7, 134, 137, 142, 148–55, 160–61, 164, 166
Arden Farms, 146

B

Babcock test, 15, 141
Bailey, Millard
    and attempts to fire Dixon, 10, 64
    as Cheese & Dairy board member,
      65–66
    as delegate to County Creamery
      board, 73, 74
    on Dixon pay raises, 93
    fired from Cheese & Dairy, 115
    and Shiveley Shippers, 101, 102
Bandon Cheese, 178
Battle Ground (WA), 27
Baumgartner, Fritz, 90, 170
Beale, J. O. "Jack," 27
Beaver Cheese Factory, 172
Becker, Ferd
    background and board membership,
      30–32
    on Cheese & Dairy finances, 132
    on Cheese & Dairy removal of Schild,
      Zweifel, Bailey, 73
    and Cheese & Dairy surety bond, 124
    and letter threat, 102
    letter to *Headlight Herald*, 93
    on loan to Roy Espe, 53
    with prize bull, **31**
    as rebel farmer, 59
Becker, Jim, 28, 57, 59, 66, 120
Becker, Pete, 30
Beeler, Anita, 156
Beeler, Joe, 59, 64, 68, 73, 74, 98, 99, 124
Beeler, Walt, 68
Bennett, Sharon, 126
biogas (bioenergy), 174, 175, 177
Blaser, Bob, 61, 91, 124, 144–45, 165
blockade, tanker, 104–6, **105**
Board Information (Cheese & Dairy)
    on County Creamery accounting, 87
    creation of, 79
    on Food Fair loan, 99
    on milk check advances, 104
    on Milne resignation, 142
    on sales trip to Southern California,
      130–31
    on unsecured lending, 93
Boardman (OR), 177, 178
Bohannon, J. S. (Judge), 69, 97
bomb blast at Dixon home, 37
bookmobile, 71, 72
Books and Pipes (Field Note 4), 71–72

brick cheese, 12
Buchanan Cellars, 122
bulk tanks, 31, 94, 164–65, 172
Burke, Ed, 86, 104, 143
butter/butterfat, 7, 12, 15, 16, 20, 98, 119,
    141, 164, 176, 177, 178

C

Cadonau, Carl, 142, 145
CAFOs (confined animal feeding
    operations), 175, 177
Cannon, Kessler, 47
Capital Press, 52, 84
Carnation Co.
    and Alpenrose, 49
    and County Creamery contracts, 104
    and discounted pricing, 8, 61
    Dixon on pricing for, 135
    and Grade A milk, 7
    and House Bill 1752, 47
    and loan programs, 55, 66
    preference for County Creamery, 70
Carnation-Damascus producers, 79
Central Cheese Factory, 172
Certified B Corporations, 179
Champion, Joe, 1
Chatelain, Joe, 124
cheddar cheese, 12, 49, 91, 128, 157, 179,
    180
Cheese & Dairy (Tillamook Cheese and
    Dairy Association)
    accounting lawsuit, 152–55
    ads, cheese industry, **50**, **51**, 94
    antitrust lawsuit, 148–55
    attempts to fire Dixon, 58, 62–65
    and Bailey and Schild as County
      Creamery reps, 74
    and board member recall, 76–77
    and Bob Ely, 64, 86
    business relationships of, xii
    and Carnation Co., 61
    and County Creamery accounting, 65,
      87–91
    and County Creamery board, 93
    and County Creamery marketing, 65,
      109–15
    and County Creamery payments, 121
    and County Creamery, return to, 143,
      144
    and County Creamery, split from,
      115–16

and County Creamery, structure of, 7
and declaratory judgment, 68–69, 95,
   103–10
description of, xiii
financial struggles, 145
formation of, 40
and Granny Goose, 100
influence of, 92–93
injunction against County Creamery,
   132
and loan programs, 7–9, 52, 54–55,
   58, 65–66, 69–70, 73–75, **75**,
   115–18, 121
Los Angeles broker, letter to, 147
and market share, 50
meeting minutes ledgers, final,
   169–70
member benefits, 24
power struggles, internal, 73–77, 74,
   75–76
Premium Brand Tillamook cheese,
   128–32, **129**, **130**
production costs, 49
public relations, 79, 117
and quota law, 79
refusal to ship to County Creamery,
   121–25
reopening of cheese factory, 147
setbacks from court battles, 140–48
and Shiveley Shippers, 104, 106, 121,
   122–23, 133, 144
surety bond, 124
trademark lawsuit, 132–37
See also Dixon, Beale; Milne, George
cheese factories, small
   Alder Vale Creamery, **13**
   Beaver Cheese Factory, 172
   board support of Dixon, 90–91, 93
   and bulk tanks, 172
   Central Cheese Factory, 172
   closure of, 171–73
   Clover Leaf factory, 26
   Cloverdale Cheese Factory, 101
   consolidation of, 16
   Hebo Cheese Factory, 172
   Holstein factory, 26
   Maple Leaf factory, 26
   Meda Creamery, 111
   Mohler Cheese Factory, 77, 114, 172
   north/central Tillamook County
      cheese factories, **18**

   Oretown Creamery, 11, 172–73
   as outdated economic model, 21–22
   south Tillamook County cheese
      factories, **19**
   See also Red Clover Creamery
      Association
cheese making process, 15–16
cheese milk. *See* Grade B milk
cheese spread, aerosol, 99–100
cheese styles
   aerosol spread, 99–100
   brick, 12
   cheddar, 12, 49, 91, 128, 157, 179, 180
   Colby-Jack, 181
   Monterey Jack, 24
   mozzarella, 181
   Swiss, 12
Cheese War
   aftermath, 166–68
   beginning, 3–10
   final settlement, 159–64, 170
Cheese War Truce (Field Note 6),
   138–39
cheese weight, 87
cheese wheels, giant, 128, 130–31, **130**
Chilton (WI), 179
Christensen, Fred, 12, 15
Christensen, Harley, 61, 124, 142
Christensen, Kermit, 35
closed pools, 34, 82, 83–84, 118–19
Clover Leaf factory, 26
Cloverdale (OR), 180
Cloverdale Cheese Factory, 113
Colby-Jack, 181
Columbia River Processing Plant, 177
Columbus Day Storm, 1962, 23, 67–68
Combs, Avery (Judge)
   and declaratory judgment, 108–9,
      112, 115
   Linda Kirk's recollections of, 95, 96,
      97
   and tanker blockade, 105, 106
   on Tillamook factory, 119
confined animal feeding operations
   (CAFOs), 175, 177
Congressional Record, 35
co-op consolidation, 26–40
corn, 125–27, 140, 174
coronavirus pandemic, 181
county, 172

County Creamery (Tillamook County
Creamery Association)
  accounting issues, 87–91, 122
  and accounting lawsuit, 152–55
  ad attacking Cheese & Dairy, 133
  and Alpenrose, 49, 52, 53–54, 104,
    108, 117–19, 142, 149–50
  Annual Report, 1959-60, 36
  and attempts to fire Dixon, 8–10,
    63–64
  board member cap, 92–93
  and Cheese & Dairy marketing
    agreement, 65
  and Cheese & Dairy reps, 74
  and Cheese & Dairy's proposal to
    return, 143
  on closed pools, 84
  commingling of cooperatives' milk,
    104–5
  debt to Cheese & Dairy, 115
  and declaratory judgment, 68–69,
    103–10
  description of, xiii
  early activities, 12–13
  and GASA, 20, 29–30, 32–33, 38
  and Grade A milk, 17, 33–34, 164
  lack of oversight, 94
  and loan programs, 52
  and manure management, 174–75
  marketing of Tillamook cheese,
    recent, 176–81
  Minnesota cheese, purchase of, 134
  newsletter February 1962 issue,
    83–84
  and Red Clover files, 120–21, **120**
  and Shiveley Shippers, 101, 103–5,
    109, 112, 115, 123, 133
  structure of, 6–7, 29
  and Teamsters strike, 34–35
  Tillamook factory, move to, 26
  trademark lawsuit, 124, 132–37
  veto power of, 32
  vote counting, fraudulent, 110–15
  See also Dixon, Beale; loan programs;
    Milne, George
Court of Appeals Ninth Circuit, US, 136
Cow Milkers Incorporated, 148
Craven, John R., Jr., 110–15
Culberson, Helen & Marie, 14
Curly's Dairy v. Mayflower, 52–53

D

Dairy 100 (producer list), 179
Dairy Co-op. *See* Mayflower Dairy
Dairy Foods, 179
dairy organizations, key to, xiii
DAR (Daughters of the American
  Revolution), 138–39
Darigold (Farmers Cooperative
  Creamery), 79, 165, 172
Daughters of the American Revolution
  (DAR), 138–39
Deadly Wind, A (Dodge), 68
death threats, 102–3
declaratory judgment, 68–69, 95–97,
  103–10, **119**, 131
Department of Agriculture, OR, 46, 48,
  61, 78, 86, 123–24, 165, 175
Department of Environmental Quality,
  OR, 175
Department of Transportation, OR, 66
digesters, manure, 175, 177
distributors, 17–19, 44–45, 47, 48, 80
Dixon, Beale
  arrival in Tillamook County, 5–7
  attempts to fire, 8–10, 58, 62–65
  and Bob Ely, 64–65, 86
  bomb blast at home, 36–37
  Carnation, deals with, 61–62
  and Cheese & Dairy board member
    recall, 77
  and Cheese & Dairy influence, 92–93
  and Cheese & Dairy's refusal to ship,
    121
  and cheese factories, 21–22
  closed pool opposition, 83–84,
    118–19
  and County Creamery accounting, 90
  and declaratory judgment, 104, 108
  early career and reputation, 27–30
  and Grade A milk, 164, 166
  on Granny Goose deal, 100–101
  on House Bill 1752, 47
  interview with Hysmith, 1987, 1–2,
    83, 166
  and loan programs, 49–50, 53, 54–55,
    69–70, 93, 115, 146–47, 166
  on market pools, 48
  and pay raises, 93–94
  and Premium Brand Tillamook
    Cheese, 131
  and quota law, 82–83

and Red Clover files, 120–21, **120**
resistance to price increases, 20
on secret meetings, 107
and statewide pricing system, 45
on Teamsters strike, 36–37
testimony at trials, 135, 153–54
on trademark lawsuit, 133
on Warren McMinimee, 166
See also Cheese & Dairy; County
Creamery
Dixon, LaVerne, 28
Dodge, John (*A Deadly Wind*), 68
Dunn, Rome, 111
Durrer, James & Robert, 61, 128

E

East, William (Judge), 132, 134, 135–36
Edgar, Gordon, 171
Elliott, Harry C., 2
Ely, Bob, 46, 64–65, 77, 86, 165
environmental concerns, 173–75
Environmental Quality, Oregon
Department of, 175
EPA (Environmental Protection Agency,
US), 174–75
Espe, Roy, 53
Eugene (OR), 78
Eugene Plan, 84

F

Fairview Grange Hall, 76, 115
Farm Chores (Field Note 3), 41–43
farm pollutants, 173–75
Farmers Assuring Responsible
Management, 175
Farmers' Collection cheese, 180
Farmers Cooperative Creamery
(Darigold), 79, 165, 172
FBI (Federal Bureau of Investigation),
102
Federal Milk Marketing Order (FMMO),
48, 171–72
FFA (Future Farmers of America), 16, 81
Field, Shirley, 84
Field Notes (Kirk)
note 1, Treasure Hunt at the
Museum, 1–2
note 2, From Milking Pit to Ice Cream
Counter, 23–25
note 3, Farm Chores, 41–43

note 4, Books and Pipes, 71–72
note 5, Once Again to the
Courthouse, 95–97
note 6, Cheese War Truce, 138–39
note 7, Tourists Swarm the Factory,
156–58
note 8, I Was a Teenage Creditor,
169–70
final settlement, Cheese War, 159–64,
170
First Citizen of Tillamook honor, 66
First National Bank of Oregon, 54, 122,
131, 142–43, 144, 148, 170
FMMO (Federal Milk Marketing Order),
48, 171–72
Foland, Merriman, 11
Food Fair grocery, 99
Ford, Guy, 13
Foremost Milk Company, 146, 147–48
fraudulent vote counting, 110–15
Fred Meyer grocers, 128
From Milking Pit to Ice Cream Counter
(Field Note 2), 23–25
Fry-Matson, Ruby, 1
Future Farmers of America (FFA), 16, 81

G

Gallagher, Hugh, 47
GASA (Grade A Shippers Association)
and Alpenrose Dairy, 54
and Cheese & Dairy, 54–55, 56
and County Creamery, 20, 29–30,
32–33, 38
description of, xiii
formation of, 17
George Milne as board member, 20
and loan programs, 49, 53, 54, 56–58
and Mayflower price cuts, 46
member benefits, 24
and small cheese factories, 21–22
and statewide pricing system, 45–46
and Teamsters strike, 35
giant cheese wheels, 128, 130–31, **130**
Gibson, Howard, 45, 53
Gienger, Bud, 77
Gipson, Fred (*Old Yeller*), 72
Goodwin, James, 68, 95, 97
gourmet cheese, 180
Grade A milk
certification, 166
changes in standards, 164–65

and Cheese & Dairy debt crisis, 144
County Creamery handling of, 103
and Grade B farmers, 172
internal quota, County Creamery, 33–34
introduction to Tillamook farmers, 16–17
Mayflower purchase of Cheese & Dairy, 7, 46–47, 146
minimum price of, 48
pool, 34
production of, 19–20, 21–22, 37
quality crisis at Tillagem Farm, 140–41
and quota law, 78–79, 82–83
and Shiveley Shippers, 101–3
statewide pricing system, 46
at Tillamook factory, 29
Grade A Shippers Association (GASA) See GASA
Grade B milk
Cheese & Dairy inventory to Red Clover, 145
and cheese sales, 8
and County Creamery, 21
and Grade A pricing, 17, 19, 34
producers, 21, 92, 94, 102, 165, 172
production, 15, 19, 98, 164
and quota law, 82
and Tillagem Farm, 141
and Tillamook factory, 29, 37
Granny Goose deal, 1, 99–101, 120, 135
Great Western National Bank, 148
Guernsey cow breed, 15, 126, 165

H

Haberlach, Carl, 12
Hall, Bruce, 97
Hanrahan, Bonnie, 96
Hatfield, Mark, 36, 47, 158
Headlight Herald
on 2017 sludge release, 174
Becker letter to editor, 93
on Bob Ely, 86
and Cheese & Dairy marketing, 128–30, **129**, **130**
on closed pools, 84
on conclusion of Cheese War, 159
on Dixon pay raises, 93
Glenn Johnston letter to editor, 56–57
on Grade A milk marketing, 164

on letter threat to Becker, 102
on milk price stabilization, 83
on tanker blockade, 105, **105**
Hebo Cheese Factory, 172
Hiestand, Edgar W., 35
Hoffa, Jimmy, 35
Holstein cow breed, 15, 126, 175
Holstein factory, 26
House Bill 1752 (Producer Milk Stabilization Law), 46–48, 52, 166
House of Representatives (OR), 52, 84
Hurliman, Bob, 128
Hurliman, Clem, 59, 106–8
Hurliman, Liz, 108
Hurliman, Max, 128
Hysmith interview with Dixon, 1987, 1–2, 83, 166

I

I Was a Teenage Creditor (Field Note 8), 169–70
ice cream, 23, 25, 119, 156, 157, 172, 178, 179, 181
Idaho, 177
industry changes after settlement, 164–66
interview with Dixon, Hysmith 1987, 1–2, 83, 166

J

J. C. Penney Co., Inc., 43
Jack, Glenn, 97
Jenck, Donald "Hooker"
and Cheese & Dairy return to County Creamery, 143, 165
and Cheese & Dairy surety bond, 124
on conclusion of Cheese War, 167
as County Creamery board member, 101–2
on George Milne, 20
and Granny Goose deal, 99–100
image of, **67**
police officer incident, 68
as rebel farmer, 59, 60
and Steve Steiner, 126
Jenck, Joe, 20, 60, 111, 168, 174
Jenck, Ken, 61, 114
Jersey Cattle Club, 59
Jersey cow breed, 15, 30, 175
Johnston, Filbert "Fib"

on attempts to fire Dixon, 10
on Dixon, 28
and farm work during conflict, 127
and loan programs, 57
on Millard Bailey, 64
on the rebel farmers, 60–61
on Vern Lucas, 89–90
on Warren McMinimee, 66
Johnston, Glenn
  and Cheese & Dairy board member
    recall, 73, 77
  and Cheese & Dairy contracts,
    cancellation of, 146
  and Cheese & Dairy publicity
    committee, 79
  and Cheese & Dairy surety bond, 124
  on conclusion of Cheese War, 167
  and Craven's vote count, 112
  and Food Fair lawsuit, 99
  image of, **56**
  and loan programs, 56–58
  and milk price stabilization, 83
  and quota law, 78
  as rebel farmer, 59
  and sales trip to Southern California,
    131
  and Shiveley Shippers, 101
Johnston, Rita, 60, 169
Jud, Frank, 33

K

Kaufman, Douglas, 97, 153
Kennedy, John F., 128
key to dairy organizations, xiii
Kilchis River, 173
Kilkenny, John F., 52–53
Kirk, Linda
  changing irrigation at Tillagem Farm,
    71–72
  childhood jobs at Tillagem Farm,
    41–43
  as creditor to Cheese & Dairy, 169–70
  at DAR meeting, 138–39
  and declaratory judgment, 95–97
  early life at Tillagem Farm, 23
  meeting minutes ledgers, final,
    169–70
  visit to Tillamook County Pioneer
    Museum, 2011, 1–2
  work at Tillamook factory, 156–58
Koehler, Glen, 124

L

Landis, Mrs. Ed, 145
Landolt, John, 73
Larson, Joe, 143, 144, 145, 146
Lawson, George, 26–27
lawsuits
  accounting lawsuit, 152–55, 160–61
  antitrust lawsuit, 7, 134, 137, 142,
    148–55, 160–61, 164, 166
  declaratory judgment, 68–69, 95–97,
    103–10, **119**, 131
  Food Fair v. Cheese & Dairy, 99
  multiple against Cheese & Dairy, 121,
    123
  nonpayment lawsuit, 123
  Oregon Department of Agriculture v.
    Cheese & Dairy, 123–24
  trademark lawsuit, 124–25, 132–37
Leuthold, Dave, 17, 28, 67, 99, 111, 165
Leuthold, Hans, 115
  on attempts to fire Dixon, 63
  and Cheese & Dairy board member
    recall, 73
  on Cheese & Dairy finances, 145–46,
    148
  and Cheese & Dairy publicity
    committee, 79
  and Cheese & Dairy split from
    County Creamery, 113–14
  and Cheese & Dairy surety bond, 124
  on conclusion of Cheese War, 167
  and declaratory judgment, 108
  on First National Bank of Oregon, 144
  and Food Fair lawsuit, 99
  and Grade A milk, 17
  and Granny Goose deal, 100–101
  and local terrorism, 102
  and milk price stabilization, 83
  and quota law, 78, 82–83
  as rebel farmer, 59
  and sales trip to Southern California,
    131
  support for Ferd Becker, 33
Lincoln City (OR), 53
loan programs, County Creamery
  and aftermath of Cheese War, 166
  and Alpenrose Dairy, 52, 65, 66, 74,
    108, 117–18, 142, 145
  and Carnation Co., 66
  and Cheese & Dairy, 7–9, 52,
    54–55, 58, 65–66, 69–70, 74–75, **75,**

115–18, 121
and declaratory judgment, 103, 108,
   110
and Dixon, 49–50, 53, 54–55, 69–70,
   93, 115, 146–47, 166
establishment of, 49–55
and GASA, 49, 53, 54, 56–58
opposition to, 56–58
and Portland grocers, 8–9, 145, 147
Longview (WA), 74
Los Angeles (CA), 130, 147, 179
Lost Valley Dairy, 177
Lower Columbia producers, 79
Lucas, Vern
and antitrust lawsuit, 152
and attempts to fire Dixon, 114
and Cheese & Dairy, basement
   meeting of, 115
and Cheese & Dairy board member
   recall, 73
and Cheese & Dairy publicity
   committee, 79
and Cheese & Dairy sales committee,
   128
and Cheese & Dairy surety bond, 124
and County Creamery payments, 121
on First National Bank of Oregon, 144
and Food Fair lawsuit, 99
and loan programs, 69
and local terrorism, 102
and quota law, 78
as rebel farmer, 59
and Red Clover files, 120–21, **120**
reputation, 89–90
and sales trip to Southern California,
   130, 131
and tanker blockade, 105–6
Lucerne Foods, 104

M

manufacturing grade milk. See Grade B
   milk
manure management, 174–75
Maple Leaf factory, 14, 26
maps, small cheese factory
north/central Tillamook County
   cheese factories, **18**
south Tillamook County cheese
   factories, **19**
market pools, 45–46, 47–48
Masons in Oregon, 66

Maxwell, Merrill, 120, **120**
Mayer, Del, 135
Mayflower Dairy
and Cheese & Dairy, 7, 122, 144–46
Curly's Dairy v. Mayflower, 52–53
and GASA, 46
and Grade A milk, 7, 46–47
McCall, Tom, 138
McIntosh, Peter, 12
McMinimee, Louise, 138–39
McMinimee, Warren
and antitrust lawsuit, 153–55
and Bob Ely, 86
as County Creamery attorney, 93,
   111–15, 166–67
and Hurliman testimony, 107
image of, **67**
letter in *Tillamook Cheese News*, 70
Linda Kirk recollection of, 97
and nonpayment lawsuit, 123
reputation and career, 1–2, 66–68
and tanker blockade, 106
on Teamsters strike, 35
McMullen, Donald E., 153
Meda Creamery, 111
milk, Grade A. See Grade A milk
milk, Grade B. See Grade B milk
Milk Audit and Stabilization Division
   (Dept. of Ag., OR), 61
milk checks, 104, 110, 122, 125
Milk Control Act, Oregon, 52
milk distributors. See distributors
milk for cheese. See Grade B milk
milk grades. See Grade A milk; Grade B
   milk
Milk Marketing Act, 123
milk pools. See pools, milk
Milk Stabilization Act, new (quota law),
   78–85, 171
Milk Stabilization Law, Producer (House
   Bill 1752), 46–48, 52, 166
milk tanker blockade, 104–6
milking procedure, 14
Milne, Barbara
and antitrust lawsuit, 154–55
on Bass Tone, 92
and Cheese & Dairy board member
   recall, 73, 76–77
cheese factory, visits to, 23–25
on conclusion of Cheese War, 167–68
on County Creamery, 22, 88

on farm work during conflict,
125–26, 128
on First National Bank of Oregon, 132
on Food Fair lawsuit, 99
on formation of Cheese & Dairy, 40
on hired hand difficulties, 141
on House Bill 1752, 166
on Hurliman testimony, 107, 108
on Leuthold testimony, 108
on loan programs, 93
and Otto Schild, 33, 74, 76
photos of, 165
on Vern Lucas, 89–90
on Warren McMinimee, 167
Milne, Cathy, 41–42, 156, 158
Milne, George
and antitrust lawsuit, 153
arrival in Tillamook County, 5–6, 16
and attempts to fire Dixon, 8–10
and Cheese & Dairy board member
recall, 73, 77
and Cheese & Dairy contracts, 146
on Cheese & Dairy finances, 145
and Cheese & Dairy publicity
committee, 79
and Cheese & Dairy split from
County Creamery, 116
and Cheese & Dairy surety bond, 124
on closed pools, 84
on conclusion of Cheese War, 167
on County Creamery, 88, 171
on declaratory judgment, 68–69, 103,
106
and farm work during conflict,
125–26
and Farmers Cooperative Creamery,
165
financial struggles, 44–45
on Food Fair loan, 99
and Granny Goose deal, 100–101
and hired hand difficulties, 141–42
on House Bill 1752, 166
and local terrorism, 102–3
as manager of Cheese & Dairy,
140–42
and meeting nights, 71
and milk price stabilization, 83
on Oregon State University, 80
photos of, 6, 165
as president of Cheese & Dairy, 40
and quota law, 78, 79, 80–82

and Red Clover files, 120–21, 120
reputation, 20–21, 59–60
and sales trip to Southern California,
130, 131
state hearing, selected to attend, 61
and statewide pricing system, 45
on tanker blockade, 105–6
and Teamsters strike, 34–35
and trademark lawsuit, 135
See also Cheese & Dairy; County
Creamery
Mohler Cheese Factory, 77, 114, 172
Monterey Jack, 24
Montgomery Ward & Co., 42
Moody, Valerie, 170
Morning Star (ship), 137
Morrow County, 177
mozzarella cheese, 181
Mt. Angel producers, 79
Multnomah County, 152
Musick, Albert R. (Judge), 97, 152, 153,
154

N

Naegeli, Casper, 124, 143
National Labor Relations Board, 36
Neah-Kah-Nie High School, 138
Nehalem Bay, 173
Neilson, Anita, 29, 56–58, 56, 115, 169
Neilson, Bob, 169
Neilson, C. R., 115
Nestucca Bay, 173
Nestucca Bay Creamery, 180
Nestucca High School, 138
Nestucca River farm scene, 5
Netarts Bay, 173
Nielsen, John, 128
Northwest Dairy News, 29, 40, 53, 82–83,
93, 103
Northwest Environmental Defense
Center, 174–75

O

ODA (Oregon Dairymen's Association),
80–82, 141
ODI (Oregon Dairy Industry group), 47,
80–81
Ogden, Harry, 12
Old Yeller (Gipson), 72

Once Again to the Courthouse (Field
    Note 5), 95–97
open pools, 45–46, 49, 79, 84
Oregon Coast Foods, 178
Oregon Dairy Industry group (ODI), 47,
    80–81
Oregon Dairymen's Association (ODA),
    80–82, 141
Oregon Department of Agriculture, 46,
    48, 61, 78, 86, 123–24, 165, 175
Oregon Department of Environmental
    Quality, 175
Oregon Department of Transportation,
    66
Oregon Farm Bureau Federation, 78, 99
Oregon Food Bank, 177
Oregon Journal, 109, 133, 136
Oregon Milk Control Act, 52
Oregon State University (OSU), 46, 80,
    158
Oregon Supreme Court, 124, 153
Oregonian
    on bomb blast at Dixon home, 37
    on Cheese & Dairy finances, 145–46
    Craven on Cheese War hostilities,
        114–15
    on declaratory judgment, 103
    on strife in the milk industry, 7
    on tanker blockade, 105
    on Teamsters strike, 35
    on trademark lawsuit trial, 135
Oretown Creamery, 111, 172–73
organic milk, 180
organizations, key to dairy, xiii
OSU (Oregon State University), 46, 80,
    158
Owens, Thomas, 17–19

P

Pangborn, Esther, 128
Pangborn, Marvin, 28, 73, 83, 128
Parks and Recreation Advisory
    Committee (OR Dept. of Trans.), 66
pasteurization, 14–15, 100
Perry, C. J. (Chief Justice), 124
Persistent Callings (Taylor), 13n14, 207
Peterson, Edwin, 97, 153
Peterson, Roy, 57
police officer incident, 68
pollutants, farm, 173–75

pools, milk, 12, 33–34, 45–48, 49, 75,
    78–79, 82–84, 118–19
Portland distributors, 17–19
Premium Brand Tillamook cheese,
    128–32, **129**, **130**, 145, 147–48, 157
Premium Farms, 126
price fixing, distributor, 17–19
Producer Milk Stabilization Law (House
    Bill 1752), 46–48, 52, 166
Puget Sound (WA), 46
Pure Milk Products Company, 134

Q

Quick, Bert, 91, 98, 120, **120**, 124
quota law (new Milk Stabilization Act),
    78–85, 171
quota pool, 33, 78

R

ragwort, tansy, 141–42
rBGH (recombinant bovine growth
    hormone), 180–81
rebel farmers, 59–61, 73–77, 90, 125–26
Red Clover Creamery Association
    and attempts to fire Dixon, 9, 58, 64
    and bulk tanks, 172
    on Cheese & Dairy finances, 145
    and Cheese & Dairy marketing
        agreement, 109–11
    on Cheese & Dairy return to County
        Creamery, 144–45
    and Cheese & Dairy split from
        County Creamery, 115–16
    and County Creamery accounting,
        89–90
    files at County Creamery, 120
    and fraudulent vote counting, 111–15
    merger with Cheese & Dairy, 148
    opposition to Dixon, 91–92
    public relations, 117
    secret meetings, 107–8
    and trademark lawsuit, 134
Redberg, Ralph, 73, 74, 78, 113
Redberg, Roy, 124
refrigeration requirement, state, 164–65
Richards, Bob, 11
Ridderbusch, Ed, 47
Robert's Rules of Order (Robert), 81
Rocha, Joe, 176–77, 180
Rood, Frank, 81

Rulifson, Bob, 113

S

Safeway Inc., 43, 177
Satterfield, Archie (*Tillamook Way*), 12, 27, 28, 93, 118, 164, 167
Sayles, Dale "Doc," 57–58, 79, 98, 124
Schild, Harold, 12
Schild, Otto
    and antitrust lawsuit, 152
    and attempts to fire Dixon, 64
    and Barbara Milne, 74, 76
    and Cheese & Dairy board member recall, 73
    on declaratory judgment, 69, 104
    and formation of Shiveley Shippers, 101
    as GASA president, 33–34
    image of, **33**
    on loan programs, 53
    and nonpayment lawsuit, 123
    support of Dixon, 62, 65–66, 77
    and Teamsters strike, 35
Scotts Mills (OR), 27
Sears, Roebuck and Co., 42
secret meetings, 107–8
settlement, Cheese War final, 159–64, 170
Sheldon, O. N., 170
Shiveley, Gaylord, 101, 112
Shiveley Shippers (Tillamook Fluid Milk Shippers Association)
    and Cheese & Dairy, 104, 106, 121, 122–23, 133, 144
    and County Creamery, 101, 103–5, 109, 111–12, 115, 123, 133
    and declaratory judgment, 109
    description of, xiii
    formation of, 101–3
    and tanker blockade, 105
    and trademark lawsuit, 133
Shopping Smiles (newspaper), **50–51**, 133
small cheese factories. *See* cheese factories, small
Solomon, Gus (Judge), 133, 134
spills, waste, 174–75
St. John's Episcopal Church, 28
Stabilization Law, Producer Milk, 46–48, 52, 166
State Parks Advisory Committee, 138

statewide pricing system, 44–48
Steiner, Nick, 28, 59, 66, 90, 126, 127
Steiner, Steve, 28, 58, 124, 126–28, **127**, 167
strike, Teamster Union Local 569, 34–37, 99
Strunk, Harold, 177, 178
Super-Valu Food Stores, Inc., 74
supreme courts, 124, 136, 153
surety bond, Cheese & Dairy, 124
surplus milk
    Dixon's efforts to sell, 61
    Grade A, 39, 62
    Mayflower purchase of Cheese & Dairy, 146
    and milk checks, 34
    in Pacific Northwest, 46
    and quota law, 79
    and statewide pricing system, 45–46
Sutton, Pete, 28
Swett, A. J., 146
Swiss cheese, 12

T

tanker blockade, 104–6, **105**
tansy ragwort, 41–42
Taplin (Mohler Factory rep.), 77
Taylor, Joseph E., III (*Persistent Callings*), 13n14, 207
TCA (Tillamook Cheese Association), xiii, 26–27, 37–38, 90
TCCA/T.C.C.A. (Tillamook County Creamery Association). *See* County Creamery
TCDA/TC&DA/T.C.&D.A. (Tillamook Cheese and Dairy Association). *See* Cheese & Dairy
Teamster Union Local 569 strike, 34–37, 99
terroir, 179–80
terrorism, local, 36–37, 102–3
TFMSA (Tillamook Fluid Milk Shippers Association). *See* Shiveley Shippers
Thompson, Bruce (Judge), 136, 166
Threemile Canyon Farms, 177
Tillagem Farm, 16, 23, 41–43, 71–72, 95–96, 125, 140–41, 175
Tillamook Bay, 173, 175
Tillamook Catholic Church, 57
Tillamook Cheese and Dairy Association (Cheese & Dairy). *See* Cheese & Dairy

Tillamook Cheese Association (TCA), xiii, 26–27, 37–38, 90
Tillamook Cheese News (County Creamery), 69–70
Tillamook Coliseum, 122
Tillamook Country Smoker, 178
Tillamook County cheese industry, early, 11–19
Tillamook County Creamery Association (County Creamery). *See* County Creamery
Tillamook County Library, 1, 71
Tillamook County Pioneer Museum, 1
Tillamook dairy industry, 11–22, 175–76
Tillamook factory, 26, **26**, 34–37, 105–6, 119–21, **119**, 156–58, 172, 173
Tillamook Fluid Milk Shippers Association (Shiveley Shippers). *See* Shiveley Shippers
Tillamook High School, 138
Tillamook pool, 82
Tillamook River, 175
Tillamook Way (Satterfield), 12, 27, 28, 93, 118, 164, 167
Tone, Basil "Bass," 59, 91–92, **92**, 107–8, 113, 120, **120**, 124, 130–31, **130**
Tone, Tom, 125, 168, 174
Tourists Swarm the Factory (Field Note 7), 156–58
Townsend, T. S., 12
trademark lawsuit, 124–25, 132–37
Transportation, Oregon Department of, 66
Trask River, 174
Treasure Hunt at the Museum (Field Note 1), 1–2
Trumpy Cheese, 146

U

University of Wisconsin, 15
US Court of Appeals Ninth Circuit, 136
US Supreme Court, 124, 136
Utah, 177

V

Vanderzee, Yelta, 73, 128
VanLoo, Art, 128
vote counting, fraudulent, 110–15

W

Waldron, Arnold, 63, 73, 124
Walker, Arnold, 107
Walker, Mrs. Arnold, 168
Wall Street Journal, 35–36
Washington County, 152
waste spills, 174–75
water usage issue, 87–88
welfare, animal, 175
Wetzel, Mr. and Mrs. Don, **130**
whey, 15–16, 24, 173–74, 178
widow's land incident, 68
Willamette Plan, 78, 84
Willamette Valley farmers, 118
Willamette Valley pool, 82–83, 84
Willamette Week, 178
Williams, J. B., 128
Wilson, David, 11
Winslow, George, Sr., 113
Wisconsin, University of, 15
Wisconsin cheese industry, 128, 146, 178–80
Woodward, Floyd, 61, 102, 147
World's Fair, 1964, 128
Wyss, Lorraine, 89
Wyss, Mida, 145, 146

Y

Yakima Valley (WA), 46
Yates, Ed, 28, 164
YMCA, Tillamook, 66, 107

Z

Zweifel, Karl, 64, 65, 73, 101